WELLNESS CENTERS

Wiley Series in Healthcare and Senior Living Design

Alfred H. Baucom
Hospitality Design for the Graying Generation: Meeting the Needs of a Growing Market

Sara O. Marberry
Healthcare Design

Elizabeth C. Brawley
Design for Alzheimer's Disease: Strategies for Creating Better Care Environments

John E. Harrigan, Jennifer M. Raiser, and Phillip H. Raiser
Senior Residences: Designing Retirement Communities for the Future

Clare Cooper Marcus and Marni Barnes
Healing Gardens: Therapeutic Benefits and Design Recommendations

Joan M. Whaley
Wellness Centers: A Guide for the Design Professional

WELLNESS CENTERS

A Guide for the Design Professional

Joan Whaley Gallup

JOHN WILEY & SONS, INC.

New York • Chichester • Weinheim • Brisbane • Singapore • Toronto

Copyright © 1999 by John Wiley & Sons, Inc. All rights reserved.

Published simultaneously in Canada.

Library of Congress Cataloging-in-Publication Data:

Gallup, Joan Whaley.
   Wellness centers: a guide for the design professional / Joan Whaley Gallup.
      p.   cm.
    ISBN 0-471-25337-5 (alk. paper)
    1. Hospitals — Health promotion services — Design and construction.
   I. Title.
   RA975.5.H4G34   1999
   725'.5 — dc21   99-11574

Printed in the United States of America.

10 9 8 7 6 5 4 3 2 1

Contents

Preface

About twelve years ago, my mother was diagnosed with breast cancer. It was a virulent form of the disease, which took her life less than two years later.

My brothers, Richard and Jay Whaley, along with our father, John, decided on the day of her diagnosis that we would do everything we could to try to save her life. The journey that we all traveled during that period of time led us into unfamiliar territory—the world of traditional and complementary medicine.

Endeavoring to try all avenues of cure, we met with famous physicians as well as knowledgeable people in the fields of healing, nutrition, and all manner of therapies.

Although we ultimately lost our fight, the experience was not without value. I, as an architect, gained keen interest in using my design skills in the area of healthcare architecture. In the coming years, the lessons I learned about the value of prevention and taking ownership of one's own health were applied to the exploration of the design of integrated health facilities—places where maintaining health and preventing disease are as important as curing it.

At this time in history, our contemporary cultural values and the economic forces that impact them appear to support the thesis of this book: that healing is holistic, that people can, through maintaining a positive spirit, prevent a good deal of suffering they or their loved ones might otherwise endure, and that the creation of new places that promote and maintain health—centers of wellness—is the key to the future of healthcare.

A large percentage of the population of the United States is reaching middle age. The members of this "baby boom" generation are keenly aware of the importance of self-care and, perhaps because of their coming of age in the 1960s and 1970s, are also attentive to a sense of the spiritual, to the combined mind-body relationship.

This worldview influences many life choices, not least among them the decisions this population makes in terms of healthcare. One has only to gaze at a newsstand for a quick view of what the populace appears to think is important. Not a week goes by without a new exercise system, dietary alternative, psychological methodology, or environmental warning hitting the news and being explored in the popular press.

Physician-authors who formerly wrote about medicine for the lay public with a distinctly traditional view are now embracing alternative medicine in great numbers. Every new popular medical book is about mind-body medicine, alternative therapies, or anti-aging medicine.

Well-respected institutions have heard the call. Harvard University in Boston, Massachusetts, created a "Mind Body Institute" dedicated to exploring alternative healing methods and bringing these alternatives into the mainstream by offering courses for physicians on acupuncture, massage, the influence of spirituality, homeopathic medicine, and other forms of complementary medicine. The National Institutes of Health has created a department charged with exploring the benefits of complementary medicine, including the influence of spirituality on the healing process.

In the business world we see managed care companies increasingly moving toward reimbursement for alternative therapies and exercise programs. There is an obvious reason for this trend: it is less costly for insurance companies and the entire healthcare system to keep people well. Certain companies are responding to this incentive by supporting customers as they join wellness center programs, offering a "wellness benefit," as much as several hundred dollars, to clients who join exercise programs.

On a global level, it is vital for every community to make the health of citizens the number one priority. Healthier people will have a better quality of life, will be able to contribute positively to the arts, to culture, to science, and will be empowered as a more productive work force.

As an architect who has specialized for many years in the design of healthcare facilities, I have witnessed how social trends have influenced design. As much as 15 years ago, we saw the removal of certain medical services and departments from the main hospital building, relocated like so many satellites revolving around the sun. These ancillary buildings were and are less expensive to build and more convenient for patients, staff, and physicians to use. Located primarily in suburban areas, closer to the population that uses them and free of parking difficulties, medical office buildings and other ambulatory care buildings began to proliferate, supported by technological advances.

We are living at a time when there is a compelling need to create community centers in suburban areas where a greater percentage of the population are spending their lives. Suburban corporate office development and the trend toward "the virtual office" are creating a need for individuals who are not tethered physically or psychologically to a "downtown" to find a community's center. Often this need is haphazardly served by the suburban mall. With the lack of a better central location for meeting other people, malls become the central locations for charity events like "heartwalks" and the beginning and end points for community-sponsored field trips for senior citizens and scout troops. How much better is life in a community with a wellness center (which is less focused on commericalism) that provides services such as well and sick baby day care to support busy parents?

As baby boomers age and technology progresses, we will continue to see acute care facilities ministering to the needs of the very ill. At the same time, technological advances are enabling people with cardiac problems, diabetes, and other so-called chronic challenges to live longer, so there is a natural need in the system to provide pleasant and affordable chronic and rehabilitative care environments. This need can frequently be addressed in the wellness center.

The wellness center is the most positive, nurturing, life-affirming building type ever to evolve in the history of health-care facilities design. The opportunity to provide people with a social center that will affect their lives in such a positive way is at the heart of this idea. The ability to provide a healing environment for those in need of rehabilitation within a facility dedicated to preventive medicine is a powerful incentive. It is the reason for this book.

At the turn of the road into the new century, some dynamic elements in our culture have combined to produce a change in the way we live and maintain our health, the starting point for the rest of our lives. A new sense of spiritual awareness, personal responsibility, and empowerment, supported by evolution in the world of business and technology, an awareness of what is truly important in life, and a return to basic values have all led to this moment in time. We have become a culture that is able, now more than ever in the history of the world, to control our quality of life. By turning inside out the trends of past centuries, we can now focus on wellness. We can create buildings that will nurture and sustain us, healing environments that will serve to support happy, life-enhancing activities.

Centers for wellness are centers for life. This book is dedicated to my mother, Valorie Aurigemma Whaley, and to my husband, John Gallup.

WELLNESS CENTERS

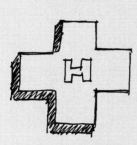

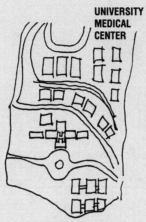

UNIVERSITY MEDICAL CENTER

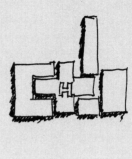

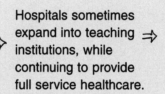

Hospitals evolve into institutions, central to the life of the community. ⇒

Hospitals sometimes expand into teaching institutions, while continuing to provide full service healthcare. ⇒

Hospitals expand again—adding beds and services, extending their mission to provide the full "continuum of care."

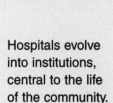

ASSISTED LIVING CAMPUS

AMBULATORY CARE CENTER

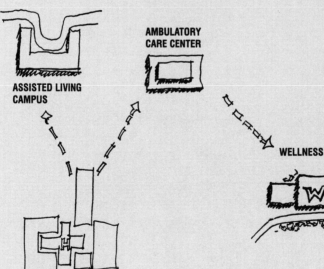

WELLNESS CENTER

Hospitals reach out to the community, following the population shifts— enabled by new technology, ambulatory care centers, adult day care, skilled care. ⇒

The "Center of Wellness" emerges, shifting the emphasis from healing the sick to prevention.

Completing the
Continuum of Care

Wellness centers are facilities that incorporate clinical and fitness components into a comprehensive healthcare center. The advent of managed care and the advancing age of the baby boom generation, among other socioeconomic forces, underlie the trend toward building such centers.

The American healthcare system, with all of its faults and shortcomings, is the best in the world; it is also a quintessentially American institution. Only in a country that advances constantly in the direction of freedom and innovation and rejects the imposition of authoritarian rule, whether by governments or powerful economic entities, will innovation continue to flourish.

Alexis de Tocqueville reflected on the American spirit in *Democracy in America*:

> From the time when the exercise of the intellect became the source of strength and of wealth, it is impossible to consider every addition to science, every fresh truth, and every new idea as germ of power placed within the reach of people. Poetry, eloquence and memory, the grace of wit, the glow of imagination, the depth of thought, and all the gifts which are bestowed by Providence with an equal hand, turned to the advantage of the democracy.

In *Cities and the Wealth of Nations,* author Jane Jacobs states, "Economic life develops by grace of innovating."

The development of the wellness center is perhaps the thin end of a wedge that will broaden into a completely new definition of healthcare delivery. Advancing into unknown territory, the American citizen is voicing discontent with the status quo in terms of the methods and quality of healthcare delivery. The trend toward self-management, directing one's own fate in the realm of healthcare, harkens back to the essential elements of the American character that formed our early government, which so impressed de Tocqueville in 1835.

The entrepreneurial spirit is alive in America and is influencing, in a very beneficial way, the quality of life in this country. This is the first country to pursue with vigor preventive medicine, borrowing the best research, practical knowledge, traditional practices, and innovations from other countries and cultures. The wellness center, and indeed the whole movement toward complementary medicine, borrows the best from the entire pool of knowledge and blends its techniques and practices with the best of advanced traditional medical practices.

This holistic approach, incorporating what is good and beneficial in traditional or "hard" medicine and in alternative medicine, is expressed in physical form in the wellness center. Many posit that the wellness center will become the hospital of the twenty-first century.

THE HOSPITAL OF THE TWENTY-FIRST CENTURY

As advances in medical procedures result in the need for increasingly smaller exam spaces — except for certain surgeries, such as organ transplants, for which the size of the medical team has expanded and outgrown the limits of a typical operating, room — the concept of the modern hospital is being reconsidered.

The evolution of wellness centers began with Ken Cooper's Cooper Aerobics Center, Houston, Texas, in the early 1970s and with the new emphasis on diet as it related to health pioneered by Nathan Pritikin. Up to this point in time, with the exception of healthful eating programs set up within the Adventist Hospital Systems, hospitals were serving food that was nutritionally unsound for the most part and, in some cases, with a high content of substances now considered taboo.

Academic medical centers across the nation took small steps in the right direction 25 years ago; the results of the now classic Framingham Heart Study in Massachusetts were among the first to relate cardiovascular disease to risk factors. This study revolutionized medicine by postulating that there were controllable, changeable behaviors that could influence the risk of cardiovascular disease. High cholesterol levels and the ingestion of a high-fat diet, along with smoking, lack of exercise, and stress, were among the factors considered in the study. Here was a turning point in the history of self-responsibility and self-care: Changing habits could result in avoiding a heart attack.

In 1982, the Riverside Health System in Newport News, Virginia, began one of the first wellness center programs and projects. In Melrose Park, Illinois, Gottlieb Hospital was the first in the nation to create a freestanding wellness center facility, followed by the Sports Med Center for Fitness, suburban Chicago, developed by a group of orthopedic physicians who created a 55,000-square-foot center. In 1991, the Galter Life Center, also in suburban Chicago, built the first freestanding urban center in the United States.

From 1972 to 1997, just over 350 wellness centers have been built, and today it is projected that by the year 2000 there will be 700 such centers in the United States. The trend of recent years in moving healthcare out of the acute hospital setting toward more outpatient facilities can be projected even further. There is already talk in the industry of "virtual hospitals."

Twenty-seven percent of today's U.S. population is over the age of 50, and in the year 2000 there will be nearly 80 million Americans more than 50 years old. Members of this population, who will consume more than 70 percent of the nation's healthcare services, have high expectations about living well far into their senior years.

Bruce Clark, M.D., writes of the baby boom generation: "In 1990 Americans made 425 million visits to providers of unconventional therapies, such as chiropractors and massage therapists, exceeding the 388 million visits to conventional physicians who provide primary care. These statistics suggest that so-called alternative therapies are more mainstream than conventional medical care."

The healthcare consumer has become more demanding. Capitation demands the creation of integrated delivery systems. Clinical integration involves the mapping of a clear pathway that delivers healthcare most efficiently. In a well-organized system, a specialist will see people whom they can help directly. For example, a neurosurgeon will see patients who require neurosurgery, but not those with neurological problems that may involve chronic or degenerative disease.

Primary care doctors will send patients directly to the specialists who can help them. Technology supports the walk down the clinical pathway that is most likely to yield results for the patient and achieve economies for the healthcare delivery system. A fully clinically integrated system will include alternative therapies. It will also strengthen the process with the inclusion of education, wellness promotion, and preventive medicine at the beginning of the continuum of care.

With the continuing advances in telemedicine and the improvement in information systems technology, it is conceivable that patients will be able to track their medical profiles through a central database, identify their records by use of a retinal scan, dance from insurance company to insurance company as jobs change or as companies renegotiate with managed care providers on a quarterly basis, and negotiate their way through government programs such as Medicare, Medicaid, or the military's Tri-Care system, all with the click of a button.

In the future, physicians and the growing number of nurse practitioners may come to be viewed as we view the mechanic who services our car, and the powerful status that medical professionals have gained through the centuries may be altered. Their social standing may become more akin to that of healers in more primitive, but not less wise, cultures.

The ultimate healer, may then, in fact, be oneself. Taking responsibility for this change in thinking is at the core of the philosophy of complementary medicine. Yet the healer is not the self alone; supporting this idea of autonomy is the recognition of humans in the spiritual sense as well. Spaces designed for meditation or prayer, such as meditation gardens, should be included in all wellness centers if the scope of work permits.

It is no accident that the Office of Alternative Medicine at the National Institutes of Health (NIH) in Bethesda, Maryland, supports research into the spiritual side of healing. Larry Dossey, M.D., has done considerable research into concepts such as remote healing and the efficacy of prayer in altering a medical condition.

Elisabeth Targ, M.D., of California Pacific Medical Center in San Francisco, California, is also involved in cutting-edge research at the Medical Center's Complementary Medicine Institute. Here, a traditional, accredited medical institution and medical school not only offers alternative therapies as an option or enhancement for the healing of certain medical conditions, but also conducts in-depth research into the viability of different systems of alternative medical therapy.

Exciting alliances are being formed between hospital systems and complementary medical practitioners. Nearly every major hospital system in the United States today is either already offering some form of complementary treatment within the hospital setting or is considering such treatment as part of an expanded program in the form of a wellness center.

Jeff Bensky, a leader in the development of wellness centers across the country, reiterates the driving force for the development and success of wellness centers in "Wellness, the Health Club/Medical Connection":

> Managed care creates powerful incentives to control cost by placing a premium on illness prevention; prompt treatment at a cost-effective price, rehabilitation which will return patients

to the workplace as quickly as possible. Now, increasingly, a real reward exists to help people maintain and improve their health—so that they are less likely to become sick in the first place. Under capitation, for example, there is a financial incentive to do fewer (very expensive) heart bypass operations and more (relatively inexpensive) smoking cessation programs.

Bensky points to the free-spending habits of hospitals and healthcare systems as a thing of the past under managed care: "Few hospitals are in the position to build multimillion dollar wellness centers on their own, especially if appropriate facilities already exist. Hospitals will be looking to share any risk with the right partner."

He suggests that fitness club entities seek out relationships with hospital partners. Calling for a spirit of collaboration and positive thinking, Bensky suggests that fitness club owners "learn to talk the language of healthcare." Fitness clubs, he says, must begin to think of themselves as hospital outreach centers.

Unique to the healthcare field at this writing is the alliance of the Community Health Centers of King County (a private nonprofit organization providing community healthcare in six clinics in King County in the state of Washington) and Bastyr University, a university devoted to the education of doctors of naturopathic medicine. The Seattle, King County, Department of Public Health has provided funding for these clinics. The

Mayo Clinic, Scottsdale, Arizona.
Ellerbe Becket Architects.

purpose of the clinics is to offer both conventional family medicine practice services and natural medicine services with an emphasis on serving immigrant and refugee populations, as well as those with low incomes or no insurance.

A survey was conducted in 1995, showing that 60 percent of patients in King County were interested in receiving natural medicine services. Patients enrolled in the Community Healthcare King County/Community Health Plan of Washington may be covered by its Basic Health Plan or Healthy Options Plan.

King County Councilman Kent Pullen, in a recent interview on CNN, said that he doubts interest in the new clinics will fade. "We want to learn enough to be the seed to encourage other communities to do the same," Pullen said. "This is the start of a revolution that is going to sweep the country."

In January 1996, the City Council of Kent, Washington, took a visionary step toward revolutionizing the availability of alternative healthcare in that city by passing Resolution 1449, which reads:

> Whereas, policies at all levels of government are changing to properly acknowledge the efficacy, professionalism, and licensure of natural medicine practitioners, the City of Kent desires to become home to the most comprehensive array of alternative and natural medicine Services in the United States.

The first accredited multidisciplinary institution of natural medicine in the United States is Bastyr University in Seattle, Washington, an internationally recognized leader in natural medicine education, research, and clinical services. Bastyr University, the first NIH Office of Alternative Medicine Center for Alternative Medicine Research, provides fully integrated medical care for HIV/AIDS patients. Each patient is interviewed by a medical doctor, a naturopathic doctor, an acupuncturist, and a nutritionist.

In 1995, the *Los Angeles Times* reported on the opening of the Seattle Clinics' Homeless Youth Clinic, supported by collaborative agreements with Bastyr University and the Northwest Institute of Acupuncture and Oriental Medicine. The Homeless Youth Clinic offers help to young people between the ages of 12 and 25 who are homeless, street involved, or at risk for homelessness. Services include primary medical care, mental health counseling, HIV testing and counseling, STD testing and treatment. Substance abuse counseling and other services are provided on a drop-in basis.

Across the country, individual states differ in regard to how the practice of complementary medicine is viewed. A move to license naturopathic doctors is gaining ground in Minnesota, in Texas three consecutive attempts at obtaining licensure have been thwarted, and in Iowa attempts have not been successful. However, in New Hampshire, Maine, Montana, and New Jersey, ground is slowly being broken.

Legislators in Montana signed a bill into law licensing naturopathic physicians but are resisting permitting them to prescribe drugs or perform surgery. Montana, at this time, requires a certification of specialization for those assisting in natural childbirth, and it recognizes those professionals who hold a Ph.D. degree in Natural Health.

Viderkliniken, a healing center near Jarna, Sweden, was built according to a spiritual science developed by Austrian Rudolph Steiner (1861–1925). Anthrosophic medical treatment is offered in low-rise buildings designed largely by Erik Asmussen, a local resident architect, and illustrated in his book, *Erik Asmussen: Toward a Living Architecture.*

Vidaerkliniken was designed to support the anthrosophic goal of engaging the patient in a conscious process of self-healing and spiritual growth. The design of the buildings involves few rectilinear spaces, ceilings are formed from more than one plane, all rooms bring in natural light and have windows that open to provide fresh air, special wall-painting techniques provide color and texture to the interior spaces, and the interior consistently maintains its relationship to the outdoors, and nature. As the assisted-living building type in this country has borrowed heavily from Scandinavian healthcare building types like Viderkliniken, so might other healthcare facilities in the near future.

Trends in the development of wellness center designs continue to evolve. For the most part, what we are seeing flourish in the United States are hospital-based wellness centers that have healthcare systems as equity partners. Risk is shared among the healthcare system, the developer, and the investors, whether private individuals or an investment group such as a real estate investment trust.

Projects like The Dow Chemical Employee Center, designed by Ellerbe Becket in 1989 for the Dow Chemical Corporation, remain successful today, without a health system partner but with a clinical functional element, in this case, as in most cases, sports medicine and rehabilitation medicine.

We are also seeing a resurgence in the development of employee wellness centers. Mark Nadel, an experienced and successful developer of wellness centers and originator of the Healthplex concept, is already seeing a spin-off—corporate-sponsored wellness centers—as one of several niche market trends.

At this writing, the Steelcase Company of Michigan, known for its high-end corporate office systems furniture design and manufacture, is developing, with Nadel's Health Equities Group, a corporate health facility in western Michigan. Projects are also in the planning stages for a major steel company in West Virginia, and there are a series of federal and local government-sponsored projects (including one at Fort Bragg, North Carolina, for the Army Corps of Engineers).

Sinai Health System in Baltimore, Maryland, having developed the spectacularly successful Sinai Wellbridge wellness center under the leadership of Warren Green, CEO, and Executive Director Darryl McKay, is developing sports-specific centers in conjunction with baseball star Cal Ripken of the Baltimore Orioles, as well as corporate centers for such clients as Legg Mason in downtown Baltimore. Sinai has active corporate wellness programs in many federal facilities in the Baltimore area, including the healthcare Financing Administration (HCFA) itself. Ellerbe Becket Healthcare architects are the architectural designers. The sports wellness centers were developed under an agreement between Cal Ripken and Sinai Health, by Sinai Corporate Health executive Susan Heiser, who will manage the centers. Sinai Health owns a franchise for these sports centers, purchased from Frappier Acceleration. Jim Frappier, an exercise physiologist, developed the acceleration training programs in 1986 after attending a training education course in Moscow that demonstrated many of the principles now incorporated into his program.

Mark Nadel of the Healthcare Equities Group Inc. (HEG), cites the new Sportsplex he is developing in Orlando, Florida, with the Orlando Magic basketball team as an example of the next generation of sports and health centers. The Sportsplex, larger in scale and with more diversified sports programs, is an interesting part of the evolution of this building type.

The community demographics and geography needed to support this iteration of the wellness center are important considerations. In the coming years, it will be interesting to see whether the sportsplex concept succeeds outside destination resort areas of the country, such as in Orlando, where Disney is opening its Celebration Health wellness center within the Celebration community. This center might well prove to be quite successful.

In Canada, there are a plethora of large-scale sports/entertainment facilities. Many include multiple lap, therapy, and amenity pools, indoor tracks, multiple indoor basketball/volleyball courts, squash, tennis, and other sports. Often, they include indoor ice rinks where hockey, speed skating, and ice dancing are enjoyed. Some include sports medicine clinics, but rarely do they seem to offer the full complement of clinical services available at the present time in the United States.

Other parts of the world interpret the concept of wellness and wellness centers with a wide degree of diversity. In Japan, fitness centers flourish, with attention to wellness primarily related to physical therapy and massage therapy. Executive clubs for corporate clients abound. The Shisedo Club is an executive fitness club primarily geared to the executives of this multimillion-dollar cosmetics empire. Spa amenities abound in all centers, with particular attention given to massage and therapeutic baths of various kinds.

In various parts of the world, such as Istanbul, wellness center clubs are being designed that are aimed at a high-end corporate market. Lacking the economic imperatives of managed care and the U.S. healthcare reimbursement strategies, these private clubs are in a position to offer programs that make sense for their unique markets.

Club Industrial, designed by Ellerbe Becket Architects and Engineers, is a state-of-the-art facility with an interesting program mix. Developed and financed by an investor, this wellness club holds no hospital affiliation, yet has a clearly defined sports medicine and therapy program. Design architects Michael D. Jones and David Rova created the wellness center in an existing factory building, located in the suburbs of Istanbul, formerly used for the manufacture of heavy machinery.

Istanbul experienced a population boom from two to three million people in the 1950s and is currently approaching fourteen million. To date, nothing like Club International exists in an area with such apparently positive demographics. The facility will be developed into a sports-health club, retail, and entertainment complex of 12,000 square meters.

Unique in this wellness center is the separate Executive Area, which has its own elevator entrance, concierge, gallery, theater, manual and air massage, oxygen room, artificial sun treatment room, and salon. Club Industrial's retail area includes a sports shop, general retail, beauty/hair salon, chiropractor's office, and a separate Therapy Salon with lobby, reception, offices, staff, first aid, manual and air massage rooms, and artificial sun treatment room.

Probably the most extraordinary variation of what we consider a wellness center, worldwide, is the development of the project for the City of Moscow, Hospital 31. Programmed and designed by Ellerbe Becket International in a collaborative effort with the Moscow city government, Moscomarchitecture, a Moscow research and design institute, Hospital 31 is a mixed-use development.

Formally called the Rehabilitation Hospital and Hotel Complex for Moscow Hospital Number 31, the project includes a 200-bed rehabilitation hospital, a 120-suite apartment-hotel, a full-service fitness center, a medical office building, a 500-room three star hotel, and several areas of structured parking.

The benefits of the project to the hospital are many: the new rehabilitation hospital is critical to the continuing success of Moscow Hospital 31, the master planning of this mixed-use project is beneficial in the synergistic effect it will have in establishing a unified medical center complex, the development project creates financial support for the hospital and provides for growth.

Moreover, the neighborhood benefits because the complex's professionals, patient families, and fitness center users are good neighbors. The project will create construction jobs and infrastructure and site improvements, including restoration of the local stream and park. The district will benefit from its identification with a world-class hospital as well as the renewed vitality to a prominent site, provided by the ripple effect of its wonderful architecture.

Interestingly, this project includes clinical therapies that are just now becoming mainstreamed into contemporary American medicine: a programmed physiotherapy function that includes medical inhalation, specialty inhalation (salt room, mountain air room, aromatherapy); electrotherapy; a massage block (zone) that includes manual therapy, horizontal spine stretching, a laser room, and classic massage; a psychological rest block that includes music therapy, light therapy, artificial sun therapy, Vichy shower, and sleep therapy; and a water treatment block that includes a medical bath with dressing area, automatic underwater massage, a plunge pool, a motional pool, an exercise pool, an amenity pool and a walking pool.

TECHNOLOGY AND HEALTHCARE

As former competitors become collaborators, enabling greater freedom in the delivery of healthcare, the question at hand is, Is the linking of all patient information records a viable process?

According to the National Committee on Quality Assurance, as quoted in a recent *Healthcare Forum Journal* (HFJ) article by Nat Heimoff, the evolution of the linking of healthcare patient information may be as follows:

1. Standardize the set of data elements collected by all health plans and providers.
2. Link all systems.
3. Standardize the way all information is defined and encoded.
4. Screen and monitor all data constantly.
5. Build protocols that ensure confidentiality and security of patient records.
6. Fully automate patient record keeping.
7. Share data completely among health plans, providers, and public agencies in support of performance measurement and improvement.

Based on the Social Security number, the U.S. Department of Health and Human Services is developing a unique identifier for use by seemingly everyone, everywhere.

In his HFJ article, Nat Heimoff points to the impact of the Internet as having a profound effect on the notion that all computers, everywhere, could develop a common interface, which would make patient information translatable and usable everywhere.

Lance Lang, M.D., a vice president of the Permanente Company, is responsible for designing and implementing a National Clinical Information System for all of Kaiser Permanente. His task involves linking multiple Intranets into an Extranet, which involves the records of more than 8.5 million patients.

Decision Support is the use of preprogrammed protocols that make automated clinical decisions. It tracks trends by scanning all of a health facility's or system's records and intervenes by utilizing push technology, which alerts physicians to variances in a patient's personal data that may red-flag a serious condition. Such systems can automatically track a patient's diagnosis and check to see whether he or she has filled the appropriate prescription, anywhere in the country.

This interconnectedness can be used to benefit humankind, or can be abused. In the move toward self-care and wellness as a way of life, information systems technology can support a move in the direction of the positive.

Public health officials have long dreamed of creating community health information networks (CHINs). The Internet has become the tool that, at little cost, is allowing the interfacing of healthcare databases to become a reality.

When push technology becomes more widespread, the link to the wellness center will become vital in assisting healthcare professionals in the monitoring of patients, whether or not they are in an at-risk category. For instance, suppose that a cardiopulmonary patient is following an exercise prescription on a piece of equipment at a wellness center and his progress is being monitored with a system like Fitlinxx (which sends data back to a central computer concerning the range of motion achieved with the machine). If this information is tied in with the patient's medical records and additional databases that provide diagnostic support, the patient can be immediately red-flagged with great accuracy if he is running into danger. Reduction of full time employees (FTEs) with the improvement of safety is a definite step in the right direction.

INFORMATION SYSTEMS AND TECHNOLOGICAL LINKS

Another factor, in the world of sophisticated management information systems, sparking growth of the wellness center concept is the advantage in linking medical information and patient profiles to the managed care system's comprehensive patient files.

Insurance companies love information. The information provided to patients about their physiological status and their progress—results of basic tests such as blood pressure and cholesterol level, along with nutritional testing, weight loss analysis, stress testing (treadmill), and the more sophisticated tests developed to measure muscle strength, endurance, oxygen utilization rates, and flexibility—all contribute to a better understanding of the state of the patients' health and, for insurers, a better profile of the risks associated with their state of health.

Physicians and personal trainers are now able to tap into a patient's electronic data file, the creation of which is available to most medical consumers, if the patient is consistent and thorough in the maintenance of the file, and obtain a snapshot of how well the patient's rehabilitation is going, how strength is being gained by following a prescribed series of exercises, how often and how thoroughly a patient is following his or her doctor's orders, and to what effect.

If adjustments must be made by a physician or trainer, they can be made before the patient goes down the wrong path, and minor adjustments to the routine itself, or to the way it is being carried out, can be quickly made. Some exercise machines have built-in data access capability so that a patient can type in her PIN number, gain access to her data file, see what she needs to do that day in order to maintain her routine, see a history of where she was, where she needs to be, and where she is in terms of strength. Similarly, a nutritional profile can be entered into the data file, analyzed with the use of readily available software programs, and prescriptions for optimum nutrition tailored to

Lobby of Sinai Wellbridge Wellness Center, Pikesville, Maryland.

the individual patient—taking into consideration present nutritional habits, age, weight, life-style patterns, family history, and current stresses—and deliver in an uncannily specific way an order to guide the patient in optimizing her nutritional habits. Along with a computerized diet analysis, a patient's current diet can be compared against specific nutrient requirements for a patient of a specific age, weight, sex, life-style, and exercise habits.

Menu planning can be developed to meet the needs of a patient's particular goals, most often concerning overall health and optimum weight. Nutrient analysis identifies the protein, carbohydrate, sodium, vitamins, and mineral (including trace mineral) content of the suggested menu items. Although current software is predicated on the American Dietetic Association's "food pyramid" and recommended daily allowances (RDA), the classically low levels of nutrients required by the RDA are being updated and supplemented by current thinking in the field of nutrition.

The advantage to the client is one-stop shopping. A person's knowing that he can gain access to his own records to chart progress and provide a general understanding of the state of his health is tremendously empowering. The individual attention provided by such access is vitally important. No longer is weight loss left to the five-minute conversation in the doctor's office: "You have to take off some weight or you are in danger of having a heart attack." The patient typically leaves the physician's' office with the same photocopied diet given to all patients, regardless of age, weight, body type, life-style, or current mental or emotional stress, medication, intake of vitamins and minerals, or lack thereof.

Technology is best applied when it supports, but does not direct, human life. In the medical facility setting, it is enormously useful in improving accuracy of diagnoses, enhancing medical imaging and other procedures, and fostering communication among healthcare professionals. Technology, then, provides the tools for accomplishing more with less, and better tools at that.

Evidence-based medicine, the practice of medicine supported by computerized databases, helps in the diagnosis and treatment of illness. It does not, however, supplant primary medicine, the one-on-one relationship between doctor and patient that results in healing. The irony is that as technology accelerates, the need for human contact seems to accelerate, as well. There are more massage therapists in this country today than ever before.

John Yates, Ph.D., in *A Physicians' Guide to Therapeutic Massage*, says that massage can benefit such conditions as muscle spasm, spinal curvature, muscle soreness, headaches, temporomandibular joint dysfunction (TMJ), and bronchial asthma. A massage therapist recently noted a steady rise in the number of people, from all walks of life, coming to see her. She credits the surge in business to the growing acceptability of massage as a viable healthcare treatment and, she says, to the fact that "people like to be touched, and it [massage] is an acceptable way to connect with another human being."

CORE PROCESSES

It is clear that healthcare organizations, systems, and providers are reexamining who they are and just what business they are in. This shift in thinking is occurring at the strategic planning level at every institution we have contacted. Author Peter Drucker cautions us to decide what business we are in. Is the core process of the hospital to solve the problem of illness or to promote and create wellness? If it is the latter, what basic ways of looking at the business of healthcare have to change to reflect the transition of the mission? What strategic filters have to be included in the decision-making process of every institution when important choices are at stake?

Determining the basic focus of a business is a challenging task. Once the primary direction is set, who we are and what we do as a corporation or institution, then the *how* of things begins to fall into place.

Blue Cross–Blue Shield of Minnesota (BCBSM) is making strides in the direction of redefining who it is as a company and what it does. It is working on a next-generation healthcare system, that is focused on prevention to ensure a healthy community.

The underpinning of this new orientation is education. BCBSM is creating a knowledge base that the consumer/patient can tie into. A pilot program has been developed with Direct Medical Knowledge (DMK) of Sausalito, California, which offers on-line in-depth consumer health information. Health plan members can receive medical reports relating directly to their areas of interest and concern. The customized reports contain information about treatment options, self-care, and complementary treatments, if applicable.

BCBSM is holding a series of forums across the state to encourage community stakeholders to identify issues related to a series of challenges, the first being the epidemic of tobacco usage. BCBSM is joined in this effort by the American Cancer Society and local health systems, hospitals, clinics, and Chambers of Commerce.

In a recent article in *Healthcare Forum*, MaryAnn Stump, R.N., of BCBSM said, "Responding to illness has been the principal focus of healthcare plans and providers [and the principal category of reimbursable service.] For the past thirty years customer-related focus at BCBSM takes a broader, consumer-focused view that redefines the territory from 'Take care of me' or 'Fix me' to 'Help me become and stay as healthy as I realistically can.'"

As healthcare providers reexamine their core business processes, they will begin to redefine how they will deliver their product over the next 10 years. How they do it is intimately tied to where they do it, and this calls for a redefinition of the master planning of healthcare campuses.

It is not an easy challenge for healthcare executives. They are working on survival, against increasing economic, political, and technological pressures. healthcare executives are a special group of talented individuals who must balance such forces and lead the systems entrusted to them to future success. Architects and planners can help greatly by acknowledging these forces and the difficult challenges that these executives and healthcare systems face.

Architects must become knowledgeable about the shift from illness care to wellness care in order to absorb the paradigm shift that will lead these institutions successfully into the next

Networked Diagnostic Life Cycle machines, Springfield Healthplex, Springfield, Pennsylvania.

century. A focus on the wellness-providing system and the needed flexibility of all healthcare buildings are the keys to understanding what is available to us in the future of healthcare.

Architects must continue to listen. It has always been arrogance and folly to impose a design standard on a client with an I-know-better approach. We architects do not know better, we have enormous skills and talents and can help a customer define the scope of what he or she wants, measured against the experience of ourselves and others. Engaging the client's own skills and talents, we can co-create an environment that will serve and support the daily business conducted there, and have fun doing it. To have skills, talents, and experience is not enough. The architect must have a knowledge of the customer's business, in this case healthcare/wellness care, in order to communicate well. At the end of this book, there are appendices that provide information resoures which will aid in this communication.

Health insurance is the wave of the future. Today, we spend twice as much per capita as other nations achieving outcomes that are the same.

Rising healthcare costs and a greater number of uninsured Americans are charactreistic of our society today.

David Eddy, M.D., in a speech to the American College of Surgeons, said the following: "For centuries, the practice of medicine has been based on one huge assumption: that physicians instinctively know the right thing to do. That myth has been shattered. We are all coming up with different answers and it is impossible for all of us to be correct. Our practices are way out in front of our intellectual lines of supply."

THE IDENTIFICATION AND BRANDING OF WELLNESS

Hospitals and healthcare systems have become sophisticated users of advertising programs to obtain and maintain market share. Identification with a wellness product is not only fashionable, it appears necessary in order for a healthcare system to survive. Wellness programs that start by providing community education quite often develop into full-fledged programs that blossom into defined product lines for a hospital and necessitate a building to house them. All hospitals interviewed for this book are striving, to one degree or another, to counteract the negative perception of managed care associated with all of healthcare and to create market awareness of wellness programs.

Markets around the country are demographically fragmented, and this is reflected in the speed with which wellness centers as a viable building type are evolving. Suffice it to say that if a market does not have a hospital-based wellness product, it soon will. The greatest regional variation is in program emphasis and the degree to which complementary medical treatment is embraced.

The market penetration of wellness center products appears to be nonlinear, and does not follow the typical four-stage model: emergence, growth, maturity, and decline. For this reason, perhaps, healthcare systems in more conservative markets have been reluctant to join the wellness trend. Market demand, however, seems to be coaxing even the most conservative entities into the fold.

Surprisingly, a number of sophisticated hospital systems have not embraced the concept, yet smaller suburban hospitals have, taking with them the communities they flourish in which they flourish. Individuality appears to be the characteristic of the wellness center product. Unlike the assisted living facility or the freestanding ambulatory care center, the wellness center, because of this individuality, means different things to different people.

There is no cookie-cutter solution for wellness center design, but there are common starting points, definite logic and suggested programs that will help to create the best products for individual markets. Chapter 3 offers guidelines and basic programming advice. Throughout the chapter, there are examples of how others have handled the design challenge, providing insight and allowing some basic conclusions to be drawn. Each center, however, is very individual in its design reflecting the mission of the hospital and the values of the community.

MARKET DEMANDS AND MARKET TRENDS

What is important to healthcare consumers at the turn of the century ?

The Center for Health Design is a nonprofit organization whose mission is to be an industry facilitator, integrator, and accelerator of the widespread development of health-enhancing environments, and to promote the benefits that these environments bring to human wellness, health, and well-being. In December 1997 the preliminary results of a study on American consumers' thoughts and perceptions about the healthcare environment were presented. These findings represent Phase I of a multiyear study begun by the Center for Health Design in conjunction with the Picker Institute in Boston. These initial results were presented in at the Tenth Symposium on Healthcare Design in San Diego, California.

The investigating team organized focus groups consisting of patients and family members at acute care, ambulatory care, and long-term care facilities in Boston, Massachusetts, and St. Paul, Minnesota. They used expert interviews with local architects, design professionals, and healthcare executives, as well as an initial literature review, to serve as resources in planning the focus group interviews. The preliminary results indicated that consumers want a healthcare environment that has the following attributes:

1. Provides a connection to others
2. Is conducive to a sense of well-being
3. Is convenient and accessible
4. Demonstrates caring for the patient's family
5. Is considerate of the patient's impairments
6. Is clear in its expectations
7. Is close to nature

Susan MacRae, R.N., a research and development associate with the Picker Institute, presented these findings at the symposium.

The completed investigation is expected to provide information enabling those who are responsible for making facility decisions in acute care, ambulatory care and long-term care settings to better understand what matters most to consumers. [It is hoped that] by knowing this, those planning facilities can make design decisions that will enhance overall consumer satisfaction and thereby improve the overall quality of care.

Hospital-provided alternative healthcare is a burgeoning market. At California Pacific Hospital in San Francisco, Elisabeth Targ, M.D., heads the Complementary Medicine Research Institute, which studies the effects of alternative therapies on patients suffering from a number of disease constellations.

Last year California Pacific Medical Center was the first in the country to revive the concept of the labyrinth as a tool in healing. Patients are guided through a 36-foot in diameter, one-third mile long series of twists and turns, designed to soothe the mind and spirit and calm the body in times of crisis. The hospital patterned its labyrinth after one built in France in the twelfth century. Committed to serve the community by offering alternative therapies, California Pacific Medical Center is a leader in the country in integrating traditional and complementary medicine.

On the other side of the country, in Baltimore, Maryland, several hospitals are taking steps in the same direction. The St. Joseph Center for Health Enhancement is one year old. Founder Sister Anne P. Hefner says that alternative medicine practices, which she defines as including spirituality, have become popular in Catholic hospitals. She says that the trend makes sense if you look upon Jesus as a healer. "People are looking for something that taps into the spirit."

Sophie Fineran, office manager for St. Joseph's Center, says that she is surprised at the number of older people who participate in programs at the center, taking acupuncture for pain relief and t'ai chi to strengthen their bodies. She surmises that there may always have been interest in complementary medicine, but that many people thought it was inaccessible until now.

At the Life Style Center, one of two wellness centers owned and operated by Chesapeake Hospital in Chesapeake, Virginia, one can see cardiopulmonary rehabilitation patients working out on exercise machines guided by healthcare professionals employed by the hospital. Beth Reitz, M.S., director of the lifestyle center and prominent health educator, says that this group represents a portion of the population that would not otherwise have access to a formal exercise program.

The availability and the legitimizing of complementary medicine therapies has created a market that heretofore did not exist. This is a market segment and healthcare service unaccounted for in traditional hospital planning. People who may not have been served at all by the medical establishment or by the fitness establishment suddenly have easy access to programs in which they have been interested and therapies they have wanted to try.

Greater Baltimore Medical Center in Baltimore, Maryland, has on its main campus the Alternative and Complementary Health Center. In an article in *Baltimore* magazine, Robin Prothro, the center's director, said:

> There is the whole movement toward managed care—people are being encouraged to become more proficient at self-care. There are national presentations like Bill Moyers' mind-body television series. And [there is] that liberated hippie group who are now middle-aged and experiencing health difficulties and [are] open minded enough to say, "I want the best of everything."

What is the profile of the medical professionals who serve in complementary care clinics? More often than not, hospitals train traditional medical professionals to administer nontraditional therapies. For example, hospitals typically hire physician acupuncturists. In Maryland, physicians are required to complete 200 hours of continuing education in order to practice acupuncture; practitioners (healthcare professionals trained only as acupuncturists) are required to have 1,800 hours of training.

Ball State University in Muncie, Indiana, offers a degree in Wellness Management, recognized nationally as an outstanding training program by the Association for Worksite Health Promotion. The Fisher Institute for Wellness, established in 1986, includes programs in wellness management and gerontology, a campus wellness program for university students and faculty, and the Center for Gerontology and maintains the National Wellness Information Center.

Graduates from the Institute receive a master's degree in Wellness Management and are employed by hospitals, health cooperatives, insurance companies, Fortune 500 companies, YMCAs, universities, colleges, and public schools. The emphasis of this program is health of the mind, body, and spirit. Course work includes physical education, health science, nutrition, psychology, communication, and business. It is a truly interesting example of the application of systems theory to human health.

Andrew Weil, M.D., a physician who writes extensively on the subject of nontraditional medicine, recently discussed the delivery of healthcare. He stated that he thinks many hospitals will go bankrupt in the next decade, leaving regional centers with tertiary capability as the primary resource for crisis medicine. He suggests that both doctors and patients should be involved in the decision of which symptoms should direct the patient to conventional or to alternative medicine. He asserts that approximately 20 percent of all patients seen by a physician have conditions that can be healed by complementary medicine.

When asked whether he could see any way in which HMOs could centralize the delivery of healthcare, could become true wellness centers, Weil said that he would like to see a new kind of healthcare facility, whose function falls somewhere between a spa and a hospital. "I think a lot of people who go into hospitals could be much more readily served by a facility of that sort where they could learn about healthy life-styles and come out knowing more than when they went in about how to keep themselves healthy." He further suggests that Germany and Switzerland are ahead of the United States, as in those countries there is a greater interest in natural medicine, more physicians who practice it, and a reimbursement system for stays in spas.

Weil proposes that state regulatory agencies create new ways to examine the practice of alternative medicine. Arizona, where he practices medicine and teaches at the University of Arizona, has liberal laws in regard to the practice of alternative treatments. Arizona is one of two states (the other is Nevada) that have a Homeopathic Board of Examiners from which people practicing nontraditional medicine can obtain licensure. He suggests that state boards engage consultants who are experts in alternative medicine to review those who practice it, so as to prevent nonlegitimate practices.

The *New England Journal of Medicine* recently stated that one of three Americans routinely uses some form of alternative medicine. Representative Peter DeFazio of Oregon's Fourth Congressional District (D) said recently, "Not only do we need comprehensive, quality healthcare for all, but we must generate effective new approaches to treating illness and increase the types of healthcare available." DeFazio is working to increase American's access to nonharmful alternative treatments and by-products by calling for greater healthcare access.

On February 3, 1998, DeFazio introduced legislation giving the Office of Alternative Medicine at the National Institutes of Health authority to provide funding for independent research into alternative healthcare methods. Representative Joe Barton of Texas (R), joined DeFazio and a bipartisan coalition in introducing a bill to give Americans more options in choosing their healthcare.

In a recent speech before the American Preventive Medical Association, DeFazio stated that approximately 90 million Americans suffer from chronic illness, which costs society approximately $659 billion dollars a year in healthcare dollars, lost productivity, and premature death. He points to studies conducted by the Centers for Disease Control (CDC) and the Robert Wood Johnson Foundation pointing out that taxpayers spend $26.6 billion dollars a year on treating diabetes alone. Diabetes, DeFazio says, is a disease that can be treated with low-cost, nonharmful alternative therapies. Medicare has spent $42.5 billion dollars on patients for the treatment of diabetes, and the incidence of diabetes has risen exponentially relative to other diseases.

A Robert Wood Johnson Foundation Study recently published in the *Journal of the American Medical Association* (JAMA) revealed that the current healthcare delivery system is not meeting the needs of the chronically ill in America. The study goes on to conclude that such trends reveal a dysfunctional system of care that perpetuates rising costs, a lack of effective treatments, inadequate research efforts, and a disproportionate number of people needing specialized care. Patients and doctors are demanding more from the current model of care, but are not getting results.

Representative DeFazio asserts that although commercial pharmaceuticals have been proven effective in treating many infectious diseases, they have not proven effective in treating chronic illnesses. He called for the nation to devote more attention developing effective healthcare for patients who do not respond to conventional medicine.

DeFazio is encouraging the National Institutes of Health's (NIH) Office of Alternative Medicine (OAM) to become more proactive and dynamic in its efforts to explore ways in which alternative therapies can relieve the healthcare crisis. He is calling for the OAM to be given the status of a center, which would enable it to administer grants and studies for clinical research on alternative medicine. Center status would also give OAM the degree of autonomy and authority needed to oversee sound scientific research.

He is also examining the way in which the Food and Drug Administration's (FDA) approval process discourages innovation and prevents patients from receiving access to nonharmful, low-cost alternative treatments. Because alternative treatments often include combinations of natural substances and are therefore not eligible to receive a patent, researchers cannot raise the funding they need to perform the studies necessary to submit a treatment to the FDA approval process.

The "Access Bill" that DeFazio proposes would not alter the FDA's mandate to protect the public health and safety, but would open the system to the utilization of low-cost treatments. There is a strict claims restriction in the bill that is designed to make sure there is no incentive for any manufacturer to market a product that has not been approved by the FDA.

An anecdote illustrating the importance of this issue perhaps best tells the story. Former Representative Berkley Bedell contracted Lyme disease, which forced him to leave Congress. He tried several rounds of conventional treatment but these proved to be unsuccessful. Turning to an alternative treatment that involved nothing more than the drinking of processed whey from cow's milk, he was cured. The treatment took two months, and the total cost was no more than a few hundred dollars. Yet, in spite of the effectiveness of this treatment, it can no longer be administered because it has not gone through the FDA approval process.

Educating the public about the politics of medicine and how alternative therapies were heretofore kept out of the mainstream is a subject of its own. The importance here in regard to the development of a wellness center building is that alternative therapies are coming into the mainstream as never before, and a clear view of what within complementary medicine is valuable and what is not is becoming clear.

Moreover, educating physicians about the value of alternative medicine, once a trying process, is now becoming easier, as the value of nontraditional medical practice in the universe of healthcare becomes apparent.

Columbia University in New York City has recently been given a grant to start a center for alternative medicine. At Harvard Medical School, in Cambridge, Massachusetts, the Department of Continuing Education is offering courses for physicians in the area of alternative medicine. The current curriculum includes the folowing courses:

- Clinical Training in Mind Body/Medicine
- Three-Day Training in Mind/Body Medicine
- The Future of Psychotherapy: Integrated healthcare
- Complementary and Alternative Medicine in Rehabilitation
- Spirituality and Healing in Medicine

At the University of Arizona College of Medicine, Andrew Weil, M.D., is starting a program in Integrative Medicine, offering one-year fellowships to people who have completed family practice and internal medicine residencies. They will receive training in how to combine the best ideas of traditional and nontraditional medicine; this program is the first of its kind in the country. According to Weil, there will be a strong emphasis on natural healing, mind-body interactions, and healing in general. He anticipates that this program will grow into a residency program, and eventually, into a track in the medical school curriculum.

HEALTH EDUCATION AND THE PUBLIC

Today's interest in wellness, self-education, and self-care is great, if the evidence supplied by current magazine articles and books can be taken as a measure. The focus on wellness itself implies a proactive, nonpassive way of relating to the healthcare system in general. For this reason, it is important for individual communities to respond to this need for knowledge, supplement the outpouring of information available from all contemporary media, and make an effort to meet the interest of people with action. One way to do this is by developing community-based programs in health education. Not all wellness centers are as active as others in this area. Health education was once purely the milieu of educators in hospitals who created programs that, with tightening budgets, were the first to go. Marketing departments at hospitals often touched on this issue by setting, as part of their mission, a goal to get semihealthy individuals into the hospital environment by offering free blood pressure or diabetes screening, classes on childbirth, or programs for smoking cessation.

Entrance to Lifestyle Health and Fitness, Chesapeake Hospital, Virginia. *Ron Whorley Associates, Architect.*

The thinking was, and in many areas of the country still is, that exposing healthy individuals to the availability of services within the hospital setting is a way of educating the public to services offered by the hospital. Yet this approach does not necessarily educate people in any great depth as to how to take care of themselves, how to prevent disease, or how to stay healthy. A more in-depth definition of health education is needed to keep up with public interest, to serve the community, and to truly effect the improvement of healthcare delivery.

Beth Reitz, M.S., director of Community Health Services, who directs the Lifestyle Health and Fitness Center Program at Chesapeake Hospital, is a leader in developing health education wellness programs. Hospital president Donald Buckley, F.A.C.H.E., is credited by Reitz as having supported the concept of wellness education long before it was fashionable in the acute care environment.

By the broadest definition, preventive medicine includes all areas of practice in medicine, because all physicians have a mission to prevent disease, to keep people well. In recent years preventive medicine has been defined as the prevention of the spread of infectious diseases and has traditionally been the field of medicine concerned with epidemiology. Physicians who practiced preventive medicine have concentrated on populations in danger of contracting and spreading disease.

Even today a physician who specializes in preventive medicine, as defined by the American College of Preventive Medicine, focuses on public health, occupational medicine, or aerospace medicine and works with large population groups to promote health and understand the risks of disease, injury disability, and death, seeking to modify these risks. Doctors specializing in preventive medicine may further specialize in general preventive medicine and focus their skills on health and safety in the workplace. These physicians undertake postgraduate training in any of 85 residency programs accredited by the Accreditation Council for Graduate Medical Education.

The definition of *preventive medicine physician* is becoming increasingly broad; today it includes physicians who are actively engaged in prevention of disease for individuals, rather than just populations. Classically trained physicians, such as leaders in the field of alternative medicine Andrew Weil, M.D., Deepak Chopra, M.D., and Christine Northrup, M.D., are living examples of this broader perspective.

Medical directors are now being selected to direct and manage wellness centers and prevention programs within the acute care hospital setting, as they would any other departmental specialty. Celebration Health Wellness Center in Orlando, Florida, part of the Florida Hospital and Adventist Systems, has a medical director whose specific charge is to manage wellness center activities. Celebration Health Wellness also has its own psychoneuroimmunologist on staff.

The trend toward legitimizing the practice of alternative approaches to medicine and combining these valuable practices with traditional medical practices is the wave of the future. The physician of the future might well be trained in a program like that which Andrew Weil is leading at the University of Arizona School of Medicine. Eventually, we may see the American College of Preventive Medicine recognizing these physicians and their valuable programs, bringing to the community the best healthcare choices available.

NONTRADITIONAL MEDICINE

Preventive medicine physicians, who may be specialists in general preventive medicine, public health, occupational medicine, or aerospace medicine, work with large population groups as well as with individual patients. Their aim is to promote health and understanding of the risks of disease, injury, disability, and death, seeking to modify and eliminate these risks. These are the key players in addressing risk assessment for the global environment, crafting healthcare systems for the future, and working to prevent and control the spread of HIV, tuberculosis, and other diseases.

Physicians in preventive medicine, a medical specialty fully recognized by the American Board of Medical Specialties since 1948, report high and continuing job satisfaction and compensation equal to the earnings of other primary care specialists. There is, however, a serious shortage of physicians in all areas of the specialty.

Those who enter the field of preventive medicine find that it offers rewarding, plentiful, diverse, and challenging careers, as well as the following benefits:

- A chance to make a significant contribution to society
- A wide variety of practice settings
- A balanced and satisfying life-style
- Upward and lateral mobility and advancement

Chesapeake Hospital, the aforementioned 200-bed independent community hospital located in the Tidewater area of southern Virginia, started its wellness program in 1988, designing a small fitness center adjacent to the main hospital building. In 1996, the hospital expanded its health education programs and its hospital campus wellness facility and established an additional, freestanding 44,000-square-foot facility, Western Branch, 20 miles from the hospital campus.

The importance of this hospital's efforts in developing programs for community wellness lies in its uniquely designed health education component. Along with weight training areas, machines, and aerobics rooms, Director Reitz has included in her program four classrooms in each of the facilities, intended solely for educating the community on matters of health.

Reitz has even designed a computer lab area where patients and members can conduct research on the Internet, guided by a health educator who has developed links into Internet sites that supply valuable information regarding healthcare issues in which the member may be interested.

Living with Diabetes is a diabetes education program at Chesapeake. Certified diabetes educators work closely with all diabetes patients, and continuing education is available in a program called "Diabetes University." This four-part series teaches the basics of diabetes self-management and complication prevention. (It is important to note that most insurance programs offer 80 percent reimbursement for classes.)

Located within the Lifestyle, Health, and Fitness center adjacent to the hospital is a diabetes store that sells diabetes supplies: meters, strips, and cookbooks. In addition, the chief hospital dietician holds cooking classes that have become so popular that Director Reitz has had to develop additional class times. Community members, even those not involved in diabetes care with a family member, are enjoying these classes. Adults' and children's support groups for people living with diabetes, as well as personal counseling, are available through the health education programs offered at the wellness center.

Another major program at most facilities is cardiac rehabilitation. This program is, generally, along with physical therapy, a primary program included in the wellness center complement of services.

At Chesapeake Hospital the Cardiac Rehabilitation Program involves exercise, education, and counseling. Often, wellness centers offer cardiac rehabilitation as a clinical service, but neglect or downplay the educational side of the equation. Key components of Chesapeake's Cardiac Rehabilitation Program are education and counseling in a group setting, as well as exercise. The program is self-reinforcing. Cardiac rehabilitation patients derive benefit from the group counseling setting, and group members encourage one another, reinforcing the exercise program. One patient, in the program since October 1996, says he works out five days a week and looks forward to spending time with people in his group. "I've been able to keep up faithfully with my workouts because of the other people," he said. "Cardiac rehabilitation has helped me both mentally and physically. Mentally, I feel much better about myself, and, physically, I am taking better care of my body and have a lot more energy."

This patient works out at the wellness center in a specially designated area for cardiac patients, who work under the supervision of a healthcare provider. Adjacent to this area is a general membership workout area that serves the general public. In this center, the areas are visually separated by a movable partition, which enables the center to open all equipment to the general members at times when cardiac rehabilitation patients are not exercising.

The rehabilitation program addresses the physical, nutritional, and vocational needs of the patient. Key to the program's success is the supervised, regular progression of activity designed to strengthen the cardiovascular system as well as increase muscular strength and flexibility. Benefits to the patient include loss of body fat, lowered blood pressure, lowered blood cholesterol, and increased tolerance to stress. The phases of treatment include the following:

- *Phase I*. In-hospital education and low-level exercise, designed to identify the risk factors associated with heart disease and begin rehabilitation from the cardiac event.
- *Phase II–III*. A natural progression from the inpatient program. More in-depth and structured exercise and an educational program designed to help the patient control the disease. Enrollment in Phase II–III requires a physician's referral and includes individual exercise prescriptions and guidelines, group exercise sessions with warm-up and cool-down periods, aerobic circuit exercise, weight and flexibility training, and continuous or intermittent heart and symptom monitoring during exercise by the hospital's rehabilitation staff. There are educational sessions on medications, risk factors, smoking cessation, stress management, and exercise safety. This phase lasts from 6 to 13 weeks, three days per week, one hour each, with an additional one-hour lecture each week.
- *Phase IV*. Phase IV is a higher-level cardiac fitness and maintenance schedule designed for graduates of Phase II–III and people with cardiac risk factors. The Phase IV program meets at various times during the week and is supplemented with ongoing lectures and intermittent monitoring of vital signs during exercise.

Weight training at Chesapeake Lifestyle Health and Fitness, Chesapeake, Virginia. *Ron Worley Associates, Architect.*

Cardiac rehabilitation programs such as this are typically reimbursed by most insurance companies.

Chesapeake Hospital's cardiac program, developed by Beth Reitz, is a supervised exercise and education program for people who want to exercise but who have special needs or risk factors or desire individual attention. Exercise specialists evaluate fitness levels, discuss goals, and design individualized programs. A staff member monitors blood pressure and acts as an informational resource.

Chesapeake Hospital also has programs for maternal/child health and women's health. Like many other programs focused on women's health, it offers information and guidance in regard to breast health, menopause, and prevention of osteoporosis.

In January 1998, the state of New Hampshire's legislature was expected to confirm a vote to study a measure that would involve reevaluating its naturopathic licensing law. There are bills in the New Jersey State Senate, currently being contested, which discriminate against nutrition counselors, consultants, and educators involved in the field of integrative medicine. Lobbying groups that support research and the dissemination of information regarding good practices for complementary medicine practitioners are enthusiastically working at the local, state, and federal levels to increase awareness of the benefits of alternative medicine and the value of mainstreaming it into the American culture.

The National Library of Medicine and the Medical Subject Headings Term Working Office of Alternative Medicine, both located within the National Institutes of Health, classify alternative medicine as "an unrelated group of nonorthodox therapeutic practices, often with explanatory systems that do not follow conventional medical explanations." This definition is a departure from the National Library of Medicine's original classification, which was "nonorthodox therapeutic systems which have no satisfactory scientific explanation for their effectiveness."

The Office of Alternative Medicine (OAM) was established by Congress in 1992 within the National Institutes of Health. OAM operates as an intermediary between the alternative medical community and the federal research and regulatory communities.

As interest in alternative (or complementary or integrative) medicine increases, strategies are beginning to evolve that not only reinforce the growth and value of wellness centers, but provide new ways of targeting and managing income streams for nontraditional medical care. Growing consumer confidence in alternative therapies has sparked the interest of insurance companies, and new insurance companies have been formed to take an early lead in what is potentially an extremely lucrative market for investors.

The following is a sampling of insurance plans that now cover alternative therapies, some more generously than others:

American Western Life Insurance Wellness Plan   In operation since 1993, this comprehensive plan that emphasizes preventive care is available only to residents of California, Utah, Colorado, New Mexico, and Arizona who are less than 65 years old. Members pay what they would for a standard managed care plan and are covered for major medical expenses, hospitalization, prescription drugs, lab tests, and surgery. However, they also are covered for up to 12 visits per year each to a variety of alternative healthcare providers, including naturopaths, chiropractors, homeopaths, acupuncturists, ayurvedic doctors*, nutritionists, massage therapists, hypnotherapists, and others. The plan also pays for vitamins and herbal and homeopathic supplements when prescribed by these practitioners.

A special feature of this plan is the Wellness Line, a 24-hour hot line that offers phone consultations with a health professional who can suggest natural self-care remedies for minor complaints or recommend an appropriate specialist if the situation is more serious. The staff is also trained to advise members about the side effects of prescription drugs and how to choose vitamins. This part of the plan is available nationwide for a small monthly fee. *100 Foster City Boulevard, Foster City, CA 94040. 800-925-5323.*

Health Partners Health Plan offers plans which cover alternative therapies.

Alternative Health Plan   Available to subscribers nationwide, this plan comprises a wide range of conventional and alternative healthcare providers, including those practicing acupuncture, ayurvedic medicine, homeopathy, naturopathy, chiropractic, and traditional Chinese medicine. Vitamins are not covered, but the plan does pay up to $500 a year for homeopathic and herbal remedies prescribed by a "licensed physician." Up to 12 visits per year to a bodyworker** are also covered if prescribed by a physician. *P.O. Box 6279, Thousand Oaks, CA 91359-6279. 800-966-8467.*

Mutual of Omaha   Impressed with the cost-cutting potential of Dean Ornish's life-style heart disease reversal program, Mutual began covering the $5,500 program more than two

---

*Medical system developed in India.
**Bodyworker is a healthcare practitioner specializing in healing through Feldenkrais massage or other physical therapy modalities.

years ago and is very pleased with the results. Company officials estimate that they have already saved $6.50 for every dollar paid to subscribers, and because of the repeated operations required by many bypass patients, the Ornish approach could eventually save them up to 20 cents on the dollar. At present Mutual also reimburses for chiropractic visits and some acupuncture. *Mutual of Omaha Plaza, Omaha, NE 68175. 402-342-7600.*

CommonWell Health Plan This comprehensive preventive and wellness plan has been available in eastern Massachusetts since early in 1996. It offers benefits for conventional, complementary, and alternative healthcare services. In addition it offers Wellness Education Seminars covering nutrition, fitness, and stress management. Members can access information on appropriate self-care or referral to an alternative or conventional provider through a 24-hour toll-free number. *P.O. Box 1705, Brookline, MA 02146. 617-566-9355.*

In metropolitan Washington, D.C., a company has been created solely to take advantage of the alternative care market. "Society is changing, and more people are more interested in alternative care than they have been in the past, due maybe to some fantasized expectations," said Charles Duvall, M.D., a Washington-based internist who is a member of the District of Columbia Medical Society. There is a growing awareness and this new group has identified a niche and a way of repackaging a smorgasbord of medically related services.

The group is now building alternative healthcare facilities in four states. Each facility has 12,000 to 15,000 square feet of clinical space, which is divided among doctors, chiropractors, acupuncturists, massage and physical therapists. Owner Mark Pacala's background is the hospitality industry, and he intends to bring that service-oriented focus to healthcare.

In the world of managed care, the primary care doctor is the gatekeeper, the primary player in the referral chain. The importance of such physicians is not to be overlooked. Primary care doctors refer patients to hospitals and specialists. Hospital systems typically buy up smaller physicians' groups to increase inpatient revenue and to ameliorate their negotiating position with managed care companies.

A rule of thumb is that a single primary care physician represents roughly a half million dollars worth of inpatient care annually. Paul Katz, M.D., chairman of Georgetown University's Department of Medicine, said in a recent newspaper interview, "For every dollar billed by a primary care doctor, six dollars are billed downstream either from inpatient business, referrals, or other services stemming from the patient's primary care visit. As primary care physicians align themselves with wellness centers or collocate medical office buildings with wellness centers, they are reinforcing the income stream." We can see why the wellness center as a freestanding entity becomes increasingly important.

Wellness centers provide hospitals and hospital systems with for-profit income. Although not all wellness centers are for-profit facilities, the number of for-profit centers is on the rise. In a *Chicago Tribune* article dated February 9, 1997, Arthur Knueppel, president and chief executive officer of St. Lawrence Hospital in Lansing, Michigan, spoke of the success of St. Lawrence's Healthplex wellness center, which opened in 1992. The Healthplex idea originated in Michigan when Michigan State University received a large grant to house a biomechanics laboratory.

Steve Robbins, executive director of Crozer-Keystone Hospital's wellness center in Springfield, Pennsylvania, who helped develop the Lansing facility, said that the idea in Lansing was to "meld sports medicine with a large outpatient center and diagnostic areas to create a sort of medical mall. After that, we would implement phase two, an outpatient surgical center, a birthing center, and some inpatient beds to create a hospital without walls."

Robbins continued this idea as he helped Crozer-Keystone develop the Springfield Healthplex. "Since the end of World War II, this country has done a great job at creating a sick care system. We're great with crisis and emergency care, but few health systems really practice healthcare," he remarked.

CEO and president of Crozer-Keystone John C. McMeekin said recently,

> I remember the Pennsylvania Railroad. They went under because they thought they were in the railroad business, instead of realizing they were in the transportation business. If we only see ourselves as an industry that treats the sick and injured, healthcare is going to be a very difficult and challenging business...
>
> This concept of a Healthplex is centered around healthy behavior. It came about when we tried to define where our business was going and what our business really was. We're an industry that has always taken care of the sick and injured. Now we are beginning to see ourselves as a system concerned with the health of the population as well as caring for the sick. There is greater emphasis now, due largely to increased managed care, on keeping the population healthy, independent, and out of the hospital. This is where healthcare is headed.

St. Lawrence was expected to generate $1.8 million in revenue its first year, resulting in a deficit of $414,000. The projection was $2.5 million for the second year, with a profit of $109,000, and for 1996, revenues of $3.2 million and a profit of $373,000.

St. Lawrence Center actually brought in $3.8 million the first year, with a deficit of $159,000. Second year revenues totaled $4.1 million, with a profit of $327,000. Last year, revenues reached $6 million, with a profit of $840,000. Membership is at 3,953 people, and St. Lawrence is expanding.

With more than 50 hospital-based wellness centers in Illinois, it is not surprising that the concept has sparked the interest and support of the financial community. The Citadel Group, which finances the construction of ambulatory care and other medical facilities, was quoted in the Chicago Tribune, February 9, 1996 article as saying that Citadel is "pregnant in" this trend. Citadel has put $84 million toward four centers in the past four years. "We thought this is just like when hospitals originally got into the long-term care business, and they didn't know what they were doing," said David Varwig, senior managing director and chief executive of the Citadel Group.

Varwig relates the growing number of hospital-based wellness centers to hospitals' desire for the latest in medical technology, such as magnetic resonance imaging devices: "If their neighbors are doing it [establishing wellness centers] and it's working, they'll do it."

According to a survey conducted by Harvard Medical School physician David Eisenberg and published in the *New England Journal of Medicine* in 1993, one in three Americans used an alternative therapy, there were an estimated 425 million visits to alternative providers, and $13.7 billion were spent, only 25 percent of which was covered by insurance. $12.8 billion was spent out of pocket for hospital stays.

In the southwest, the University of Arizona has established a program in integrative medicine, among the first of its kind in the country to incorporate alternative with traditional medicine. There are now 42 medical schools offering some type of integrative therapies, and approximately 137 hospitals nationwide include integrative medicine therapies alongside traditional or hard medicine. In a concept pioneered by the Planetree group in San Francisco, California, Mid Columbian Hospital in The Dalles, Oregon, is one of a few hospitals that has embraced integrative medicine totally.

The American Hospital Association recently reflected on its 100-year anniversary and how a century of serving the nation has been electrified by change in the hospital industry. In an article in *Modern Healthcare* (January 26, 1998) there was a discussion of a task force put together by the Florida Hospital

Garden on Big Island, Hawaii.

Association. The task force issued a 41-page report "to help hospitals concretely measure what they are doing for their communities." The report stated that hospitals should begin now to design and address community needs and to implement new community benefit programs. It cautioned hospitals to document and quantify those community benefits. "The exercise is touted as a way to survive the healthcare changes of the time, including shrinking inpatient stays, increasing competition, and demands from the public that outcomes data be made available." As of this writing, short stays include, for example, an approximate length of stay for kidney transplant patients of less than four days, according to Thomas Peters, M.D., of the Methodist Jackson Transplant Center in Jacksonville, Florida.

Whether a hospital is a for-profit, a nonprofit, or a not-for-profit facility, the symbolic nature of the institution as the centerpiece of the community can be used to the industry's advantage and benefit the community as well. If programs of health education expand, growing out of small programs for smoking cessation and weight control, and if they blossom fully into community-centered active programs, with local chefs holding cooking classes, exercise physiologists and personal trainers demonstrating how they have built strength in older women who had osteoporosis, and kid fitness programs are available that use interactive learning programs to develop hand-eye coordination, balance, rhythm, and control, they would become the dynamic focus of the hospital community.

Encouraging this concept, which speaks to the spirit, as well as the body and the mind, can revolutionize the way citizens view healthcare.

In 1988, Presbyterian Behavioral Health opened its Center for Integrative Medicine in Charlotte, North Carolina. The center offers alternative healing options. Patients may engage in touch therapy, yoga, stress management courses, meditation, and hypnotherapy. The Duke Endowment has given the center a grant of $100 milion.

Griffin Health Services Corporation, the parent company of Griffin Hospital in Shelton, Connecticut, plans to build a $10 million health and fitness center that will include two pools, a track, a fitness room and a gymnasium. Griffin president John Bustelos has remarked, "The Center continues Griffin's transformation from a hospital to a health system focused on providing preventive and wellness services which enhance life, as well as restore the life of the ill."

A GENERATION OF CHANGE

H. Popik, M.D., of Cigna Healthcare was quoted in a recent article, "Alternative Medicine Moves into the Mainstream": "Consumers want high touch medicine… alternative medicine represents that and traditional medicine has gotten away from it."

A recent study conducted by Press/Ganey Associates, a South Bend, Indiana, consulting firm, illustrates that individuals born between 1946 and 1964, the so-called baby boom generation, are not satisfied with their healthcare services. Data were analyzed for more than one million patients, which

showed that older people were generally more satisfied. According to Press/Ganey, baby boomers' mean satisfaction levels were 87 out of a 100, as compared with mean satisfaction levels for older patients, which ranged from 88 to 90.

The advent of the new information age made possible by the Internet should, in theory, create a better-informed healthcare consumer. Not all individuals seek this method of investigating healthcare options for themselves. With that in mind, it is still important to realize that the consumer is assaulted with information from media of all kinds. In terms of helpful print material available, there is a constant stream of health-related books and magazines being produced in this country, many of which reinforce the concept of self-responsibility in healthcare choices. There is much good information available, but the consumer must take responsibility for his or her own search for knowledge.

With the information readily available to an individual on any given day, a person may be able to investigate the best possible program for diabetes management, find a physician who accepts a particular managed care plan, and engage in an electronic exchange of knowledge with a number of credible, and sometimes incredible, sources. In her Community Health Education Program at Chesapeake Hospital, Beth Reitz is creating a computer access room at one of the hospital's two wellness centers, where patients and members can be linked to the best health-related sites under Reitz's guidance.

KPMG Peat Marwick Healthcare conducted a study with Northwestern University, which was mentioned recently in *Modern Healthcare* magazine. The study, which canvassed 321 executives at 70 leading healthcare organizations nationwide, showed that Americans are making more demands about healthcare and the business of how it is delivered.

Quoted in the article, Senior Vice President Kathy Swenson of Kaiser Permanente, an Oakland, California-based company, said that change is occurring because consumers are shouldering more of their own healthcare costs, employers are giving them more choices, and there has been a consumer backlash against managed care.

The study found that across the industry most healthcare executives believe consumer demands are increasingly influencing the business decisions made by healthcare companies, in areas ranging from policy and strategy to investment decisions. The article further pointed out that, in general, where populations are denser, there is less emphasis on patient education (this notion has been borne out in the research for this book), but there are certain densely populated pockets of the country that are advanced in patient/community health education. One such area is Atlanta, Georgia, where Emory University operates a mini-medical school that educates patients about the healthcare process. Randy Martin, M.D., associate dean for clinical development at Emory Healthcare, remarked, "The educated patient is a good doctor's best weapon to keep that patient well."

Approximately 50 percent of all insured Americans received healthcare through managed care organizations in 1997. The American Osteopathic Association (AOA) defines the different types of managed care delivery systems as follows:

Health maintenance organization (HMO). Provides coverage of agreed-upon health services needed by plan members for a fixed, prepaid premium. There are four basic models of HMOs: group model, individual practice association, network model, and staff model.

- The group model HMO involves contracts with physicians organized into groups, who receive a fixed payment per patient to provide specific services. These physicians typically see only HMO patients.
- The individual practice association (IPA) model HMO involves contracts with independent physicians who work in their own private practices and see fee-for-service patients as well as HMO patients.
- The network model HMO involves contracts with multiple physicians groups, sometimes with multiple specialties. Physicians work in their own offices and may also treat fee-for-service patients.
- The staff model HMO employs physicians to provide healthcare to its members. The HMO rewards physicians with salary and incentive programs.

Preferred provider organization (PPO). Contracts are established with care givers, referred to as preferred providers. Usually, the benefit contract requires significantly less copayment for services received from preferred providers so as to motivate enrollees to use these providers.

Exclusive provider organization (EPO). Similar to a preferred provider organization; however, whereas a PPO provides coverage for nonpreferred provider services, as well as provider services, an EPO reimburses only for services rendered by a preferred provider.

Point of Service Plan (POS). This plan structure allows the patient to decide at the time of service whether to choose a participating or nonparticipating provider; there are different levels of benefits associated with using the participating providers. The plan may be delivered in several ways:

- An HMO may permit limited services from nonparticipating providers.
- An HMO may offer a supplemental major medical policy to provide nonparticipating member benefits.
- A PPO may be used to provide both participating and nonparticipating coverage.
- Various combinations of these services may be used.

The AOA also neatly describes the basic current methods of healthcare services reimbursement as the following:

Explanation of benefits (EOB). The statement sent to patients by their health plans listing services provided, amount billed, and payment made.

Capitation (CAP). A fixed dollar amount established to cover the cost of healthcare delivered for a person, usually paid monthly to a healthcare provider. The provider is responsible for providing all health services required by the covered person under the conditions of the provider contract.

Fee maximum. The highest amount a provider may be paid for a specific healthcare service provided to a person on conditions as set forth in a contract.

Fee schedule. A listing of codes and related services with fixed payment amounts, which can be percentages of billings' flat rates or maximum allowable rates.

Fee-for-service equivalency. The difference between the amount a provider receives from an alternative reimbursement system such as capitation versus fee-for-service payment.

Modified fee for service. A policy that pays providers on a fee-for-service basis; however, there are maximums for each procedure.

Prospective reimbursement. Any method of paying hospitals or other healthcare providers for a defined period of time, usually one year, based on a fixed rate agreed upon in advance.

Reasonable and customary (R&C). The commonly charged or prevailing fees for health services within a specific geographic region. A fee is deemed reasonable if it falls within the limits of the average or commonly charged fee for that service for that specific community.

Resource-based relative value scale (RBRVS). Introduced by HCFA, this fee schedule reimburses physicians' Medicare fees based on the amount of time and resources expended in treating patients, with adjustments made for overhead costs and geographical differences.

It is obvious from the preceding description of healthcare delivery systems that there is a business incentive in this country to keep people well. Managed care, good or bad, is fueling the drive toward wellness; thus the concept of alternative treatments and the development of wellness centers as a building type created to house that need.

If capitation allows a certain amount of healthcare dollars to be reimbursed to the healthcare professional and/or healthcare institution, whether the capitated dollar comes from private sources, managed care organizations, or the federal government, the resulting economic force is the same. Keeping people well keeps dollars in the pockets of providing companies and the government. Dollars kept in the hands of the government and lower healthcare costs should have a beneficial effect on the overall American economy.

One in three Americans utilizes alternative therapies, and more than 50 percent of HMOs in this country intend to offer alternative therapies within the next two years. Alternative therapy patients tend not to be members of managed care groups, and they tend to be healthier as a group, paying more than 70 percent of their medical expenses out of pocket. These findings point to an underserved market, ready for responsive managed care companies to enter the arena, offering benefits to this population segment while increasing their healthcare delivery market share.

The revolution in electronics and communication in the twentieth century has forever altered the way we live. The next century promises further acceleration in the improvement of all sorts of technologies. The delivery of healthcare is advanced with each technological improvement and so, also, is the benefit to the consumer/patient.

Standard diagnostic and treatment techniques in the medical center have changed, allowing services to be provided outside the usual places. Surgery, as well as cardiopulmonary rehabilitation, and physical and occupational therapy are often provided on an outpatient basis. Certain techniques, such as endoscopy, perform the same function that invasive surgery used to, at a reduction of cost to the hospital, patient, and third-party payer. Outpatient surgery and endoscopic procedures can often be practiced more economically in a setting off the main hospital campus and can, therefore, make more money for the hospital, physicians, and third-party payers.

The key to the change is technology, and the trend will continue. In the wellness center setting it means that procedures and therapies that were once the product of inpatient, hospital-based practices are moving to ambulatory care buildings and multiuse off-campus buildings such as wellness centers.

Within the wellness center, advanced information systems are revolutionizing the industry. One program links fitness machines with computers, creating interactive data programs that give a clear, precise picture of how the patient/member is using the machine. This enables the machine itself to coach patients and members who follow an exercise prescription, which provides motivation and a self-reinforcing feedback loop to exercisers. An additional benefit to patients is that their physicians and therapists can download information about their progress, allowing the physicians and therapists to adjust the exercise therapy programs and provide better, more individualized, and more specialized care to their patients. (This particular system is capable of detecting changes in range of motion of 0.1 inches every 40 seconds).

The link between monitored exercise machines and medical information systems is where the revolution begins. The information link will serve as a conduit of data, linking the fitness element of the wellness program to the healthcare system. Cardiopulmonary patients, as well as physical and occupational therapy patients and others, will benefit by the additional flow of information.

Insurers and other third-party payers will also have a new data link that provides additional information for patient profiles. The Fitlinxx program developed by Keith Camhi of Stamford, Connecticut, offers a computer data link between patients and physical therapists, providing information that allows a therapist to better manage staff time without sacrificing the quality of care. The fitness information link thus helps in the allocation of resources, and in every healthcare setting, saving FTE time helps to maintain the profit center of the system. Detailed patient programs, coupled with outcomes data, allow support of a variety of protocols designed for people with widely diverse needs.

Measurement of outcomes, another feature of such programs, provides physicians and managed care companies with

Model of Yon Sei Hospital and Wellness Center, Seoul, Korea. *Ellerbe Becket Architects.*

vital information. Patient followup, predictably hard to determine once a patient is discharged from a formal physical therapy program, now becomes manageable. The patient also benefits in being able to relate to and maintain a sense of control over a continuing physical therapy program and transitioning into a lifetime fitness program.

Systems such as this can be retrofitted into existing wellness center fitness areas and health clubs; they can also help to reduce administrative costs. This creates design options for hospitals. Suppose for instance, that a hospital system is unable to build a new wellness center but wants to take the first step in exploring this revenue stream. The hospital could retrofit an existing health club with this sort of computerized system, add a series of examination and treatment rooms, create aerobics and locker room areas, and begin functioning. Once the revenue stream is established and the added value created by the wellness program begins to gain credibility with hospital management, expansion of the center is the next step.

As hospital programs continue to move outward from the acute hospital setting, information system links will tie them together into a virtual hospital. We have already seen this trend grow by leaps and bounds.

However, there have been setbacks in the trend toward integration of medical information systems. Hospital system clients continue to be dismayed at the lack of communication among all of the information systems within a given facility and/or system. As this dilemma is resolved and another element of information, the fitness link, is established, the possibilities of success and advancement in the industry are great.

As advances in medical imaging technology continue, digital information can be added to the medical profile of a patient. In a wellness center, digital mammography results can be communicated over fiber-optic or phone lines.

Because digital information can be transmitted easily, as in the preceding example (being used at this writing at Disney's Celebration Health Wellness Center in Florida), many more hospital-based programs can be delivered in the outpatient setting, and the wellness center can be solidly established as the final link in the continuum of care.

In Denmark, the Institute of Electronic Systems (IES) is conducting research on spoken language processing, imaging, and medical information. Its Medical Decision Support System Group researches tools to support complex decision making. The group has developed several successful medical decision support systems, including human-computer interaction issues.

This group asserts that "intellimedia" systems, systems that integrate interface components and the underlying knowledge structure, will play a central role in the dissemination of medical information. Advanced medical diagnostics systems, virtual operating rooms, and telemedical praxis will require use of knowledge-based techniques for efficient interfacing.

HCFA statistics illustrate the change in the utilization of healthcare services. For example, they show that discharges from acute care hospitals numbered 10.5 million in 1990, and in 1995 there were 11.7 million. The days of care recorded for this time period show that in 1990 there were 94 million care days, and in 1995 there were 83 million persons with average lengths of stay reduced to 7.1 million in 1995 from a previous 9 million in 1990.

Persons served by Medicare in skilled nursing facilities numbered 252,000 in 1982, increasing to a record 1,068,000 in 1994. The following table shows the costs for total healthcare spending in the U.S. in 1994, including that for skilled nursing.

This trend will continue as the baby boom generation matures and retires. As healthcare technology continues to improve the quality of life for many Americans and as we become a nation that stays healthier longer in life than most other countries in the world, there will be an obvious impact on the ability of both private insurers and the federal government to manage a growing group of individuals who will enter the system in the next several years.

Healthcare Spending in the U.S. (1994)

Item	Amount ($ Billion)
Gross domestic product (current dollars)	7180.7
Percent gross domestic product	21%
Department of Health and Human Services	665.2
HCFA Budget	
Medicare benefit payments	176.9
Medicaid medical assistance payments	85.4
HCFA program management	2.1
State and local administration/training	3.7
Other administrative expenses	0.9
Peer review organizations	0.2
Total (unadjusted)	269.2
Offsetting and proprietary receipts	-20.2
Total net of offsetting and proprietary receipts	248.9
Percent of federal budget	16.4%

To ensure a that good quality of life for aging Americans, as well as all Americans, is consistent with our national ability to solve problems and advance the world culture, we must apply our knowledge to advancing and improving our healthcare system. This can only be done by encouraging and supporting the cultural trend toward self-care, fitness, and preventive medicine by reimbursing medical programs that attack potential problems before they start.

Educational programs on preventive medicine and fitness depend largely on the private sector to encourage their growth. Fully integrating preventive medicine and complementary therapies into mainstream medicine, along with federal support of such programs, will reduce the healthcare bills the country will be facing in the future. It is common sense to sanction and support integrative medicine, as the result can only be a healthier nation and world.

Hospitals in even the most conservative areas of the country are beginning to follow this trend. Integrative medicine is no longer a west-to-east trend, as has so often been the case with healthcare development in recent years; rather, it is springing up in pocket areas of the country.

There appears to be no geographic pattern to this integration of alternative therapies into mainstream medicine.

Certainly, the NIH Office of Alternative Medicine has lent a sense of credibility to the study of such programs. But the fact remains that in a society such as ours, what ultimately rises to the top in terms of trends, especially in regard to healthcare, is what makes sense.

The Seventh Day Adventist Church and its worldwide hospital affiliations have had an early lead in this country in the delivery of holistic healthcare. In Adventist-sponsored hospitals and affiliates around the world, the food service provides only vegetarian meals, in keeping with the Adventist preferred diet. We see this as an early trend in combining traditional medical care, often the best available, with simple nutrition programs whose health benefits in recent years have been discovered by the popular culture.

Consistent with its mission to serve humanity by improving the quality of healthcare, the Adventist Healthcare System includes a wellness and prevention corporate division that specializes in reaching out to other hospitals, corporations, and communities, developing courses and programs such as Disease Management, Comprehensive Health Risk Analysis, Lipid Profiles, Massage Therapy, Nutrition Seminars, Fitness Program Jump Start, and "Ask a Doctor" lectures. The Adventist Healthcare System has become involved in the design and development of wellness centers across the country and is part of the Celebration Health Medical Center Development in Orlando, Florida. In suburban Washington, D.C., the Shady Grove Adventist Hospital is planning a wellness center as part of the growth of its suburban Rockville, Maryland, campus.

TELEMEDICINE

Because advances in technology allow for such diverse applications of healthcare technology, we can easily demonstrate yet another example of trending away from the hospital setting. As the delivery of healthcare takes on new meaning in the new century, the movement toward new types of facilities, primarily outpatient, is supported by telemedicine, achieved by the technology, of stringing a network of fiber-optic cables.

Telemedicine links healthcare professionals with patients in remote locations. This is a bona fide adjunct to the full spectrum of healthcare delivery. It allows physicians and other medical professionals to diagnose and treat patient populations that would otherwise go unserved or underserved.

No longer is telemedicine merely the stepchild of the healthcare delivery process. According to an article by Deborah R. Dakins in *Telemedicine* magazine, the number of sites reporting use of telemedicine increased by 62 percent between 1995 and 1996. Dakins notes that there are 117 sites across the United States that are actively using telemedicine to deliver clinical care. In addition, she says, an increasing number of hospitals are investing their own funds in telemedicine networks and equipment. The use of telemedicine by large urban hospitals is on the rise.

The Mayo Clinic employs telemedicine technology for remote echocardiography, as do Massachusetts General Hospital, Duke University Medical Center, Johns Hopkins, and Stanford University.

Whether the implications of telemedicine greatly impact the strategies of managed care providers is yet to be seen. We do know that, as of this writing, Medicaid reimbursement for services furnished through telemedicine applications is available in some states. This is a cost-effective alternative to in-person examinations. Physician and nurse practitioner time is utilized more productively, and the savings in travel costs to patients, particularly residents of rural communities, are significant.

Federal requirements must be satisfied in regard to efficiency, economy, and quality of care provided through telemedicine. To meet these requirements, individual states may interpret federal law as to innovative payment methodologies.

The healthcare Financing Administration (HFCA) is the regulatory federal agency within the Department of Health and Human Services whose mission is to act as a purchaser of healthcare services for Medicare and Medicaid beneficiaries and to establish policies for the reimbursement of healthcare providers.

HCFA conducts research on the effectiveness of different methods of healthcare management, treatment, and financing, and it assesses the quality of healthcare facilities and services.

The HCFA urges states to investigate methods of payment in regard to telemedicine application. It is possible for states to be reimbursed for the patient at one end of the process, and the physician at the other end. States can also, according to HCFA , reimburse any additional cost such as technical support, line charges, and depreciation of equipment. Medicaid reimbursement for telemedicine is available in Arkansas, California, Georgia, Iowa, Montana, North Dakota, South Dakota, Virginia, and West Virginia.

HCFA's vision for the future is to guarantee equal access for all Americans to quality healthcare. It is well within the design of this mission, one would think, to provide preventive guidance to all Americans to better their health by taking ownership of the process.

COMPLEMENTARY MEDICINE

"The doctor of the future will give no medicine but will interest his patients in the care of the human frame, in diet, and in the cause and prevention of disease" so said Thomas Edison.

The forces that have led to the paradigm shift in the delivery of healthcare are many. In terms of the built environment, we have seen the evolution of this change in thinking reflected in the way we build.

The familiar pattern is that of healthcare architecture as monuments: institutions resembling the cold, utilitarian clinics of the 1930's where, it was generally perceived, one went when something in one's body or mind needed to be fixed. The end of the twentieth century has brought us a new way of perceiving and managing this part of human life. This new concept, wellness, is shifting our perception of how we relate to the medical community and to our own health.

The concept is not really new, but its current application is. The idea of the physician's role guardian of one's health began many centuries ago in China and is reflected in the practice of Chinese medicine today. The basic tenet of Eastern medicine is that the physician should be paid to keep a person well, through a series of office visits, and is charged with examining the individual's entire being—detecting and interpreting, at early stages, discomfort, blockages in energy, nutritional deficits, and the mental and emotional states that are present or evolving—in order to diagnose and predict possible outcomes. Through this early warning system, it is posited, an unhealthful condition can be altered before it blossoms into a disease state.

The Chinese physician practices medicine by unique forms of physical diagnosis. An examination of the eyes of an individual, for example, can prove most revealing to the Chinese doctor. Observing the eyes closely, the physician sees a small universe of signs that tell a story about the person's state of health. The eye is a map which, when correctly and sensitively interpreted, holds the keys to a possible future problem and the logical immediate preventive solution.

The holistic philosophy of Chinese medicine demands that a person be healed in a holistic way, and, through determining the optimal state, it is thought that the person can then fight off a possible disease threat. Chinese remedies and special foods help to create the optimum regulation of this internal state, and, it is thought, when balance is achieved, disease flows away from its human host.

Eastern medicine views aging and longevity differently as well. It is acknowledged in the Eastern view that people do not die from old age but from diseases. Diseases speed up the aging process and shorten life expectancy. The aging process itself, a generalized slowing down of all metabolic processes, sets the stage for the onset of disease. Thus, maintenance of the immune system by sparking the system through the wise use of nutrients, exercise, and right thinking keeps the machine active, deterring the onset of disease and, therefore, slowing the aging process.

Diseases such as the common cold are treated with balancing foods, including herbs. Treatment of chronic diseases such as gastritis are treated similarly, as are low and high blood pressure. Chinese medical treatment does not include the addition of vitamins per se but does include food and herbs that contain the vitamins needed by the person to bolster the immune system in ways specific to the ailment.

In the western world, diabetes is thought to be caused by abnormalities in the regulation of insulin produced by the pancreas, owing to a genetic disorder, inflammation, or malignant invasion. Eastern medicine begins by ameliorating certain tendencies of the person so genetically predisposed: limitation of the intake of sweet foods, avoidance of alcohol and caffeine, and limitation of fatigue and mental stress.

If signs of diabetes appear in a patient at an advanced age, certain herbs and foods are prescribed. Often, as is the case with the discovery of aspirin, these herbs and foods contain elements that Western medicine later isolates in research, sanctions, and then promotes as pharmaceutical remedies. Chinese medicine has long prescribed the eating of liver for the prevention of night blindness; it is only within the past 50 years that vitamin A, found in abundance in the liver, has been found to be useful in preventing this disease.

Homeopathic medicine, created in Great Britain in the nineteenth century but used today throughout the world, is a natural pharmaceutical system that stimulates a person's own healing abilities. Homeopathy involves the uses of extremely small doses of plant material or substances from the animal kingdom to augment a person's own defenses.

Based on the Principle of Similars, homeopathy uses substances that would, if given in large doses, cause in the patient a similar reaction to the malady from which he or she is suffering. Homeopathic remedies aid the body's own defenses, as opposed to conventional drugs that typically treat and often suppress symptoms. Homeopathic remedies are selected not simply according to the disease a person is suffering from, but on the basis of the individual symptoms of that person.

Conventional medicine attacks disease after it has reached a high acuity level and—for example, in the case of cancer—does so with a strong and serious arsenal: radiation, surgery, and toxic drugs. There is, finally, a concern about how the patient's suffering directly from the onslaught of these weapons while they wipe out cancer cells, for a time at least delaying their progress,

In *Reclaiming Our Health: Exploding the Medical Myth and Embracing the Source of True Health,* John Robbins cites this statistic: "Seventy-five percent of oncologists said if they developed cancer they would not participate in chemotherapy trials because of the 'ineffectiveness of it and its unacceptable toxicity.' "

This is not only the fault of the Western medical community. It is the fault of Western culture. People are trained to go to the doctor only when they have reached a crisis of some kind. Something has to hurt enough for them to take the time to go to a physician. Managed care, perhaps, amplifies this thinking: doctors have an incentive to order drugs over the phone for patients in their care rather than insisting on seeing them because, of course, they are allotted a certain amount of reimbursement per patient per year. When they allow a patient an office visit, they carefully contrive to ask quick questions that demand quick answers; their reimbursement codes require them to elaborate on any office visit beyond the allowed 15-minute limit.

Questions about a person's life-style, eating and sleeping habits, and state of mind rarely enter into this short exchange between healer and patient. Only the most highly attuned physician may be able to sense a greater context in which to view the patient's complaint. Managed care, in general, does not make room for whole patient care.

The other side of the coin, the positive outcome of the new managed care environment, is support of providers for the continued wellness of the insured in their charge. But to foster this approach, a new concept of prevention and maintenance had to evolve.

Energy medicine, which is an offshoot and amplification of Chinese medicine, and focuses more specifically on various techniques with the same goal: achieving balance. Qi jong, acupuncture, and shiatsu massage are among these techniques, using different methodologies.

Ayuvedic medicine, a traditional healing system in India, identifies 10 organs of the body and relates them to elements in the physical environment. By understanding these elements and their relationships to the 10 vital organs, it is thought that with attention to proper food, the immediate physical environment, bodily movement, and thought processes, a balance can be achieved that will ameliorate disease or states of physical discomfort and prevent such imbalances and, therefore, diseases of the mind and body in the future.

Exercise, viewed in the context of maintaining and treating the whole body has been prescribed in both Eastern and Western medicine as a basic need of the human body, which needs constant fulfillment. Eastern thought has for centuries considered the practice of yoga as integral to maintaining health and preventing disease. Although yoga, in its broad interpretation, is a practice that involves attention to the spiritual as well as to specific life-enhancing physical postures, the physical practice of yoga is what we in the West are most familiar with. It is also curious that many of the stretching exercises that are part of ancient yogic techniques have long been incorporated into Western exercise programs under the heading "stretching exercises" and are, in fact, specifically adhered to by members of professional football teams as well as the armed forces of Western governments. Physical therapists and rehabilitation specialists have studied and implemented many techniques derived from yoga.

T'ai chi, an Eastern system of exercise, also has its spiritual aspects. Derived from ancient Taoist writings and mimicking the movements of animals, this physical art represents philosophical interpretations of humans' relationship to their environment, to other people, and to the unseen energies that flow between them. There are many subcategories of this practice, as there are for the ancient practice of akido and the more rigorous martial arts, karate and tae kwon do, whose origins involve the preparation for battle or the psychological art of avoiding it.

All of these physical arts provide physical benefits. Several are increasing in popularity and are offered widely for people of all ages. In many centers of wellness, Eastern martial arts and yoga are practiced along with aerobic dancing and other active Western exercise systems. A basic understanding of Eastern medicine and exercise is important, because it underlies the relationship of Western and Eastern values and views of healthcare and, more specifically, explains the union of these heretofore disparate worldviews into a single aim: wellness.

Western medicine studies parts of the body separately. ("Dr. Smith is a kidney man...") Modern Western medicine sees human beings as separate from nature and their environment, and in order to study and perfect the analysis of smaller and smaller parts of the human anatomy, these parts have become isolated. Increased knowledge is the benefit of specialization; what has suffered is the ability of the physician to relate the part to the whole.

Eastern medicine, including all of the aforementioned modalities, views the entire construct: the human being (all interrelated parts) and the environment. Hence, we use the term *holistic*. It is believed that this way of thinking is beneficial because it establishes a framework that leaves nothing out. The mental and emotional aspects of the human state are examined

Women's locker area, Springfield Healthplex, Springfield, Pennsylvania.

together with the physical state, and potential problems are viewed holistically.

In recent years East and West have moved closer on the continuum on which we view healthcare. The term used to describe the current perspective is *integrative medicine*, meaning the integration of Western medicine with Eastern methodologies. As we approach the millennium, the division between these two major worldviews is blurring, which is beginning to benefit the culture as a whole. For the first time, the NIH has published what amounts to a sanction on the use of acupuncture for medical treatment.

We have only to look at newsstands and bookstore shelves to glimpse what has become an important source of information our society. The rising costs and potential threat of treatments have led to a healthcare revolution. There is greater awareness now than ever before of the importance of people's taking control of their own health and, it follows, their own lives.

Interest in attaining and maintaining a high level of physical fitness, good nutrition, mental health, and spiritual health has blossomed, and so has a key concept: the integration of all these interests. Mind-body medicine is explored at Beth Israel Deaconess Medical Center, Harvard Medical School, and the Office of Alternative Medicine at the National Institutes of Health. Serious study is continuing at many major medical research institutions across the nation, and many knowledgeable people have started down similar paths in regard to this mind-body and wellness concept.

As managed care continues to cut costs by limiting access to doctors and medication, costs are still soaring, reaching an unprecedented high. Nearly 50 million people are uninsured in this country. Invasive techniques are credited with 36 percent of deaths in the nation.

Future technology promises us greater diagnostic precision, enabling us to detect minute chemical imbalances that can lead to disease, thus allowing us to prevent or control early stages of some life-threatening diseases. Future technology will be able to accomplish more in less space, reinforcing the idea that the medical village can be a humane environment, with a minimum of the equipment that appears so menacing in healthcare institutions today.

In the realm of mind-body medicine, research over many years has reinforced the hypothesis that what is in the mind affects the body, and vice versa. Science and new technologies will allow us to quantify such hypotheses, to identify clearly the powerful relationship we have long suspected.

Internist Larry Dossey, M.D., says, "Courses in spirituality and healing are now in place in eleven major medical schools in this country...these are historic developments, and they will continue. The research documenting these effects is so abundant that it will not go away. We're going to have to deal with it, and it will find an honored place in the medicine of the future."

Dossey envisions a future in which high-tech medicine will continue its emphasis on the biochemical, physiological, and genetic approach to diagnosing and curing disease. But he also envisions a future in which mind and body are considered as part of one energy system, and in which the power of spirituality has a quantifiable impact in regard to healing.

Author John Robbins, in *Reclaiming Our Health: Exploding The Medical Myth and Embracing The Source of True Healing*, asserts that the movement toward self-care, prevention, natural healing approaches, and holistic medicine within the medical business climate is pushing healthcare in a new direction. He sees a future in which the emphasis is on the patient's ability to self-empower and self-heal, utilizing the techniques provided by both Western and Eastern medicines. People will become more responsible, agents in their own healing.

The revolutionary work of Bernie Siegel, M.D., whose books address the way in which patients see themselves in relation to their illness, is in part responsible for this medical revolution, as is the work of Norman Cousins and Carl Simonton, M.D. Siegel posits that the medical revolution will be even more significant to the way in which medicine is practiced when changes in thinking are incorporated in the medical education system.

Dean Ornish, M.D., has spent the last three years setting up training programs in nine hospitals in the United States that deal with preventive medicine, including life-style changes that specifically benefit heart patients, as an alternative to angioplasty and other surgery.

Ornish believes that as results of alternative therapies and life-style changes become more scientifically documented, insurers will become increasingly convinced of their value to patients and to their own financial outcomes.

Herbert Benson, M.D., founding president of the Mind Body Medical Institute of the Beth Israel Deaconess Medical Center at Harvard Medical School, says, "When people learn how to use self-care methods, visits to HMOs decrease.... In prepaid systems this is money in the bank."

Benson's colleague, licensed psychologist Joan Borysenko, suggest that changes in thinking within the medical community will not happen immediately;

> While it's true that there are more medical school courses being taught in alternative medicine, ... they are being taught with the old way of thinking. ... Acupuncture is used as a prescription ... it's still a very mechanical approach that relies on outside agencies for healing.
>
> What I see eventually is a complete shift in perspective, an understanding like that of many indigenous cultures that healing is about relationality—our relationship to self, others, the environment, the cosmos.... Why do men who have heart attacks live longer if they happen to have dogs or are married? Why does social support make the biggest difference in healing?

Medical writer Caroline Myss, Ph.D., believes that the crisis in medical care will reach a terminal point where some traditional hospitals may go bankrupt and reemerge as healing centers. She envisions the development of wellness villages, centers where people can go for short periods of time to be trained in life-enhancing, self-healing techniques.

Andrew Weil, M.D., physician and writer from the University of Arizona, is at the forefront of the integrative medicine movement, which advocates the integration of alternative healing methods with standard medical procedures. "By uniting philosophies that have been separate for a long time, the integrative movement will completely transform healthcare." Weil sees "managed care becoming more and more important and the corporatization of medicine continuing.…But as it does, it will create an openness to change on the part of medical institutions and further disaffection of consumers.…So I think that will drive another kind of movement, which is toward integration. In addition, there are prospects of radical reform in medical schools in terms of the training that doctors receive." Weil is pioneering the use of integrative medicine at the University of Arizona and thinks that other schools will follow quickly. He also believes that some hospitals will go bankrupt. "My hope is that they will be resurrected as healing centers." The sort Weil imagines are places where people go for a week or so and learn how to eat, exercise, and use their minds to access their own healing power. He urges the reimbursement of such treatment by insurance companies.

Edward Taub, M.D., is the Director of Wellness Services at the Western Medical Center Hospital and Regional Trauma Center in southern California. He believes that the future of healthcare will be based on intervening in the disease process before it begins, and that what we call "primary care" is an outmoded concept. He says that we should look toward a new concept called "preprimary care," which is, in effect, preventive medicine. He believes that preprimary care will open the door to a "whole new world of healthcare cost avoidance…This will be the first time in history that doctors and hospitals will make the bulk of their profits by keeping people away from doctors offices in the first place."

Taub points out that Western medicine has not promoted preventive medicine because the technology has not been available to apply scientific proof to the theories and concepts of this way of thinking. Now, with the advent of the new science of psychoneuroimmunology, we can demonstrate the causal relationship between what is in our minds to our ability to heal and our resistance to disease. "We finally have the technology to build the art of healing, the science to develop new methods of health promotion and the economic platform that will reward everyone concerned including doctors, hospitals, managed care organizations, governmental programs, and especially patients."

The economic forces that have led to the changes in the way we deliver healthcare and the consequent architectural implications of those changes are many. The current average price a health insurer pays for bypass surgery is $30,000, the current price for a balloon angioplasty procedure is $7,500. The current amount of money health insurers are committing for healthcare education and stress management is $150 per patient. Under capitation, which allots a certain number of dollars to be spent by the insurance company for an insured per year (as opposed to the traditional fee-for-service arrangement), the benefits to promoting, encouraging and reimbursing for wellness education—programs in nutrition, exercise , stress management, smoking cessation, weight loss and so on—are obvious, especially for those diseases, such as heart disease, whose links to poor nutrition, lack of exercise, and poor stress management are easily documented. It is in the best interest of insurance companies, the government, and the employer to keep people well and productive. The loss to employers and to American industry in general is regrettable when the consequences of a shift in thinking has such great potential benefits.

Add to this the evolving awareness by the medical world that environment has an influence on healing, which human beings have intuitively known for centuries. Only in the last two decades have environmental concerns become popular in the design of healthcare institutions, giving them a "residential" feel. Thus we have the setting for the building concept that is currently being expressed in the American scene.

THE FACILITY'S RESPONSE TO NEW MEDICAL MODELS

The architecture of healthcare facilities took a turn in the early 1980s, when architects began questioning some well-worn concepts. ... Why are the interior walls of hospitals always "hospital green"? Why are the floors an indistinguishable linoleum, the lighting harsh, and the total environment threatening? Part of the answer lies in the availability of materials and the limits of technology at the time, and part of the answer is cultural. We expected a hospital to be perceived as solidly institutional and therefore, trustworthy. Doctors were practicing serious medicine here, making life-and-death decisions; this was not an environment that we wanted to be in any way like our living rooms. People came to this building to be born, die, or receive treatment for serious illnesses.

Hospitals were places where people stayed for given periods of time, to get better and then leave, back to their homelike environments, their homes. The concept of home was never to be blurred or confused with that of the hospital. Indeed, the authority and majesty implying that "this is an important institution," characterized these massive brick and limestone buildings, an impression that remained in people's minds. Even today, traveling through small towns in rural areas of the United States, we find the old main hospital building in the center of town or sitting on the highest hill. Efforts to talk to administrators about physically changing the hospital with reimbursement changes, the advent of managed care, and the ever accelerating growth in technology as topics of eminent impor-

Hotel in Kona, Big Island, Hawaii.

tance, were, even two years ago, met with weary resistance. A knowledgeable architect explained, "It's like telling them you want to take away the high school football team."

In these smaller towns, the hospital was and is a cultural icon. One does not try to alter an important symbol in the lives of many local residents by suggesting a move, an affiliation with another institution, or a dramatic change in the facade or a realignment of the entrance, without encountering a strong response.

These icons are slowly disappearing as the aforementioned changes become overpowering and the population shifts. The hospital on the top of the hill can no longer survive without some serious changes to its financial and physical structure in order.

The design of healthcare facilities overall at this time is still following the trend toward residential design, but is becoming more sophisticated. The influence of the hospitality industry has made a definite mark, as has retail design. The phrase "medical mall" and its underlying concept are obviously borrowed from the retail world. The introduction of color in all healthcare environments is to be applauded and encouraged, always with the caution related to common sense. Designers do well to avoid the obviously trendy color statements, which will wear thin in just a few years time, and the use of red as a dominant color, especially in emergency department settings.

Metatrends in healthcare design follow demographic, technological, financial, and legislative dictums. It is thought that the medical center of tomorrow will include a comprehensive range of consumer choices and offer, in an expanded medical mall facility, an integrated medical campus that will relate ambulatory surgery centers with small inpatient hospitals. There will be hotels for care givers and/or recovering patients who are not yet able to perform life tasks in the home setting, and emergency services with medivac availability to easily transport a seriously ill person to a designated trauma center (if the community does not have one). These medical communities may each have a center of excellence, so that a person can take advantage of the facilities on campus for all but the most serious problems. Following times of diagnosis and treatment for serious illness, patients can easily avail themselves of the community healthcare facility for followup and rehabilitation.

The special needs of women must certainly be attended to in these community settings, as well as the special needs of the elderly. Such facilities may be expanded into "healthy villages," where the continuum of care is completed. These centers would include long term-care facilities, including assisted living, skilled nursing, independent care, and adult day care. They may also incorporate child care centers and dedicated pediatrics departments with an emphasis on well baby care.

Educational elements of the facility will benefit the community and help to integrate the healthy village. People will be able to learn about childbirth, receive guidance on parenting, become educated on the skills needed to diagnose and help substance abuse-prone adolescents and adults, learn about smoking cessation, pain management, and physical and occupational therapy. One of the most important first steps toward this new concept is the currently evolving hybrid building type, the wellness center.

In urban areas, the clustering of services and the creation of strategic alliances have accelerated the obviously necessary outreach to the furthest regions of a hospital's catchment area, where population is moving and real estate is less expensive and tax assessments are lower.

In the mid-1980s we saw the flowering of the ambulatory care center, with or without a surgical element. As doctors became integrated into networks, there was increased need for medical office space aligned with these ambulatory care centers or adjacent to suburban or regional hospitals. The economies of practice integration led physicians groups to make business decisions about collocating their practices and to look more closely at the bottom line. As technology and lessened acuity levels influenced the business of healthcare, so the stage was set for the arrival of its most important player, managed care.

The American healthcare system has been steadily moving toward an integrated system for the past 15 years. Accompanying the healthcare revolution has been a shift from specialization to primary care. Medical students are focusing on working within integrated systems to provide a full range of primary care, which includes general physical care along with general psychological care.

The American Medical Association defines "managed care" as the processes and techniques used by any entity that delivers, administers, or assumes risk for health services in order to control or influence the quality, accessibility, utilization costs and prices, or outcomes of such services provided to a defined population. A systemwide reform of payment mechanisms has been called for, as well as the reorganization of healthcare delivery. It is acknowledged that the current healthcare system is noteworthy for its fragmentation and that managed care is beginning to put an emphasis on health promotion and disease prevention. However, it is thought that managed care raises questions about the allocation of increasingly scarce resources.

As physicians' practices grow and multispeciality group practices become an increasing trend, various ways of achieving equity and tax advantages for a practice, whether physician or hospital owned, are available. In most states the beginning move is to form a limited liability corporation that will benefit all members of the physicians group.

Flexibility in terms of real estate ownership can be built into the contracts of physicians joining a group practice based on the tenets of this arrangement. In today's world of healthcare delivery, physicians move from practice to practice more than at any other point in time. Accommodations are made for physicians who have a longer time invested in a practice, with an equally significant return on their investment. By owning the building in which it practices, a group can realize obvious tax benefits. States differ as to the Certificate of Need laws in regard to certain types of surgical procedures allowed to be performed in a group practice office. In some states the number of operating rooms for purposes of outpatient surgeries and the types of procedures are the governing factors in determining what types of procedures can be offered at each facility.

Like everything else in healthcare, these rules are subject to change. The overriding logic to designing and building anything in the healthcare system is flexibility. Care should be taken to design wellness centers with as much flexibility as possible. The decision on the location of the wellness center or wellness campus should be made with this in mind. In selecting real estate, the owner/design team should consider marketability as well as potential for growth.

No wellness center should be located on a site without good access to transportation or high profile visibility. Site considerations such as parking should include future growth, as it is entirely possible for the uses of wellness centers to increase as insurers become more aware of the value of reimbursing populations for wellness activities and technology provides the means to perform a greater number of simple procedures in these environments.

The wellness center itself must be designed to be flexible. What is shell space today may be diagnostic and testing space tomorrow. It may also be an aerobics dancing space, additional locker rooms, food service facilities, or a flex space alternating education with yoga or t'ai chi classes. As new therapies come into being or old therapies find new application in the new century, new spaces to accommodate them must be envisioned. In terms of real estate, no one can predict the future with crystal clarity, but we can be the best stewards of the future by acknowledging that we do not know everything and that true benefit derives from designing structures with numerous future options.

The strategic planning initiatives of groups such as physician group practices will undertake the purchase or lease of a medical office building related to a wellness center as part of their long-term business strategy. Taken into account will be other assets owned by the various physicians who are about to join the group and whether part of their negotiation with the group involves the inclusion of these assets.

Physician-hospital organizations have a further concern about the location of a wellness center and its physical proximity to the hospital. Convenience of referrals and the hospital's overall real estate strategies must be taken into consideration. Here the initiative to build a wellness center or wellness complex requires a reality check in regard to location.

In many cases, as physician-hospital organizations (PHOs) have been formed, the hospital entity has purchased real estate from the physicians group practice, allowing the practice to reconfigure its assets and divide equity among its members and permitting some members to step out of the practice with a certain economic gain and a new start. The hospital in a physician-hospital organization also takes on the debt obligations for the group practice, again allowing the practice to reconfigure its financial situation.

If the physicians group retains real estate as part of the negotiation, the hospital will have to pay rent to the group entity for the PHO's use of the physicians offices. It is advisable for the hospital to pay full market rates for this privilege. Sometimes the physicians group will raise the rent if it is believed to be below market, in which case the income to the physicians' pool will be increased.

The least integrated model relationship for physicians with hospitals is the management services organization (MSO). This model requires all entities to work together, but the physicians are not employed by the MSO as they are in a PHO or HMO relationship. Resolution of organizational issues, purchasing economies, and a more sophisticated and businesslike approach to delivering healthcare services are achieved within such a model, but physicians retain more autonomy and authority.

An MSO structure provides access to managed care contracting. Capital expenditures, including real estate acquisition, are decided by a board formed by members of the MSO. Exclusivity is mandatory; a hospital must not actively pursue competing physicians groups.

Another model is the foundation model of integrated services. In this approach, a separate entity—a foundation—is formed, which operates differently from any of the models previously mentioned. Physicians need not be employed by the hospital or the foundation itself. The foundation provides a business infrastructure to allow sophisticated real estate transactions to occur, including the provision of capital without physicians' participation, and physicians may use the foundation as a resource to acquire capital to put into their group practices, thereby allowing them to attain senior voting positions within the group.

The foundation purchases group assets, which gives the physicians equity, a one-time benefit. The foundation provides patient-related services, such as billing. In general, it relieves physicians of administrative and business decisions related to group practice. Reorganization of the physicians group in the foundation model is also a benefit.

The medical division–employment model is another integrated service model. Physicians requiring less autonomy and more security in the new managed care environment are contracting directly with the hospital, in fact, becoming hospital employees. A physician sells stock in his or her practice to the hospital in return for a one-time benefit. The physician then enters into an employment agreement with the hospital, with the hospital paying a guaranteed income plus bonuses. Hospital-based physicians such as radiologists have typically been the first wave of physicians employed by hospitals.

Market feasibility studies based on income analysis and zip code within a circle drawn with the hospital at its center typically become the first level of information needed about location and can be a good predictor of success. Companies that perform this type of analysis can be found through architectural and engineering firms that specialize in healthcare architecture design and development.

Sharing decision making with healthcare professionals in all specialties emphasizes disease prevention and incorporates new technologies within an entire system. Such integrated delivery systems are developed in various ways to benefit members of the system. They create relationships that streamline different elements involved in healthcare delivery, providing various reimbursement benefits and tax incentives and establishing groups of physicians in physical locations that reinforce their competitive advantage in the marketplace.

Integrated delivery began flourishing in the early 1990s, spurred on by the anticipation that the political system would likely create dynamic changes for which healthcare professionals, insurers, and financial markets must be ready. Although change did not come from on high, the economic forces leading to change motivated healthcare systems to protect themselves against potential massive changes—global realignment of the entire system.

There are many models of integrated delivery systems. A comprehensive model is a system that groups physicians, hospital(s), and other medical facilities, completing the contin-

Pool at Springfield Healthplex, Springfield, Pennsylvania.

uum of care. The benefit to all members of this system is cost control. Hospitals may or may not purchase physicians' practices in order to achieve an integrated delivery system. Physicians and hospitals enter into managed care contracts together in order to control costs. Occasionally, physicians and hospitals have contracts with each other, sometimes forming companies that are the result of joint venture agreements. These companies then provide a united front in dealing with managed care contracts.

An integrated delivery system is created to control costs. Medical providers group themselves in various ways with other physicians, hospitals, and other medical facilities, in order to increase their market power, reduce their administrative costs, and allow themselves to perform utilization reviews and quality reviews internally. These new groups then can attract capital for improvement and growth and can take advantage of group purchasing.

In *Transforming the Delivery of healthcare*, Kenneth Kornuchuk likens present-day delivery of healthcare in the United States to the manufacture of machinery prior to the development of mass production. In this model, different stages of production were physically located in different places, not necessarily in any logical geographical proximity. As the development of this industry progressed, the assembly line was created, reducing costs and raising productivity. Although the delivery of medical care is a service model rather than a product model, the analogy as it relates to efficiency is a good one. The integration of the delivery of medical care and the future of the industry depend to a great extent on the ability of the system to be efficient and, at the same time, flexible.

By integrating hospitals, physicians' practices, insurers, and other elements of healthcare delivery, many cost-cutting measures can be effected, which should increase profits for the industry and, theoretically, benefit the consumer by providing consistent service of a certain quality at a certain price level.

As technology advances, enabling ever more procedures to be undertaken with minimal or no inpatient hospital stay, the system becomes increasingly flexible, because it is no longer necessary to cluster patients in hospital rooms. Medical facilities with shorter stays can have higher staff-to-patient ratios and require less infrastructure and real estate.

Service today already means that a patient may or may not go near an acute care hospital for diagnostic testing, surgery, or treatment. The difficulty is that the ability of the healthcare system to deliver service in a variety of nonacute hospital locations has not caught up with the economies available to offering these services in just one place. That one place, in the future of medicine, may indeed be the wellness center.

We will have changed, then, from the acute care hospital model (where nearly all medical diagnoses and treatment took place in single building or location), to the community outreach model (where a growing number of services, diagnostic, surgical, and treatment, are clustered around the central hospital core), to the integration of these hospitals into regional systems (where duplication of services is reduced and real estate benefits are realized), to the development of the wellness center concept. The wellness center refocuses the energy of healthcare on the preventive, rehabilitative, and educational realms, while clustering preventive and rehabilitative services with diagnostic and treatment services. The future may see a centralized, community-based wellness campus that replaces the traditional hospital and becomes the focus of healthcare delivery well into the next century.

The wellness centers that exist in the country today are attached to hospitals and hospital systems. They benefit from referral patterns and the halo effect of the hospital system's reputation, its ability to obtain financing, to coordinate with managed care companies, and, in general, to share the pool of participants/patients with the medical professionals and systems in the community. In certain areas of the country, these centers might well be developed into wellness villages, where long-term care and ambulatory surgery centers and medical hotels established on campus complete the continuum of care.

Demographic analyses show that baby boomers will reach retirement age at the beginning of the twenty-first century. It is important to note that even now, as baby boomers select assisted living, skilled, or subacute care for their aging parents, marketers are building their business strategies around this population and have realized the financial benefits of appealing to this market. They seek locations for these facilities close to baby boomer homes rather than in far-flung communities in Florida or Arizona. They reduce the anxiety of placing one's parents in a nursing home by identifying current architectural design trends, with residential layouts and furniture, elegantly concealed medical equipment, and hotelstyle food service.

Integrated delivery systems offer entities a distinct advantage: an enhancement of the referral chain. Critical to the success of healthcare institutions is the way in which patients are referred within the system. No other business entity has quite this extraordinary dependence on the domino-like effect of business referrals passing from provider to provider. Indeed, the consumer is only partially aware that a suggestion that he or she go to a certain radiologist or laboratory for tests (or, if in a hospital, to a subacute or skilled care facility) is part of a well-choreographed plan, designed to enhance the revenues of all the providers along the way.

Within this new climate, the healthcare revolution, the benefit to integrated systems in enlarging the menu of healthcare services offered is obvious; there is the potential for more referrals. As wellness centers proliferate, their menu of services will grow and with such growth, the enhancement and broadening of referral patterns.

For example, if a patient joins a wellness center motivated by a desire to stop smoking and to get more exercise, as recommended by his family physician, he may take advantage of other programs offered at the center. If his daughter sprains her ankle at soccer, he will take her to his primary care physician, who may refer him to an orthopedist, who will likely be recommended by both the primary care physician and the sports medicine doctor (orthopedist) on staff at the wellness center.

Consider another illustration of the referral pattern. A woman in her mid-forties joins a center to enter a weight loss program and begins to develop relationships with staff at the center. If she becomes pregnant and needs a good obstetrician, she may naturally ask the advice of the doctor who is helping to monitor her progress in the weight loss program.

The idea grows out of the methodology that has proven successful for hospitals in recent years. In order to market hospital services to well people, a hospital proceeds to create community outreach and educational programs. These programs, for the most part involved with smoking cessation, prenatal education classes, diabetes and cardiac care classes, exercise programs, and, most recently, stress management programs, have all led to increased visibility for the hospital within the broad market. They have planted the idea in the consumer/patient's mind as to where that person would go if he or she needs help of a more serious nature.

Conversely, physicians may refer patients in need of physical rehabilitation to a wellness center as part of the hospital referral link. The patients, engaging in their rehabilitation in spaces adjacent to the workout areas used by well patients, are often inspired by the success they encounter and the exposure to the motivated people around them, exercising as a part of personal improvement and life-style enhancement. Thus, they may stay with the center as part of their personal continuing wellness program.

As physicians and hospitals have, in the past 10 years, created integrated delivery systems for the aforementioned obvious business advantages, or if they have created just strategic alliances and multispecialty practice groups, they have sought the support of a particular facility to house their newly structured enterprises and have created a plethora of medical office buildings. What we are seeing as the wellness center concept develops and grows is the linking of these generally mid-rise medical office buildings (MOBs) with the wellness center itself. Thus, in the current environment, a wellness center may have a certain number of square feet devoted to clinical spaces and, at the same time, be linked physically with a medical office building of some size, usually housing a multispecialty group practice. Another variation is the outpatient/ambulatory care mini-hospital, with outpatient surgery linked to a medical office building and to a wellness center.

CONCEPT OF COMMUNITY

Reinforcing the driving force of economics in the delivery of medical care, as mentioned earlier, is the more personal and emotional idea of wellness as both a goal and a journey, a path of life-enhancing activities and awareness that underlies the formalized, financial, and technical systems to improve the quality of life. The attraction of people to the concept of wellness is as basic as life itself; there is within human beings a positive core that affirms existence and becomes a strategic filter for the choices they make. Healthy people always choose life, and the future lies in the creation of architectural complexes that enhance, encourage, and promote environments that support this thesis.

Wellness centers that have been in existence for a year or two have, perhaps surprisingly, become gathering places for the community. Indeed, there is obvious marketing advantage to encouraging this trend. What is interesting is that it has evolved naturally, and so architects are finding, as we go back to institutions for postoccupancy evaluations and are asked to plan an addition because of the quickly growing popularity of the centers, that we are being asked to expand and develop these places in which people gather.

Such popularity may or may not be involved with food service or entertainment. Larger wellness centers are including small cafes, juice bars, or cafeterias with, of course, an emphasis on fresh and natural foods. Smaller centers tend to provide coffee bars where small snacks are available. Whether to offer food service is often a financial decision, based on the economics of the particular center and the availability of staff, suppliers, and so forth.

All centers, whether they include food service or not, appear to have a growing need for gathering places for people to meet, share experiences, or, in some cases, to rest, read, or play quiet games. As evident in the public houses in Great Britain, people seem to like to gather, to meet and talk with other people in places outside their homes, places casual enough not to demand any great planning or expense to visit, places where they may go at any time of day.

In this ambitious culture, it seems there is always another agenda to legitimize another place. In our society, the place has most frequently been the mall. But the mall does not serve well the need to develop any regularity in regard to the definition of a particular place, nor does it generally provide people with amenities such as child care or even a place to hang one's coat in order to feel comfortable, nor create a sense of routine and regularity and identification.

Golf clubs, men's clubs, and even the YMCA have been traditional gathering places. As we become more sophisticated, more knowledgeable, more able to gain access to information, we seek places that serve our human need to gather. We want to get together away from the dominating agendas of the business environment, the strain of the school environment, the pressure of the retail environment, where people can merely come and go. Health clubs have fulfilled this need in some communities, but they are often demographically targeted to narrow age and economic groups and thus become socially self-limiting.

Given that wellness centers have begun in middle-class neighborhoods, where discretionary income coupled with the reimbursements available from insurers mostly involving middle-class participants are the genesis of these centers, the concept can be made to work for a broader socioeconomic group. As the relationships of insurers change and grow, and involvement of government on the federal, state, and community levels changes and grows, it is realistic to envision the full participation of a community in a wellness center or series of centers where clinical and fitness programs flourish.

Why not have recreational centers in the inner city combine with ambulatory care clinics? Why not encourage the inclusion of educational programs that help communities to house themselves? Further laboratory testing, such as blood and urine testing for hormone levels, electrolyte balances, and so forth, can also be entered into the profile. The inclusion of laboratories, as well as pharmacies, within the wellness centers is a growing trend. Other diagnostic testing areas, such as for radiology, are also included in certain wellness centers, either in the center itself or in an adjacent medical office building. Mammograms and pap smears, as part of inclusive and preventive women's wellness programs, are included as well.

Developing the Wellness Center

The shift from the fee-for-service healthcare system to the managed care model is the primary driver for changes in every aspect of healthcare delivery. Not to be overlooked, however, is the influence, power, and driving force of technology. Technology has always been an energizer in the healthcare profession, as in other professions. The history of medicine bears this out.

Hippocrates based his medical practice on bedside observation. Telemedicine enables physicians to observe patients, to diagnose and treat them, at incredible distances. This technology enables us to bring the best medical care in the country to remote locations, including war zones. During Operation Desert Storm, the U.S. military relied to some extent on the satellite transmission of data that helped doctors in the United States to support troops involved in ground operations.

Yet how advances in medical technology relate to the practice of medicine is not simply a question of access, but of the changes in the specific requirements of medical buildings themselves. As endoscopic procedures, for example, have evolved, the number of certain more invasive procedures has declined. Thus, where once a patient would have a lengthy operation for the removal of a gallbladder, entailing significant expense and extended recovery time, this procedure can now be done with an endoscope, requiring less time, fewer hospital staff, less danger to the patient, decreased recovery time, and a smaller room, specially designed for endoscopic procedures instead of a standard operating room with its full complement of equipment and energy requirements.

As the required sizes of rooms in medical facilities shrink or, in the case of specialized operating rooms, grow, the profile of what is included in a medical facility in a given community changes greatly, and continues to change. Here, flexibility is the key. Architects should advise clients on meeting the potential of change with the best possible plans for healthcare campuses and individual buildings that reflect flexibility and adaptability.

This can be accomplished programmatically in several ways. For instance, if an existing hospital is looking for redefinition into the next century, a master plan of the campus, in broad terms, can be developed with built-in flexibility. No building should be built in the year 2000 without several potential alternative uses. This is not to say that a medical facility building should be prepared for a possible transition to a retail use, but that the locating of new freestanding building elements, as well as additions, on the land should be well-thought-out decisions, decisions made with vision.

Within existing buildings, efforts should be made to maintain whatever flexibility can be maintained, and new medical facilities' buildings should be extremely flexible. If a hospital campus has existed for a number of years and is expanding, those departmental functions that are easily relocated away from the acute care hospital should be so relocated. This is not always easy. Functions that are typically relocated include administration and departments that have evolved in size or complexity. Cancer centers, for example, especially within a university medical center campus, are likely departments to become freestanding treatment centers on their own.

Pediatric medical centers and rehabilitation hospitals, on the other hand, are likely to become freestanding facilities, but in most communities they need the support of more than one sponsoring medical center. These types of buildings are being developed in joint venture relationships with multiple hospitals, or hospital systems.

The Certificate of Need process, active in some but not all states, sets limits on the number of buildings, usually defined by a bed count for each facility in a given catchment area in each state, and the need determination of that area is based on the logic of what a community requires in terms of medical service. Legislators and regulatory bodies determine, after careful analysis of the situation, which beds go where, and community hospitals are often in stiff competition with one another for "beds," which translates into market share. This process applies only to certain types of medical facility functions, with some state to state variation.

For example, in Maryland, a medical office building can be built without benefit of a Certificate of Need unless it considers the inclusion of operating rooms. If it does, then the number of doctors practicing within a specialty and the number of operating rooms (ORs) anticipated in the design become criteria. If the number of ORs is above a certain threshold (currently, two), and if there is more than one medical specialty being practiced, then the project in question must undergo rigorous review by the governing state agency, in competition with other projects of similar nature and size.

At present, in most states there is no regulation on the creation of wellness centers, because wellness centers are medical buildings with no specific regulatory requirements other than those imposed by building codes and professional standards of care. As standards evolve for the regulation of some types of complementary medical practices, such practices and procedures may be subject to future regulation.

Physicians in the field of complementary medicine are, on the whole, in favor of some regulation, as ensuring the public safety is central to the mission of their medical practices.

The current gathering momentum for creation of wellness centers is in part due to the lack of regulation. With the proper team assembled — owner/ hospital affiliate, financing partners, architectural design team, project developer/facilitator — anyone can build a wellness center. If market studies show a legitimate need and all the elements fall into place, the process is simple. The implementation of the process runs into obstacles (challenges) typical of any new building project, but regulation is not yet one of them.

A number of factors are fueling the race to build, which seems to have accelerated recently. Among these are changes in managed care, a perception that the market is ready and will not peak for another few years, a perception by some that this is only the beginning of the healthcare revolution, the availability of capital in various markets, especially real estate investment trusts (REITS), the demographics of baby boomers and the potential in catering to this massive group, and the trends toward self-care and alternative healthcare treatments.

Allowing the acceleration of the growth of what has become the wellness industry, in terms of facilities, is the lack of regulation. There is, on one hand, no need to predetermine and over-regulate the design of a medical fitness facility. For years, fitness facilities have had no regulations other than building codes and professional standards. Incorporating healthcare elements into fitness building types requires a great deal of design finesse.

Issues of privacy and safety, which are of the utmost importance, must be addressed. Where specific medical procedures occur, these spaces must meet standards like those suggested by the Joint Commission on Accreditation of Hospital for health-care facilities.

Where alternative therapies occur, such as chelation therapy, there is an opportunity for architects to set reasonable standards for what these spaces need to be in order to create a design that adequately and graciously supports them. Where spaces for the practice of alternative therapies intersect with spaces for the practice of traditional medicine and the elements of the fitness complex are special opportunities for well-thought-out design.

Engineering considerations, such as the number of air changes needed for these wellness facilities, are significant. The high humidity of pools, locker rooms, steam rooms, and work-out areas, coupled with the inclusion of medical equipment in clinical spaces, will have to be thoughtfully designed.

The danger of transmission of pathogens, such as those that cause Legionnaires' disease, is very real in these facilities. Spa areas alone have been suspected as being the environmental hosts for Legionnaires' disease outbreaks in a number of cruise ships in recent years. Mold, a challenge in most fitness facility locker room areas, holds a potential risk for those suffering from environmental allergies, who may well be visiting the wellness center with the goal of taking steps to cure such allergies.

THE PLANNING PROCESS

In developing a wellness center, the planning process can be separated into two major areas: the evaluation phase and the implementation phase.

Evaluation

During the evaluation phase the planning process is driven by the goal of minimizing the risk accompanying a decision to expand or move selected hospital programs to a wellness center. Risk is minimized by reducing, as much as possible, the uncertainties associated with the project. The assumption underlying this approach is that the more one knows about a project and all of the elements that bear on it, the better the decisions one will make.

The starting point for an organization's decision to build a wellness center is the organization's strategic plan. The strategic plan is the framework within which the evaluation and implementation take place; it defines the broad criteria according to which feasibility will be determined.

If, for example, a strategic plan has an objective of achieving a 15 percent rate of return on program investment, then one factor in financial feasibility is defined.

The strategic filter, the fabric of criteria created to measure program additions, is typically composed of an organizational assessment and a plan development section. The organizational assessment attempts to describe the current state of the organization, and the plan development section describes where the organization thinks it should be at some point in the future and how it plans to get there.

Each component considers the programs and services the organization believes it should provide. As part of the plan development section, certain elements are addressed that become the linkage between the strategic plan and the evaluation of the wellness program. These elements may include performance goals for the entire organization, market responsiveness, the organization's plans for reacting to the quickly changing healthcare market, facility evaluation, programs the hospital system might move to the wellness center or wellness center campus, financial objectives and/or forecasts of revenue, expense, or capital requirements the organization must obtain to maintain or improve financial viability.

Management considerations include those administrative, legal, and other operational issues that require resolution during the evaluation phase. The test for deciding whether a management issue should be included in the evaluation phase is whether the issue influences the feasibility of the wellness center program.

Technological considerations are those that pertain to what will be included in the clinical program of the wellness center design and how the movement of certain clinical programs will affect the technological requirements of the system. These issues are especially important for the more technologically intense clinical programs, such as outpatient surgery and imaging, that may be included in the wellness center program.

For example, if outpatient surgery and imaging will be included in the program, a rough estimate of equipment costs should be made. It will also be important to consider exercise equipment and larger amenities such as swimming pools. Fitting these requirements into the overall budget for equipment is the first step.

Facility considerations are next. Will the wellness center start out as part of the hospital's mission to become an expanded health education service in the next century? Such a step will require expanded classroom space, perhaps within the hospital campus buildings. Or if the program requires its own space, will that space be on the hospital campus, or will it be freestanding? Will it follow population growth in the suburbs, or will it be part of a new focus on the community's center? A gross space program will reflect facility requirements and give the organization the starting point for other program considerations as sifted through the strategic filter.

The evaluation phase includes financial considerations. All elements of evaluation relate to the organization's financial goals. Determining the financial soundness of a proposed wellness center project begins with the financial objectives contained in the plan development and the strategic plan. These objectives define an organization's financial needs and the direction it plans to follow, or to alter, to maintain its financial position. The financial feasibility of the wellness center program is then evaluated within the context of these objectives.

During the evaluation phase, financial feasibility is analyzed through consideration of the following:

1. *Return on investment requirements.* The net financial gain required by the organization on dollars invested in new or existing programs or services.

2. *Reimbursement potential.* Sources of revenue from third-party payers, which include reimbursement for clinical services such as physical, cardiopulmonary, and occupational therapy; third-party reimbursement for wellness benefits; and reimbursement for integrative therapies formerly considered not reimbursable, such as massage therapy and acupuncture.

3. *Funding requirements.* The total projected amount of both capital and operational costs that require funding as part of the project.

4. *Preliminary feasibility.* The consolidation of market and financial analyses into a projection of revenue and expenses, cash flow, and profitability of the wellness center.

5. *Ownership options.* An investigation of the various alternatives for ownership of the wellness center, and the impact of these alternatives on the ability to generate necessary investment capital and on the ability to achieve acceptable profitability.

6. *Financial options.* An investigation of potential sources of funds to cover initial capitalization requirements.

7. *Financial plan.* A detailed statement of the financial feasibility of the wellness center project. The plan includes underlying assumptions regarding market demand, market share, and capital requirements and pro forma financial statements. The plan also describes the manner in which financial resources, both internal and external to

the organization, will be used to achieve the desired results projected in the financial statements.

During the evaluation phase, the final functional area of issues and questions to be resolved is the market for the wellness center. Market demand for fitness programs, spa programs, integrative therapies, and outpatient clinical procedures must be assessed.

The decision to initiate or continue clinical programs depends on the preceding factors. All market and financial feasibility data are sifted through the filter of the organization's strategic plan to determine whether the wellness center will or will not advance the organization's overall goals.

Implementation

If the evaluation process results in a decision to proceed, the next step is implementation. The critical forces driving implementation activities are schedule and budget.

If the wellness center is to include such services as outpatient surgery, a Certificate of Need will be required in most states. The certification process, which can be lengthy and complex, must be included in the project schedule at the outset. The sometimes unpredictable nature of the Certificate of Need process in some jurisdictions can have an impact on whether the project's basic market information is still valid at the time the project is brought on-line. Organizations should consult a healthcare attorney as early as possible in the implementation process if they have not already done so during the evaluation phase.

An architect can assist in the initial implementation phase by providing insights as to the buildability of a selected site and clarifying economic considerations in the construction market that may influence the project's schedule and cost. An architect can also provide rough cost estimates, based on his or her own experience or that of others.

Other management development activities that should be considered early in the implementation phase include the drafting of contractual agreements governing the provision of services, the development of staffing requirements, and the preparation of a business plan. In addition, although they may not be needed until later in the process, it is also advisable to consider policies and procedures for operation of the facility and the development of staff training materials.

During implementation, technical issues are raised in regard to the selection and installation of equipment that will

Aerobics class, Sinai Wellbridge, Pikesville, Maryland.

support the clinical, fitness, and spa components of the wellness center. This process is distinct from the construction contractor's equipment selection.

In the implementation phase, the most critical events relating to facility development are put into motion. There are several variations of the design/bid/build process available, and all have been successful in the implementation of a development plan for wellness center facilities.

One project delivery method gaining widespread popularity is the integrated services approach, in which the architect and engineer present a design/build team to the owner. The team provides fully integrated services, including construction. This method offers the prospect of substantial savings to the owner, because the construction professionals are included in the team early in the project, when their knowledge can prevent future buildability problems. Often the architect-engineer-contract (AEC) team (the design/build team) will offer the owner a guaranteed maximum price for the project. This can reduce the owner's financial uncertainty early in the implementation process and can give the owner greater confidence in securing project financing. Most design/build teams offer an open-book approach, which allows the owner to examine subcontracting arrangements and material costs at all stages of the project.

Market development activities are aimed at bringing in the market identified in the feasibility study. Specific activities may include the following:

1. *Marketing objectives.* Identification of certain accomplishments to be realized during a given period of time pertaining to reaching market potential for the wellness center.
2. *Marketing strategies.* Specific actions to be taken to achieve marketing objectives.
3. *Marketing program.* A plan for conducting marketing strategies with available resources. Included in the plan are media strategies, public relations plans, and a separate marketing budget.

Financial Development

During the facility development process, the following activities will be performed:

1. *Final feasibility.* Preparation of any formal feasibility statement or documentation to accompany a bond issue or investment prospectus.
2. *Project budget.* Preparation of a comprehensive budget based on the feasibility analysis and including construction, equipment, and operation costs.
3. *Financing.* Activities associated with actually acquiring funds required to capitalize the project.
4. *Operating budget.* Establishment of the annual operating budgets for initial operating years.

Building program elements for a wellness center campus may include the wellness center, a medical office building, and a small ambulatory care/outpatient surgery center. These three elements, when included on a single site, produce the synergistic relationships that work best economically. Although the creation, existence, and success of the wellness center building type appear very individualized in regard to the demographics of each center's catchment area and the vitality of the hospital system with which it is connected, it may be helpful to examine a single hospital system to illustrate the evolution of that system and where the wellness center building type fits in. (The XYZ system financial outline is included in this chapter.)

Typical wellness center financing is illustrated by the following example, a prototype of how the financing mechanism can be designed, with modifications and adjustments as needed according to the particular project anticipated. Ellerbe Becket's Project Development Director John Curran has successfully implemented this investment method.

Off-balance-sheet financing is a method of financing a project that allows the institution, in this case a midsize hospital, to obtain some of the benefits of ownership while distancing its credit rating and ability to borrow capital from this project activity. This is one of the three basic forms of project financing typically used in wellness center project development.

A real estate lending company that specializes in healthcare project investment can probably offer a distinct advantage over a bank or other lending institution because of its understanding of the market, the nature of the healthcare industry, and its experience with helping to develop this building type.

A healthcare–oriented investor, then, has a market advantage over other investors. Because of his or her particular market knowledge, such an investor will most likely offer up to 100 percent financing, a low cost of capital, a declining-price perpetual purchase option for the property, flexible terms on both term and amortization period, an easily expandable funding mechanism to meet future needs, and flexible fixed rate and variable rate structures with available interest rate hedging mechanisms.

There will often be no prepayment penalty. The best investors will offer the ability to match the financing structure specifically to an entity's financing needs through the use of interest rate swaps, caps, and options. They will also offer the perpetual ability to lock in a fixed rate, conversion from a variable rate structure with a few hours' notice through the term of the financing, and minimal fees and expenses that can usually be financed as well.

Often the real estate investment company financing the development also finances the wellness center investment and remains the owner until such time as the hospital or other sponsoring entity exercises an option to buy.

The support mechanism typically involved with off-balance-sheet financing is a beneficial occupancy agreement, a synthetic operating lease, or some other form of support mechanism, instead of a more stringent master lease or direct guarantee. A beneficial occupancy agreement is not a lease, but a standby arrangement. It is classified as a contingent liability. Under a synthetic operating lease, the credit entity is the primary obligor and the lease must be structured to comply with Statement of Financial Accounting System (SFAS) 13 operating lease criteria.

Lobby, Springfield Healthplex, Springfield, Pennsylvania.

The four criteria of SFAS 13, none of which can be present for an agreement to be classified as an off-balance-sheet operating lease, are as follows:

1. The lease transfers ownership of the property to the lessee by the end of the lease term.
2. The lease contains a bargain purchase option.
3. The lease term is equal to 75 percent or more of the estimated economic life of the leased property.
4. At the beginning of the lease term, the present value of the minimum lease payments equals or exceeds 90 percent of the value of the leased property to the lessor at the inception of the lease.

By leasing the property and project from the investment company, the hospital or hospital foundation preserves its credit rating and debt capacity for future needs.

A healthcare real estate investment company with good resources will offer the healthcare provider flexibility: it can either use a reputable developer and construction organization (preferably a company that offers design-integrated services including architecture, engineering, and construction services), or serve as its own developer. This flexibility gives the healthcare provider total control over the design of the building and the delivery of the finished project.

The following is a sample of a preliminary off-balance-sheet funding terms sheet for a prototype hospital-based wellness center.

XYZ Hospital Foundation

Amount	$4,500,000 (approximate)
Property Owner/Borrower	Generic Real Estate Investment Company
Property	Wellness Center containing approximately 45,000 square feet of space
Type	Construction and Long-Term Permanent Financing

Option A: Synthetic Operating Lease

Security	Mortgage on the Property Assignment of the Synthetic Operating Lease Healthcare Providers' Foundation for the Property
Lease Rate	1.1 x debt service
Lease Term	5-year extendable (up to 30 years)
Purchase Option	Healthcare Provider's Foundation will have a purchase option throughout the lease term equal to the outstanding debt plus the property owner's original 3 percent equity exposure.
End-of-Term Obligation	The Synthetic Operating Lease will contain an end-of-term obligation to make the lessor whole if the purchase option is not exercised prior to the end of the lease term and the property is sold for an amount less than the purchase option price. This end-of-term obligation will be structured with a stipulated maximum lessee exposure to meet SFAS 13 operating lease requirements.
Asset Management Cost	0.375%

Option B: Beneficial Occupancy Agreement

Security	Mortgage on Property Assignment of all tenant leases in the property Assignment of the beneficial occupancy agreement with healthcare provider's foundation for the property
Lease Rates	Minimum of 1.1 x debt service
Property Reversion	The Beneficial Occupancy Agreement will provide the Healthcare Provider Foundation with the same declining price perpetual purchase option and end-of-term obligation as the Synthetic Operating Lease described previously.
Asset Management Cost	0.375%

Debt Funding Terms

Amount	$4,500,000 (approximate)
Instrument	Commercial paper interest rate swap or cap (if desired)
Loan term	Up to 30 years, callable at credit enhancement termination
Credit Enhancement Term	5-year evergreen
Amortization	Up to 30 year amortization
Credit Enhancement Cost	Annual: 70 basis points on principal balance; up-front: 25 basis points
Real Estate Group Closing Fees	2.5 points
Other Costs	Legal expenses and other out-of-pocket costs are for the account of the borrower and guaranteed by the Healthcare Provider's Foundation.

Hypothetical Wellness Center
BALANCE SHEET
For month ended 30 June 1997

	June 1997	May 1997
ASSETS		
Cash and investments	113,087	67,855
Member receivables	51,796	34,868
Other receivables	93,779	153,048
Inventory	27,087	28,318
Prepaid expense	126,293	142,002
Current assets	**412,042**	**426,091**
Workers Compensation trust	5,700	
Property, plant, and equipment	1,218,531	1,214,301
Deposits	16,653	16,652
Organizational costs	13,320	13,320
Deferred pre-opening costs	270,354	268,242
Total assets	**1,936,600**	**1,938,606**
LIABILITIES AND STOCKHOLDERS EQUITY		
Accrued expenses	198,396	322,177
Secured deposits	1,948	1,948
Deferred revenue	11,229	26,645
Current liabilities	**211,573**	**350,770**
Capital lease obligations	650,892	661,402
Other liabilities	47,640	48,585
Capital stock	1,700,000	1,583,334
Retained earnings (deficit)	(673,506)	(705,484)
Total liabilities and stockholders equity	**1,936,599**	**1,938,607**

Hypothetical Wellness Center
STATEMENT OF INCOME
For month ended 30 June 1997

	June actual	June budget
REVENUES		
Dues	208,318	216,547
Initiation fees	40,852	53,591
Other revenue	61,548	58,277
Clinical program revenue	1,867	3,600
Total revenue	**312,585**	**332,015**

Continued on next page

	June actual	June budget
EXPENSES		
Salaries and wages	86,747	75,443
Benefits	(9,433)	9,233
Supplies and other	88,382	35,128
Rent expense	123,951	154,917
Utilities expense	23,107	24,928
Property taxes	(60,449)	39,749
Management fee	7,416	7,417
Advertising and marketing	4,899	3,876
Bad debt expense	—	1,534
Insurance expense	1,292	6,731
Depreciation expense	13,554	6,298
Amortization expense	(2,113)	2,745
Interest expense	5,232	5,132
Capitalized cost	—	—
Total expenses	**282,585**	**373,131**
Income/(loss) from operations	32,000	(41,116)
Nonoperations revenue/(expense)		
Interest income	824	966
Business privilege tax	(821)	(1,021)
Capital stock/franchise tax	(25)	(25)
Total non-operating revenue/(expense)	(22)	(80)
Net income/(loss)	**31,978**	**(41,196)**

Hypothetical Wellness Center

STATEMENT OF INCOME
For 12 months ending 30 June 1997

	Actual YTD	Budget YTD
REVENUES		
Dues	1,514,920	1,542,950
Initiation fees	652,913	670,018
Other revenue	523,806	539,004
Clinical program revenue	11,993	36,000
Total revenue	**2,703,632**	**2,787,972**
EXPENSES		
Salaries and wages	968,556	872,287
Benefits	106,068	99,995
Supplies and other	572,544	431,552
Rent expense	941,602	1,239,336
Utilities expense	193,036	234,858
Property taxes	159,949	357,733
Management fee	88,834	89,004
Advertising and marketing	67,347	104,132
Bad debt expense	—	10,616

Continued on next page

	Actual YTD	Budget YTD
Insurance expense	58,190	80,772
Depreciation expense	98,011	64,286
Amortization expense	23,000	26,074
Interest expense	54,612	51,320
Capitalized cost	(56,996)	(32,893)
Total expenses	**3,274,753**	**3,629,072**
Income/(loss) from operations	(571,121)	(841,100)
Nonoperations revenue/(expense)		
Interest income	4,212	9,660
Business privilege tax	(7,936)	(8,365)
Capital stock/franchise tax	(719)	(300)
Total nonoperating revenue/(expense)	(4,443)	995
Net income/(loss)	**(575,564)**	**(840,105)**

Hypothetical Wellness Center

STATEMENT OF CASH FLOWS
For 12 months ending 30 June 1997

	Current	YTD
CASH FLOW FROM OPERATING EXPENSES		
Net income/(loss)	31,978	(575,562)
Adjustment to reconcile net income/(loss) to net cash provided by operating activities:		
Decrease in receivables	42,341	(125,375)
(Increase) in prepaids	15,709	(114,761)
Decrease in inventory	1,231	(27,087)
(Increase) in deposits	—	68,203
Decrease in start-up cost	—	(32,196)
Increase in depreciation	13,553	98,012
Increase in amortization	(2,113)	23,000
Increase in deferred revenue	(15,416)	(48,215)
Increase in other liabilities	(945)	(2,637)
Increase in workers compensation trust	(5,700)	(5,700)
Increase in security deposits	—	1,948
Increase in accrued expense	(123,781)	123,030
Decrease in escrow account	—	109,723
Net cash provided by operating activities	**(43,143)**	**(507,617)**
CASH FLOW FROM INVESTING ACTIVITIES		
(Increase) in property and equipment	(17,783)	(1,290,086)
CASH FLOW FROM FINANCING ACTIVITIES		
(Decrease) in capital lease obligation	(10,510)	650,892
Issuance of capital stock	116,666	1,099,999
	106,156	1,750,891
Net increase (decrease) in cash	45,230	(46,812)
CASH, BEGINNING	67,856	159,900
CASH, ENDING	**113,086**	**113,088**

Hypothetical Wellness Center
MEMBERSHIP DATA
For 12 months ending 30 June 1997

OPENING MEMBERSHIP

Primary	2,214
Associate	969
Teen	673
Total	**3,856**

ADDITIONS

Primary	101
Associate	28
Teen	63
Total	**192**

TERMINATIONS

Primary	(25)
Associate	(7)
Teen	(7)
Total	**(39)**

NET FREEZES FOR MONTH

Primary	(47)
Associate	(28)
Teen	13
Total	**(62)**

ENDING MEMBERSHIP

Primary	2,290
Associate	990
Teen	729
Total	**4,009**

DUES REVENUE PER MEMBER

Primary	66.68
Associate	54.95
Teen	15.61

Hypothetical Wellness Center
PROJECTED CASH FLOW
Fiscal Year 1996 ($000)

	QUARTER			
	1st	2nd	3rd	4th
CASH BALANCE, BEGINNING OF PERIOD	113	251	404	113
Projected collections				
Total collections	290	290	300	880
Interest income	0	0	0	0
Other	100	125	125	350
Total sources of cash	**390**	**415**	**425**	**1,230**
CASH DISBURSEMENTS				
Operating expense	250	260	260	770
Capital expenditures	2	2	2	5
Intercompany				
Other expenditures				
Total uses of cash	**252**	**262**	**262**	**775**
CAPITAL CONTRIBUTION	**0**	**0**	**0**	**0**
CASH BALANCE, END OF PERIOD	**251**	**505**	**567**	**567**

Hypothetical Wellness Center
DETAIL OF OTHER REVENUE
For four months ending 31 October 1997

	Actual	Budget
Locker rental	27,314	27,840
Guest fees	21,258	20,200
Pro shop	22,117	22,500
Child care	20,832	23,400
Massage	11,755	11,500
Tennis	64,533	68,306
Personal training	26,524	21,000
Swimming	13,205	15,500
Sports camp	19,943	—
Consulting	60,893	33,333
Clinical programs	7,067	4,000
Other	21,247	24,717
Total other revenue	**316,688**	**272,296**

Hypothetical Wellness Center

MEMBERSHIP PROJECTIONS
Three-year projection for fiscal years 1998, 1999, and 2000

	PROJECTED CASE BY FISCAL YEAR		
	1998	*1999*	*2000*
Active membership	5,100	5,500	5,700
Frozen membership	670	700	725
Total membership	5,770	6,200	6,425
Average active membership	4,373	5,300	5,600
Ratio of frozen to total	11.61%	11.29%	11.28%
Ratio of terminations to total	17.54%	20.79%	24.87%
RATIO OF OTHER REVENUE TO TOTAL REVENUE			
Other revenue	1,160,052	1,218,054	1,278,957
Total revenue	4,942,306	5,796,608	6,199,641
Ratio	23.47%	21.01%	20.63%
OTHER REVENUE PER ACTIVE MEMBER	**$265.28**	**$229.82**	**$228.39**
Salary expense	1,132,381	1,166,352	1,189,679
Benefit expense	158,476	163,289	166,555
Total	**1,290,857**	**1,329,641**	**1,356,234**
Salary expense per member	**$295.19**	**$250.88**	**$242.18**

Hypothetical Wellness Center

BALANCE SHEET
Three-year projection for fiscal years 1998, 1999, and 2000 ($000)

	PROJECTED CASE		
	30 June 98	*30 June 99*	*30 June 00*
ASSETS			
Cash and investments	325,969	554,434	1,042,848
Member receivables	61,200	66,000	68,400
Accounts receivable	50,000	55,000	60,000
Inventory	30,000	31,500	33,080
Prepaid expense	130,000	133,900	137,920
Current assets	**597,169**	**840,834**	**1,342,248**
Assets whose use is limited			
Workers Compensation trust	8,000	9,000	10,000
Property, plant, and equipment	**1,360,130**	**1,621,740**	**1,823,350**
Other assets			
Deposits	0	0	0
Organizational costs	9,820	6,320	2,820
Deferred preopening costs	218,546	166,738	114,930
Total assets	**2,193,665**	**2,644,632**	**3,293,348**

Continued on next page

	30 June 98	30 June 99	30 June 00
LIABILITIES AND FUND BALANCE			
Accrued expenses	125,000	155,091	459,386
Secured deposits	1,950	1,950	1,950
Deferred revenue	12,000	12,000	12,000
Current liabilities	**138,950**	**169,041**	**473,336**
Capital lease obligations	524,772	395,652	272,532
Other liabilities	50,000	50,000	50,000
Fund balance/equity			
Capital stock	2,000,000	2,000,000	2,000,000
Retained earnings	(673,506)	(520,057)	26,939
Current year earnings (deficit)	153,449	546,996	470,541
Total fund balance	1,479,943	2,026,939	2,497,480
TOTAL LIABILITIES AND FUND BALANCE	**2,193,665**	**2,641,632**	**3,293,348**

Hypothetical Wellness Center

STATEMENT OF REVENUE AND EXPENSES
Three-year projection for fiscal years 1998, 1999, and 2000 ($000)

	PROJECTED CASE		
	30 June 98	30 June 99	30 June 00
OPERATING REVENUE			
Dues	3,246,814	4,189,579	4,512,799
Initiation fees	535,440	388,975	407,885
Other revenue	1,160,052	1,218,054	1,278,957
Total revenue	**4,942,306**	**5,796,608**	**6,199,641**
OPERATING EXPENSE			
Salaries and wages	1,132,381	1,166,352	1,189,679
Benefits	158,476	163,289	166,555
Supplies and other expenses	628,689	799,642	817,693
Rent expense	1,637,400	1,787,400	1,787,400
Utilities expense	264,000	271,920	280,078
Property taxes	440,892	454,119	467,742
Advertising and marketing	103,723	118,923	133,923
Insurance	78,204	80,550	82,967
Depreciation and amortization	263,700	293,700	383,700
Interest	74,328	74,328	74,328
Total expenses	**4,781,793**	**5,210,223**	**5,384,065**
Excess of revenue over expense from operations	160,513	586,385	815,576
Nonoperations revenue/(expense)			
Interest income	8,580	8,580	8,580
Business privilege tax	(15,278)	(17,380)	(18,599)
Corporate taxes (state and fed)	0	(30,091)	(334,386)
Capital stock/franchise tax	(366)	(498)	(630)
Total non-operating revenue (expense)	(7,064)	(39,389)	(345,035)
Net income/(loss)	**153,449**	**546,996**	**470,541**

Springfield Healthplex

An ideal example of the inclusion of different building types housing the delivery of healthcare is the Springfield Healthplex in Springfield, Pennsylvania. The facility is part of the Crozer-Keystone Healthcare System in Delaware County, Pennsylvania, a dynamic healthcare system that is constantly evolving in its service to the community and its success as a business entity. Facilities included in the system, their geographic locations, and the services they offer are presented in the following paragraphs.

Crozer-Chester Medical Center, Upland, Pennsylvania, is a not-for-profit teaching hospital with 775 licensed beds at three sites. Its unique services include:

- The Nathan Speare Regional Burn Treatment Center
- Trauma Center (the only one in Delaware County)
- The Silberman Center for specialized geriatric care
- Center for Occupational Health
- Transitional Internship Program
- Back Pain Center
- Open Heart Surgery Center
- Antepartum Assessment Center
- Neonatal Intensive Care Center
- Crozer Regional Cancer Center
- Crozer Reproductive Endocrinology and Fertility Center
- MRI Center of Delaware County
- Transitional Care Center/Skilled Nursing Facility

Community Hospital in Chester, Pennsylvania, operates as a part of the Crozer-Chester Medical Center, through which a full range of clinical services is available. Unique services include:

- Inpatient Psychiatry
- Dual Diagnosis Treatment
- Ambulatory Partial Hospital/Mental Health Services
- Substance Abuse Services
- Center for Family Health
- Behavioral Crisis Center

Delaware County Memorial Hospital is 313-bed acute care not-for-profit hospital in Drexel Hill, Pennsylvania. Its services include:

DEVELOPMENT PROFILES

- The Delaware County Regional Cancer Center, an on-site, exclusive arrangement with Fox Chase Cancer Center
- Comprehensive obstetric and gynecological services
- Neonatal intensive care nursery
- Outpatient Rehabilitation and Sports Medicine Center
- Surgicenter
- Transitional Care Center/Skilled Nursing Facility
- Healthline cervices/community education
- Orthopedic services
- Women's Diagnostic Center/mammography
- Adjoining medical office building, housing many physicians' practices, apothecary, and conference center

The Healthplex Campus, in Springfield, Pennsylvania, includes Springfield Hospital, the Healthplex, and a medical office building. Services include:

- Health Enhancement Center
- Crozer Center for Diabetes
- Nutrition Center
- Crozer Center for Wound Healing
- Foot and Ankle Center
- Hand Center
- Center for Occupational Health
- Cardiac and Cancer Rehabilitation Center
- Back Pain Center
- Center for Headache Management
- Healthplex Imaging Center (mammography, ultrasound, bone densitometry)
- Sports Medicine Institute
- Apothecary
- Outpatient Surgery Center
- Physical Medicine and Rehabilitation
- Medical Office Pavilion with more than 35 specialists and a full array of primary care services. A second 48,000-square-foot medical office building will soon be constructed.
- Healthplex Sports Club: 176,000 square feet, the official practice facility of the Philadelphia 76ers professional basketball team. The Healthplex offers therapy and lap

pools, racquetball and squash courts, tennis, basketball, indoor running track, aerobics studios, weight training, cardiovascular exercise machines, whirlpools, sauna, steam rooms, pro shop, restaurant, children's gymnasium, and child care.

LONG TERM CARE FACILITIES:

- The Belvedere/Chester, Pennsylvania, facility has 120 skilled and intermediate care beds, a 27-bed personal care unit, recreational, social, and rehabilitative services.

- Chapel Manor in Philadelphia, Pennsylvania, has 240 skilled and intermediate care beds, as well as recreational, social and rehabilitative services and respite care.

- Harston Hall in Flourtown, Pennsylvania, has 120 skilled and intermediate care beds, a 76-bed personal care unit, recreational, social and rehabilitative services and respite care.

- Pennsburg Manor in Pennsburg, Pennsylvania, offers 120 skilled and intermediate care beds, recreational and rehabilitative services, and respite care.

TRANSITIONAL CARE CENTERS (PROVIDING A VITAL BRIDGE BETWEEN ACUTE CARE AND LONG-TERM CARE)

- Delaware County Memorial Hospital, 27 beds
- Crozer Chester Medical Center, 24 beds

AMBULATORY CARE FACILITIES

- Centers for Occupational Health
- Crozer-Chester Medical Center
- Crozer-Keystone Healthplex
- Doctors Urgent Care of Havertown
- Center for Family Health, Springfield
- Center for Family Health, Chester
- Center for Family Health, Middletown
- Doctors Urgent Care of Havertown
- MRI Center of Delaware County
- ChesPenn Health Services

Federally funded community health centers providing primary care, dentistry, family therapy, substance abuse services, primary care for HIV-positive children and adults.

The Crozer-Keystone Health System is the largest in Delaware County, Pennsylvania, and third in the region ranked by the number of licensed beds. Characteristics of the population served are given in the following table.

Delaware County Population 1995

Age	Number	Projected percentage growth 1995 to 2000
0–17	128,017	-1.2
18–64	332,062	+0.5
65–84	77,033	-2.7
85+	8,836	11.6
Total	545, 948	-0.2

64,796 households, or 32.3 percent, of households in the 1995 Census had children

EDUCATION LEVEL OF ADULTS AGED 18+ (1990 CENSUS)

Element	Percent of Whole
< High school	17.9
HS grad/some college	59.1
Bachelor's degree	15.0
Graduate degree	8.0

MEDIAN HOUSEHOLD INCOME		NUMBER OF HOUSEHOLDS BY INCOME	
Bracket	Income ($)	Bracket ($)	Percent of whole
Low	25,225	<15,000	12.9
Medium	43,078	15,000–34,999	23.5
High	115,673	35,000–74,999	11.8
		100,000 and up	12.2

PAYER MIX

	Crozer-Keystone (FY 1996)	Five-County Region (1994)
Medicare	39	44
Managed care	34	19
Blue Cross	11	13
Medicaid	8	12
Commercial	2	7
Self-pay and others	6	5

The president and chief executive officer of the Crozer-Keystone Health System, John C. McMeekin, wrote in 1997,

> Finally our new vision of health and wellness incorporates important relationships with our community and the individuals who receive our care. From schools, to community health centers, social service agencies, local government and business communities as well as payers and other healthcare organizations, we are listening, learning and creating new ways to truly integrate care and improve wellness.

Springfield's Center for Preventive Medicine and Human Performance offers an Executive Health Program, which includes a more thorough health assessment than is offered through a traditional physical. A "Work Capacity Program" is designed specifically for fire fighters and police to ensure that they can withstand the rigors of their jobs. Services offered through this program also include stress testing, blood profiles, body fat measurements, cardiopulmonary testing, and wellness/fitness program design.

The Physical Medicine and Rehabilitation Transition Program is a 12-week program for individuals who are ready to be discharged from a physical therapy program but still need guidance in continuing with a physical therapy program for a short period of time. Clients are referred by physicians.

Aerobics class, Sinai Wellbridge, Pikesville, Maryland.

The Springfield Healthplex offers fitness programs in aerobics, aquatics, basketball, and personal training, programs for kids and teens, programs for women, programs for senior members, strength training, tennis, and volleyball.

Membership at the Springfield Healthplex costs approximately $900 per year and is partially reimbursed by some insurance companies in Pennsylvania.

Sinai Wellbridge

The largest and most comprehensive community hospital in Maryland and the third-largest teaching hospital is Sinai Hospital of Baltimore Sinai Health System. Founded in 1866 as the Hebrew Hospital and Asylum, Sinai has evolved into a Jewish-sponsored healthcare organization providing care for all. Sinai is a nonprofit institution with a mission of patient care, teaching, and research.

Sinai Health System is an integrated delivery system which is composed of Sinai Hospital of Baltimore, the Levindale Hebrew Geriatric Center and Hospital, and several clinical and support entities that serve the central Maryland region.

Sinai subsidiaries and affiliates include Sinai Rehabilitation, Inc., which operates rehabilitation programs in the Baltimore metropolitan area for individuals and nursing homes, and Sinai Investments, Inc., a holding company for a variety of for-profit investments, which include the following:

- Sinai Care, Inc., contracts with third-party payers for provision of health services.
- Healthstar Medical Services, Inc., accepts and administers capitated and alternatively priced contracts, including capitated Medicaid subcontracts with managed care organizations.
- Practice Dynamics, Inc., provides management services to Sinai-affiliated and independent community-based medical practices.
- Sinai Community Practice Network LLC is a growing physician group whose practices, assets, and office staff are owned, employed, and managed by Practice Dynamics, Inc.
- SurgiCenter of Baltimore is a multispecialty ambulatory surgical center in Owings Mills, Maryland, a joint venture of Sinai and a number of community-based physicians.
- Sinai Wellbridge and Fitness Center, in Pikesville, Maryland, constitute a joint venture between Sinai and the Monsanto Corporation.

- Sinai Corporate Health, Inc., provides a variety of health and wellness programs for corporations, government agencies, and community groups. It is Maryland's largest provider of corporate fitness and wellness services.
- Sinai Lithotripter, Inc., represents Sinai's investment in the Maryland Kidney Stone Center, a joint venture between Sinai, three hospital corporations, and physicians, which provides outpatient lithotripsy in Baltimore County.
- Sinai Investments, Inc., owns interests in physicians group practices in northwest Baltimore, and a one-seventh interest in the Visiting Nurses Association of Maryland and its associated companies, Libertymed Care Center in Eldersburg and the Medical Care Center in Towson, Maryland.
- Northwest Hospital, Randallstown, Maryland.

Sinai Wellbridge Health and Fitness Center opened in 1996 in suburban Pikesville, Maryland. It is located on a 110,000-square-foot medical campus, adjacent to an upscale suburban shopping center. Sinai Hospital has owned a fitness-only facility in Owings Mills, Maryland, since 1984. The first hospital-based fitness center in the state, that facility was designed to serve as a bridge between fitness and acute care. Sinai Hospital senior vice president Neil Meltzer engaged Darryl McKay, who was to become Sinai Wellbridge's successful executive director, to run the Owings Mills facility and then help to develop a health and fitness center at the suggestion of leading healthcare consultant, Jeff Bensky of the Benfield Group.

Meltzer and McKay sought a partner to share the risk. They contacted the Wellbridge Company in Newton, Massachusetts. Wellbridge, a subsidiary of Monsanto, had access to ready capital. At the time, Wellbridge owned four wellness centers in the Boston area and had valuable experience. The fifty-fifty partnership that developed gave each party representation in consensus decision making at the new Sinai Wellbridge.

Wellbridge president Larry Kreiger said,

We've always thought that a hospital partner would be a wonderful match, and Sinai was a great place to start. It has a wonderful reputation and it really needed a wellness center. The way they operate is, of course, very different from the way we operate, but every partnership is that way. You have to get used to one another. You have to be willing to sit down and clarify your goals. There were growing pains and inevitable squabbles, but we always knew that something good was waiting at the end of the process. Trust and honesty are important, and both sides lived up to their obligations. For us it's been a great experience.

Meltzer acknowledged that there was no prescribed formula for how a wellness center project should come together: "There was no contract you could pull off a shelf. We were working from scratch to formulate, and then create, a shared vision. That forced us to think through what was important to both companies."

The medical director of the center was selected first because the hospital's cardiac rehabilitation program was the first clinical program to be located at the wellness center. All of the hospital's cardiologists have their offices at the center.

Like those at the Springfield Healthplex, patients who are involved in a cardiac rehabilitation program at the center are mainstreamed into fitness programs after 12 weeks. The seamless transition from patient to client is one of the benefits to patients at wellness centers generally, and at Sinai Wellbridge particularly. Darryl McKay said, "By the time they have completed their cardiac rehabilitation, more than 69 percent decide to join Sinai Wellbridge."

Patients are constantly monitored throughout the center with the aid of a telemetry system. Notes McKay,

> Our cardiologists have their offices on-site, and during classes, cardiac nurses are on hand. We have a crash cart with the necessary medications and defibrillator. Our staff is very well trained. Our fitness director and assistant director both have master's degrees in exercise physiology, and our fitness trainers are all trained in how to handle cardiac patients. We have clinical psychologists to help them manage stress; we run educational classes of all kinds; we have a registered nutritionist to provide guidance on nutrition.

There is a very successful patient referral system at Sinai. More than 70 of the hospital's physicians refer their patients to Sinai Wellbridge. "Doctors know that we won't hurt their patients," says McKay. "We fill out an extensive questionnaire for each one. If they have health risks, we conduct an exercise stress test before permitting them to exercise. We require written guidelines from doctors indicating what their patients can and can't do. And we provide the physicians with complete feedback."

Capitation is mandated in the state of Maryland, which sets the stage for the appeal of prevention and wellness programs. There is incentive to provide preventive care programs that keep people well. Under capitation, the state sets limits on the rates hospitals can charge for beds and medication, and managed care entities in the form of health maintenance organizations (HMOs) use their leverage to negotiate stringent terms for the reimbursement of procedures. HMOs wield tremendous power because hospital systems want a piece of their business. As hospitals seek alliances to increase market share and become more interested in providing services through outpatient centers, the pressure is increased.

"All of which makes wellness centers such as Sinai Wellbridge a crucial link for, or extension of, the hospital," says McKay. "Sinai Wellbridge is, in a very real sense, a satellite of Sinai Hospital here in Baltimore; when people see Sinai Wellbridge, they see Sinai Hospital."

Within the first year of opening, Sinai Wellbridge was projecting a profit of more than a half million dollars. Since physical therapy was transferred to the wellness center, McKay has seen a fourfold increase in that product line. "We can also measure the number of patients that we refer to the hospital; some of our wellness patients don't have physicians, and we refer them directly to the hospital."

Sinai Wellbridge Health and Fitness offers wellness programs in the following areas:

Prenatal/postnatal wellness

Stress Management

Senior Wellness Programs

Lifeshape Weight Management Program

Water Arthritis/ Aquatherapy Programs

The center has distinctive competencies in several components:

Institute for Cardiovascular Disease Prevention

Rehabilitation Center

Institute for Parkinson's Disease Therapy

Institute for Osteoporosis Prevention and Therapy

Health services available at the center include the following:

Personal Training

Sports Medicine

Nutritional Counseling

Physical Therapy

Stroke Exercise

Massage

The center's Medical Advisory Board is represented by the following specialties:

General Surgery

Internal Medicine

Neurology

Obstetrics/Gynecology

Orthopedic Surgery

Psychiatry

Pulmonary Diseases

Rehabilitation Medicine

Rheumatology

Sports Medicine/Orthopedic Trauma

Memberships are approximately $900 annually, and generate 90 percent of revenues. The total area is 57,000 square feet, and construction cost $5.5 million. The program is currently under expansion.

The fitness program at Sinai Wellbridge includes, on the first floor, aerobics, a basketball/volleyball luxury locker room featuring more than 225 lockers each for men and women, whirlpool, sauna, steam room, massage therapy, heated 25-yard swimming pool, water aerobics, swimming lessons, therapeutic rehabilitation pool, playroom, and child care services.

The second floor includes a one-tenth-mile, banked, three-lane track with windows that allow for views of the outdoors as well as of the exercise area and basketball courts below, an exercise machine area including pneumatic exercise equipment, a combined weight and free-weight machine area, a stretching area, and a cardio theater, which features modern entertainment technology that allows exercisers to listen to their choice of television stations and various CDs while exercising on treadmills, airdynes, stair climbers, rowing machines, recumbent bikes, and so forth.

The Entrepreneurial Model

In this relatively new field, specialty developers abound. Several have in-depth experience and offer a full menu of services, which enables the healthcare system to benefit in a number of ways.

The Healthcare Equities Group, Inc. (HEG), of Grand Rapids, Michigan, has developed more than 20 wellness centers, including the Springfield Healthplex in conjunction with Crozer-Keystone Healthcare and Healthplex president Steve Robbins. The group has developed projects up to and including wellness centers in the 200,000-square-foot range.

Mark Nadel of HEG, Inc., has been instrumental in the creation of wellness center projects, offering a wealth of expertise as well as a staff of key people who specialize in this facility type. HEG developed the "Healthplex" concept, which has been described as an integration of ambulatory care, fitness, and health promotion. Organizations like HEG join hospitals to share risk as an equity partner.

As the business has evolved, however, Nadel's group has more often become the project developer, the major equity owner that develops the wellness center projects, which then acquire healthcare systems as participants after the initial project deal is formed. Alliances are then formed with hospital systems in a variety of ways. This method of project formation allows a hospital to have even less risk associated with the venture. A hospital may take this alternative route in order to test the waters of a market it is unsure of. Using the expertise and capital of a group such as HEG, a hospital is assured that an expert is involved in a product line of which it, the hospital, may know little or nothing. This resource can be invaluable. As program elements of the wellness center evolve, only an expert can advise a healthcare partner on which fitness, spa, or complementary medicine program may be a valuable inclusion in the program mix. He or she will also be able to advise the hospital on the feasibility of the project, and the return on investment that the hospital may reasonably expect from its involvement in the wellness center.

Other benefits of working with a group like HEG is the ability to draw from a database of existing wellness center developments and to examine the elements of those particular investments. Groups such as this one can provide a knowledge base that is critical to the success of a project's development, including knowledge of the regulatory environment. Also important is the availability of equity capital and other financial resources.

Mercy Health System

In Greater Cincinnati, Ohio, the Mercy Health System has developed the Mercy Health and Wellness Center at Fairfield. Clinical services available at Mercy are physical therapy, occupational therapy and audiology, cardiopulmonary rehabilitation, physicians' offices, and specialized pediatric services. Emerging complementary medicine services include Holistic Health Services, massage therapy, biofeedback, meditation, t'ai chi, and other experimental programs.

Fitness programs include cardiovascular and weight training, indoor track, swimming pool, tennis courts, racquetball, kids' activity areas, and a gymnasium. Health education services include a health resources library, interactive health education classrooms, child care, and a 300-seat auditorium.

Thomas Urban, president of Mercy Hospital, Hamilton/Fairfield, describes the Mercy Center philosopy:

> This center is a tangible expression of Mercy's commitment to the holistic mission and values of the Sisters of Mercy. Our philosophy states, in part, that we provide health services that recognize and address the needs of the whole person—body, mind, and spirit. These comprehensive and diverse services will enhance life and promote personal involvement in physical and spiritual well-being.

In Owensboro, Kentucky, the Healthpark, to be built by the Owensboro Mercy Health System (OMHS), will include a gymnasium, indoor swimming pool, laboratory, radiology/imaging, cardiac rehabilitation, oncology, geriatric intervention services, chapel, and offices for wellness-oriented programs. Greg Carlson of OMHS reported that the $12 million Healthpark is part of the hospital's goal to improve the health of the community. For this project, the original 1948 Mercy Hospital building will be demolished, as a feasibility study showed that it was more cost-effective to remove it to make way for the Healthpark. OMHS will keep the four-story Medical Plaza I building that houses physicians' offices and a pharmacy, and Mercy Medical Plaza II, the former maternity unit.

The three-story wellness center will include the following services:

Outpatient radiology and laboratory
Convenient care center for minor emergencies and illnesses
Outpatient Rehabilitation Center, including a warm-water therapy pool
Community Health Resource Center
Chapel
Fitness Center
Medical Office Space
25-yard swimming pool
Outpatient physical therapy
Speech therapy
Sports medicine
Rehabilitation

Carlson went on to say, "Owensboro Mercy Health System will continue to heal the sick, but we also want a new mission. The opportunities to improve healthcare in our community are not in the traditional areas. What if the hospital of the future is a place you go to when you are healthy?"

Copley Memorial Hospital

Copley Memorial Hospital was incorporated in 1886 in the state of Illinois, in downtown Aurora. In 1995 a new 142-bed Copley Memorial Hospital was built to serve the growing western suburbs. The Rush-Copley Medical Center, as it is called today, is home to Copley Memorial Hospital and its six key patient centers: Cancer Care, the Emergency Center, the Physical Rehabilitation Center, the Rush-Copley Heart Institute, the Surgery Center, and the Women's Center.

The hospital's mission is dedication to health education and wellness. A children's day-care facility, called the Children's World Learning Center; the Waubonsee Center at Copley, a satellite facility of Waubonsee Community College; and the Rush-Copley Healthplex are all within the medical center campus.

Copley, a member of Rush-Presbyterian-St. Luke's Medical Center in Chicago, affiliated in 1987 with the Rush System for Health. Rush-Copley is a community hospital with cutting-edge technology and resources.

The Rush-Copley Healthplex Fitness Center opened in 1997 in Chicago, Illinois. This center is a 160,000-square-foot facility that offers a variety of fitness activities as well as 35,000 square feet of medical office space which will house a number of hospital outpatient services and physicians' practices. Its focus is on helping members with exercise prescriptions, a health promotion and education commitment to children's fitness, integrated aquatherapy, and services for obese individuals.

The Healthplex features fitness assessment programs, cardiovascular exercise and weight training equipment, eight indoor tennis courts, a one-fifth-mile indoor track, aerobics classes, a climbing wall, a gymnasium, an aquatics area featuring a six-lane indoor pool and outdoor patio, a therapy pool, and a uniquely designed children's exercise area.

The Rush-Copley Healthplex provides a fitness plan for the member's review upon completion of a fitness assessment that includes a health history, measurement of body fat, measurement of cardiovascular fitness, and determination of muscular strength and flexibility. Recognizing that a commitment to fitness should be a lifelong process, beginning early, the Healthplex has an area for children to work out. Designed for children ages 3 to 12, a special Funfit membership is available. Kids Funfit members have access to their own fitness area, which includes a gymnasium, exercise equipment sized for children's use, and a locker room. There are a variety of children's programs and activities available in a safe and secure environment.

An interesting idea that has evolved at the Rush-Copley Healthplex was to secure a private exercise area for people who are obese. The Healthplex includes an aerobics studio for special classes geared to individuals who are overweight.

Director Kirk Kruse commented, "After touring the Healthplex and finding out that we have included a special area to address their particular needs, many people have enrolled."

Although nearly all wellness center programs have some sort of educational program, usually focused on health education, the Rush-Copley Center was one of the first to have a community college satellite program within its medical campus.

Mississippi Baptist Medical Center

Another new trend in the development of wellness centers was begun at Mississippi Baptist Medical Center and Mississippi College in Clinton, near Jackson, Mississippi. In November 1995 two of Mississippi's leading Baptist institutions, Mississippi Baptist Medical Center and Mississippi College, joined and announced plans to introduce a new concept in fitness, wellness, and community health improvement through the development of a Healthplex project on the Mississippi College Campus.

Today that project is built and is meeting with great success. Howell W. Todd, M.D., Mississippi College president, remarked,

> This facility will not only provide recreational benefits, but it will strengthen and enhance our allied health education and nursing curriculum. The Healthplex is being built because we are no longer placing our sole athletic emphasis on competitive sports, but are seeking ways to encourage students to become involved in life sports that they will be able to engage in throughout their lives.

Such activities include aerobics running swimming cardiovascular exercise and low impact competitive sports. Mississippi College, with an enrollment of approximately 3,500 students, had identified a need for expansion of its on campus facilities. In particular, there was a need to expand student recreational facilities in order for us to attract prospective students.

M. Kent Strum, CEO of Mississippi Baptist Medical Center, said of the partnership,

Fitness area/basketball court,
Springfield Healthplex, Springfield,
Pennsylvania

Because of our common interest in fitness, wellness and community health improvement we have chosen a comprehensive
approach to provide these and other healthcare and educational services in Clinton. This is truly a collaborative effort,
bringing to the student community increased opportunities
for recreation and fitness while at the same time allowing
much needed growth to serve the healthcare needs of this
growing area. Hospitals, which have traditionally focused on
sickness, are now recognizing that we have the responsibility
in preventing disease and promoting health. ... Because of
these trends the College and Medical Center have this innovative concept, combining fitness, wellness and ambulatory care
services with major emphasis on disease prevention, health
promotion and community health improvement.

President Todd concurs, "Similar linkage between the colleges
and the medical centers have worked well in other locations."
The Medical Center's patients, as well as Mississippi College's
faculty, staff, and students will be able to use the Healthplex as
part of their treatment for physical medicine and rehabilitation,
occupational therapy, cardiopulmonary therapy, and other prescribed healthcare services. "We believe the mix among the
College, Medical staff, patients and the community represents
an ideal union that will serve to promote prevention and good
health for the entire community."

The Healthplex project involved a 21,000-square-foot reno-
vation of Alumni Hall, the creation of a 64,577-square-foot fitness center, and a 20,000-square-foot medical office space.
Services available include ambulatory/outpatient services,
physical therapy and rehabilitation therapy, physical education,
occupational medicine, athletic training, coach training, sports

management, and the fitness facility itself. Various hospital programs cross utilize the fitness center equipment and space. The Healthplex is managed by Mississippi College, Mississippi Baptist Medical Center, and Healthcare Equities Group, Inc.

Memorial Leighton Healthplex

Memorial Leighton Healthplex in South Bend, Indiana, is a proposed wellness complex developed by HEG and sponsored by Memorial Hospital. This center will offer the community a full range of fitness services: four-lane lap pool, two aerobics studios, a cardio exercise area, a strength and conditioning area with circuit training and free-weight areas, a child care area, basketball/volleyball, and a virtual driving range.

The clinical support area will include pulmonary/cardiac rehabilitation, the Independent Living Center, the Outpatient Traumatic Brain Injury program, Ergonomic Consultation Services, and orthopedic sports therapy.

Akron General Medical Center

Akron General Medical Center in Akron, Ohio, is a teaching hospital that serves a catchment area including 1.2 million people. The hospital was founded as Peoples Hospital in 1914 by a group of physicians and citizens who recognized a need for a second hospital in the community. The original hospital, which had 125 beds, has since grown to include 511 beds. Akron General is a tertiary care center staffed with 740 physicians, more than 3,000 health professionals and support staff, and 550 volunteers.

Akron General Medical Center has more than 70 departments and specialties, including Emergency and Critical Care Medicine, Hemodyalisis and a Hyperbaric Oxygen Chamber Unit, a Sleep Disorders Center, a Women's Center, a Wound Center, and a research laboratory.

Akron Medical Center developed the Akron Health and Fitness Center with the assistance of Jeff Bensky, president of the Benfield Group of St. Louis, Missouri. The Health and Wellness Center a 190,000-square-foot facility, is considered one of the best in the nation and noted for its comprehensive programs.

The senior management team at Akron General perceived a need to "reinvent the way we deliver healthcare to the community." The Benfield Group saw its mission as being "to help a regional hospital develop a component of a first-of-its-kind outpatient facility, where a fitness and wellness center integrates with a complete range of rehabilitation services."

Together the team created a facility that provides outpatient services ranging from diagnostic testing, same-day surgery, physical therapy, and rehabilitation, to health and fitness conditioning. The economics here, as in many other wellness center projects, make sense; all of these services can be provided at a competitive cost because the wellness center does not have the high overhead cost found in acute care facilities.

The Benfield Group, as the hospital's consultant, helped the hospital discover how to integrate the health and fitness business product line with its outpatient rehabilitation business. The group studied the market feasibility and demand for the hospital system's catchment area, which serves Summit, Medina, Portage, Stark, and Wayne counties in northeast Ohio. The hospital also benefited from this partnership by learning how to position, operate, and strategically plan this product line for long-term financial success.

The program elements were then defined, operating assumptions considered, a financial feasibility study performed, and a business plan created, which Akron General used to develop the facility. The consultant then worked with the architect to make sure that the program and operational plan were fully communicated from the user's perspective.

This $32 million project was financed through the hospital's revenues. The facility was built off the main hospital campus, west of Akron in the Montrose area of Bath Township, Akron's fastest growing suburb. The clinical zone in this facility consists of sports medicine, physical therapy, aquatic rehabilitation, diagnostic services (including ultrasound, imaging, and MRI), a breast health center, a surgery center, four outpatient surgery suites, a recovery area, two endoscopy suites, a lab, exam rooms, presurgical testing, and cardiac and pulmonary testing.

The Cardiopulmonary Phase III is an extension of the Phase I and II programs offered at the medical center. This health maintenance program is designed to improve and maintain cardiopulmonary conditioning, endurance, flexibility, and overall strength through monitored exercise.

Northeast Ohio Sports Medicine and Physical Therapy at the Healthplex offers aquatic exercise and physical therapy in a three-lane therapy pool, orthotics, sports physicals and rehabilitation, and functional capacity evaluation. The fitness zone includes a pool, whirlpool, indoor track, aerobics studio, gymnasium, "Kidstyles" kid fitness, and more than 200 exercise machines. "Lifestyles," a medically supervised membership and exercise program, is led by exercise physiologists. Fitness programs are designed to improve members' overall health as well as to support patient recovery.

Other amenities include physicians' offices, child care, a library, a cafe, and conference rooms that are available for rental. Administrator Sonda Burns says, "The Healthplex is flourishing and we are looking forward to expanding."

The Benfield Group summarized its involvement in the Akron General Medical Center Healthplex as follows:

Consultant Involvement:
1. Facilitate decision making relating to entry into the health and fitness business.
2. Establish a unified vision relative to the business strategy and model.
3. Develop a comprehensive business plan.
4. Study market demand and determine financial feasibility.
5. Integrate fitness, wellness, and clinical components.
6. Collaborate with project architect to ensure programming and operational needs are merged with design elements to properly meet end use expectations.

Key Outcomes of the Process
1. Developed a comprehensive vision to support strategy.
2. Determined consumer preferences, needs, motivations for services.
3. Defined programming and operational needs and motivations for architectural design (with architect's comlete involvement).
4. Integrated fitness, wellness, and clinical components into a seamless facility design for a 190,000-square-foot facility.

The Life Center

In Greenville, South Carolina, the Greenville Hospital System was interested in developing a cardiac rehabilitation center on its main hospital campus. As the idea grew, the program did too. It began to include additional clinical programs and a commercial health and fitness club, which would be integrated into one facility.

The Benfield Group was instrumental in bringing health and fitness club expertise into the picture, integrating this knowledge with knowledge of clinical programs. Working as a development partner to "define a working model of people, programs and place" was the group's mission. The consultant translated market research into data that became the basis for the hospital's marketing and operational plan. Marketing campaigns promoted the facility's ability to offer medically supervised programs, personal attention, qualified staff, and a nonintimidating environment. The target audience for the marketing campaign included medical staff, corporations, former hospital patients, and other potential user groups.

Today the Greenville Hospital Life Center is one of the most financially successful wellness centers in the country. The population of Greenville, South Carolina, is 60,000 in the city and 400,000 in Greenville County, which encompasses 798 square miles. The total population for Greenville-Spartanburg is 850,000. With an unemployment rate of less than 5 percent (in 1997), Greenville is a fast growing area with a number of universities and colleges.

Greenville Hospital, established in 1912, became the nation's first hospital system in 1954. At that time, Greenville Hospital System (GHS) began building a network of hospitals. Today that network includes Allen Bennet Hospital and Roger Huntington Nursing Center in Greer, Hillcrest Hospital in Simpsonville, North Greenville Hospital in Travelers Rest, Greenville Memorial Medical Center, Roger C. Peace Rehabilitation Hospital, the Children's Hospital, and the Marshal I. Pickens Psychiatric Hospital.

Greenville is nationally recognized for its visionary programs. A nonprofit community hospital system, GHS is run by a volunteer board. Its mission to improve quality, access, and cost is being maintained by its growth into a fully integrated healthcare system.

Community wellness is defined at GHS as "going beyond traditional medical care and reaching out to the community to keep people healthy." GHS has programs that include a full range of health and behavioral health services, as well as prevention and wellness services, health education and training, and a primary care physician network.

The development of the Life Center seemed a logical step in continuing the process of providing the community with a complete continuum of care. The Life Center wellness center is a 55,000-square-foot facility . Clinical programs include Cardiac Rehabilitation, Sports Medicine, Oncology Rehabilitation, and Pulmonary Rehabilitation. The fitness program includes aerobics, weights, volleyball, outdoor track, sauna, 25-meter swimming pool, indoor walk/run track, circuit weight training equipment, and computerized exercise logging program equipment.

Educational programs include "healthy heart" cooking classes and supermarket tours that guide people in the selection of good nutritional choices, nutrition consultation for adolescents, and programs for weight management and smoking cessation. Amenities include a cafe, serving low-fat nutritious meals, and child care.

The Marsh

The Marsh, a Center for Balance and Fitness, in Minnetonka, Minnesota, has a clear mission. In a recent magazine article published by International Health and Racquet Sports Association (IHRSA) Ruth Stricker, owner and director, said, "When we opened our doors twelve years ago, people wondered what we were trying to do. ... The Marsh exists to help people balance their lives. We believe that fitness and wellness involve much more than a physical workout. If your body is fit and your mind isn't, you can't be balanced."

The Marsh has eight core departments: fitness center, spa, physical therapy department, kids' center, full-service restaurant, conference center, sports shop, and guestrooms.

"The physical therapy department is staffed by outside professionals who lease space and operate the clinic as a freestanding business," says Mary Crawford, M.S., exercise physiologist at the center. "Their services are integrated, in a nearly seamless way, into what I do here; it's pretty unique, I think. Similarly, the psychologist, who works with us on a contractual basis seems very much like a member of our own staff. He does clinics and workshops, and sees people one on one, billing their insurance plans."

The center has a sleep disorders clinic and a nutritionist on staff who teaches cooking classes and gives lectures on topics such as food fads and the need for antioxidants in the diet. There is also a special reconditioning program that provides a transition to wellness for patients who have been working with

Pool at Sinai Wellbridge, Pikesville, Maryland.

a cardiologist, orthopedist, or physical therapist. New members are evaluated by an exercise physiologist . Members who are at risk for cardiac problems take an EKG stress test on a treadmill under the supervision of cardiologists who work with the center on a contractual basis.

For about half the patients, insurance reimbursement is utilized. An advantage that Ruth Stricker had in creating this wonderful, vital business was that it was self-financed. This meant that she had and has control of the program mix, which in the case of The Marsh is unique.

Had Stricker's center been partnered with a hospital, it might have gained credibility earlier in its presentation to the market because of the formal healthcare affiliation, but it would not have allowed her to maintain her intended mission as purely as she has.

The Core Method, an offshoot of the Pilates strength training method (developed by Joseph Pilates for professional dancers) is the basis of the exercise program at The Marsh. The Core Method's philosophy is that all physical conditioning begins at the core of the body, the trunk and abdomen, and that every area of the body should be worked as an extension of the core. Stricker is faithful to this philosophy, as it is reflected in every facet of every exercise program at the center.

Unique to this wellness center is the inclusion in the program of six overnight guest rooms. Added in an expansion program five years ago, the guest rooms were designed as a profit center to offset areas of the club that were not showing a profit.

As described in the IHRSA article, the attentive, thoughtful, responsive, and rewarding atmosphere makes The Marsh more than just a place to exercise. Mary Crawford characterized this further:

> Many of our members treat the center as a second home. They come here to socialize or to just while away a few hours of their day. We've tried to create a comfort level that reflects respect and tolerance. ... We support and encourage. With our new members, our focus is on posture and core strength. We help them design a manageable program viable both physically and in terms of their time. Our goal is to assist and guide them so they can achieve balance in their lives.
>
> Obviously our members come here for different reasons than the ones attracted to commercial gyms. Our members tend to be a bit older, although now we are getting people in their 20s and 30s. And they are looking for a moderate, health oriented, centering place. They want something more than fitness. They are seeking answers to the questions in their lives.

Ruth explains:

> People exercise as a way of dealing with existence pain, which is what I call living. At the other end of the spectrum is joy. But if one's mind-set, the psychological and emotional setting, is as important as the physical aspects of exercise, why do people work out in dirty, noisy, smelly, cramped places ? Here, we don't have posters all over the walls; we have plants and windows. The Marsh is a place where people come to connect rather than disconnect. We don't want them to do things that isolate them, cut them off from everyone else. Today, people feel a constant need to set priorities, achieve agendas, but why should everyone be in such a hurry? At The Marsh we give them permission to relax and look around.

The Marsh has programs in basic fitness, wellness, spa services, and sports-specific alternative medicine. Membership is in the 2,400 range. Annual revenues, as reported in the IHRSA article, are $4.5 million.

Conclusions

There are many considerations that influence the selection of programs for inclusion in a wellness center program, all with great impact on the economic feasibility of building the initial project and, after it is built, watching it flourish.

Steve Robbins of the Crozer System suggests that off-balance-sheet financing, the financing method that has supported about half of the wellness centers around the country, still ends up with recourse to the hospital. He advises hospitals that if they are master-leasing a facility, they might as well buy it. This view varies within the financial community.

The most important issue at stake in developing a wellness center, according to Robbins, is control. If a hospital does not have financial control of a facility, the hospital will not be able to control the programs that will located within the facility.

Owners or investors who have a non-health-care perspective, that is, a retail perspective, are looking for very different things when they consider the programming and design of a wellness center. A retail-oriented investor may endeavor to control programming so that there are no programs that include patient populations they may not consider "fitting," such as those for developmentally disabled children. They may pressure the building committee and architect to create separate entrances for "sick"and "well" populations, which defeats the purpose of the entire concept of integrated wellness services.

The retail-oriented investor may elect to put rehabilitation programs such as cardiopulmonary rehabilitation in areas secluded from the main fitness areas, encouraging an "us" and "them" atmosphere, rather than capitalizing on the synergies of wellness center program integration.

For the architect, understanding that this hybrid facility is at once a dynamic opportunity to project a new healthcare model for the future, and a challenge in the sorting out of agendas and politics of two very different businesses, healthcare and retail, is of the utmost importance. The architect must educate the healthcare executive to the nuances of retail design and the advantages of various design approaches that will benefit the healthcare component, and at the same time, instruct the retail (club) executive on how vital the healthcare component is to the facility's success and the special needs of such programs. The following table summarizes the programming issues of the typical wellness center.

Wellness Center Programming Issues

Issue	Question	Facility Implications
MANAGEMENT STRUCTURE	What will the ownership of the wellness center be?	Owners control program mix.
	How will ownership affect management and operations?	Managers may have objectives that are different from those of owners.
	What future programs are planned?	Identify future programs to ensure flexibility of space.
CLINICAL PROGRAM	Which programs will move from the hospital to the wellness center (e.g., cardio-pulmonary, physical therapy)?	Identify specialized requirements associated with each clinical program.
	Which physicians are likely to relocate to the wellness center or to share space there?	Are dedicated physician offices required?
FITNESS PROGRAM	What are the goals of the program?	Will phasing for future development be included?
	What age groups will be served?	Adult/senior/children fitness facility balance. Day care, children's lockers, fitness areas.
	Will the age demographics change over time?	Will more adult or senior-oriented programs be required in the future than there are now?
	How will clinical rehabilitation and fitness exercise machinery be selected? Will rehab patients be separated from fitness clients?	Are separate areas required for rehab and fitness equipment?
	Will there be a separate area for obese patients?	May be combined with others.
EDUCATIONAL PROGRAM	Will classes be mostly small or large?	Space accommodations range from 5 to 7 persons through auditorium size.
	Will there be cooking classes?	Fume hoods, additional mechanical requirements.
SPA PROGRAM	What level of spa services will be included?	Sauna, steam, whirlpool, therapeutic massage, Vichy showers, and salon services.
COMMON AREA PROGRAM	Will a retail program be included?	Pro shop, salon, library or bookstore, nutritional supplement sales.
	What type of food service is desired?	Juice bar, snack bar, cafe, cafeteria, full-service restaurant.

Designing the Wellness Center

An environment can be powerful medicine. We are affected every day by the choices made by others as to the ease, joy, and comfort we feel in our travel through spaces.

The environment that speaks most powerfully to us is home, and we see everything through the oculus of this important center. How close to home an environment is has dramatic effect on how comfortable we feel within it, the degree to which we are drawn back to it.

If home is the center of our comfort zone, whose home are we talking about when we decide to impose a "homelike" residential design on an environment that is obviously not home? If this transformation could be magically performed, and we translated to the healthcare setting all the cues—visual, auditory, aromatic—of home, whose home are we using as the standard?

Culture has everything to do with a sense of comfort. Edward Hall suggested decades ago that people needed "personal space" and posited that this personal space changes dramatically from culture to culture.

Around the world, the use of large spaces can be meant to diminish the individual, such as in the great public spaces of China. They can also be intended to help us soar into the heavens, in places like Chartres Cathedral, to give us an indication of the magnitude and power of God.

Space is used to create emotions. A "sense of the processional" is often created, through skillful design, to walk the user through an outdoor space into an indoor space while building expectations about what might be hiding inside.

As the use of space varies from culture to culture so does its meaning. Often the importance of a space is symbolic—for example, the Oval Office. The actual size and position of a space within the greater context of a building has great impact on our perception of the activities within, and this too is a reflection of culture.

A common example in the United States today is the perception that in the corporate setting, one is going to see someone important when the space changes—becomes larger and filled with better art, softer lighting, padded carpeting, a quieter environment. The sudden transition to the "important space" of an important person is designed to evoke certain emotions in the visitor, while enhancing the comfort of the person whose office it is. Corner offices shout *power* because of their position in a building, as well as the possibility of viewing the outdoors on two sides.

What is interesting in the open office environment is that here the cues to power begin to break down. A person's boss may be only a couple of cubicles away. Here the symbolic meaning of a closed door does not go without notice. Even in open office environments there is need for privacy and time alone for demanding tasks that require concentration.

In the healthcare setting, waiting areas have typically been designed as an afterthought. These areas appear to produce no actual revenue, yet as support areas they are key to the flow of patients that fuels the engine of the healthcare delivery business. It is good business to make these rooms important and comfortable, reasonably lighted for reading or casual conversation, pleasantly designed with warm colors and tasteful artwork. Views to the outdoor are welcome reminders of a world of life, nature, and activity beyond attention to one's illness.

Worry can be ameliorated in a positively designed space. Uplifting environments are not merely pleasant settings for people suffering from pain and anxiety, they can be used as part of the treatment of these maladies.

HEALING BEGINS AT THE DOOR

The very concept of the wellness center speaks to people on a very basic level. The expectation of wellness can be a self-fulfilling prophecy. Going to a wellness center instead of a "sickness center" has more than a superficial impact on a person's being.

Our culture is beginning to shift and change with the new emphasis on wellness. The idea that a wellness center offers other things to do besides seeing a physician is itself uplifting. When positive emotions are evoked, positive changes on the cellular level are set in motion.

The ability of people to focus on elements of life that are not about illness, even when they are ill, has a great positive impact.

In wellness centers, human beings are not consigned to age- and illness-related categories, and this is more reflective of the natural order of life and therefore has an impact beyond the immediate comfort provided.

A patient's going to a wellness center can affect the patient's family as well. No matter how educated or sophisticated a person is, it is likely that each has a negative memory of family illness associated with a hospital. For many, the hospital symbolizes the place where, except for the birth of a new baby, bad (or at least difficult and trying) things happen.

The survivors of illnesses may have had hospital experiences that, in the final analysis, were positive—someone was cured or a medical emergency situation was dealt with effectively. Even a major operation, such as a heart transplant, may have a happy outcome for a family. Yet, more than likely, the worry and anxiety the family experienced to come to that happy point will, on some visceral level, be connected with the hospital environment.

The most worldly hospital administrators, when asked about their hometown hospitals, often flash back to their emotional response to the hospital itself before refocusing on the hospital as it fit into a system, a place that made money or not, a place that is linked with other hospitals or not. Their first reaction is often personal: "I remember when my mother went for treatment there. ..."

The case can be made, then, that hospitals as places symbolic of important moments in a person's life, are associated in people's memories with unsettling events, anxiety, and, often, emotional turning points. This is what will change in the next century. Beyond the bricks and mortar, financial analyses and marketing, lies the symbolic nature of the wellness center. It will be a center of healing rather than illness, a place where new memories and associations begin.

The idea that healing, although positive, is also trying and demands great discipline—hours of steel-jawed determination, as is the case particularly with physical therapy—will be modified, shifted, changed with the building of wellness centers. Recreation and relaxation, spa amenities and places to rest or meet friends, places to learn about health or share in the fellowship of community, these are the new images of wellness centers. A true benefit of the wellness center is patients' ability to connect, both consciously and subconsciously, healing with fun, recreation, fellowship, and beauty—of the environment and of an enhanced self.

Conceptually, the move toward healing and spirituality has already begun in our culture. All religions have experienced an increase in membership and have developed new ways of reaching out to the secular community. The community is reaching back. At no other time in the history of humankind have so many people sought healing on a combined physical and spiritual level. Wellness centers are not churches, but, in fact, there is some similarity in the mission of wellness centers to heal the sick. Never before have buildings been created to heal the sick on physical, mental, emotional, and spiritual levels.

The first hospitals were started by religious orders, primarily women. The idea of attending to the physical while ministering to the spiritual has been popularized throughout history. Only in recent years has medicine in Western cultures become split off from the spiritual aspects of individuals in order to perfect the specialized technology of what medicine has become.

We have come full circle. Wellness centers attend to the whole human being. They encompass physical healing, behavioral medicine, social healing, the mix of different people and generations in a given community, education, and through these vehicles, a healing of the sprit.

Mind-body medicine is the wave of the future, and the wellness center is the primary environment in which it will be practiced. Increasingly, spaces will be set aside for the practice of behavioral medicine and for complementary or alternative healing methods.

What we know to be true intuitively is now documented. In a recent article in the *Healthcare Forum Journal*, Roger Ulrich states that there is mounting scientific evidence that certain design studies or choices can work for or against the well-being of patients. Research, he says, has linked poor design with anxiety, delirium, elevated blood pressure levels, increased need for pain medication, and longer stays in the hospital following surgery. Good design has been shown to reduce stress and anxiety, lower blood pressure, improve postoperative courses, reduce the need for pain medication, and shorten hospital stays.

We know that stress is manifested in a sense of helplessness and lack of control. The physiological effects of stress are devastating, depending on the person's ability to recover. In his book, *Toughness Training for Life*, James Loehr, M.D., who specializes in the training of world-class athletes, examines and suggests ways of dealing with stress that can be life changing. He says that a program that develops toughening, physically, mentally, and emotionally, will help people cycle through hard times and improve their ability to handle stress.

The designers of a wellness center will take into consideration that this unique environment will support the activities of well people, ill people, and people in recovery. Designers should be aware that a basic objective in supporting the emotional states of such clientele is to give them a sense of control within an environment.

People need to know where they are and where they are going. An environment that creates confusion, or does not actively support control and clarity, is an environment that is not likely to succeed. Large hospital complexes that have grown organically over the years, attempting to organize themselves with signage, quite often miss the mark. In such cases, people designated as "concierges," a term borrowed from the hospitality industry, must be engaged to act as hosts for the hospital, whose job is to help patients and visitors negotiate the environment. This has a benefit, in that there is a human face identified with what can be an inhuman environmental experience, and so it is a step in the right direction. But the wellness center, a building type that is manageable in size, quite often freestanding and in most cases entirely new, offers an opportunity to do something wonderful in terms of design.

People in weakened physical condition, such as those requiring cardiac rehabilitation, physical therapy, occupational therapy, or oncology therapy, need to trust the environment they are entering. As practitioners in any of the physical therapies will attest, ease of movement is key. These patients should not experience the additional stress of having to figure out where they are, where they should park, where to leave their coats, where to find a rest room, how to check in, how to pay a bill, where to wait.

INCREASING CONTROL THROUGH DESIGN

As discussed earlier, a basic objective of wellness center design is to give patients a sense of control within the environment. To this end, the following elements should be incorporated into any design plan:

1. Privacy
2. Control of room temperature (in appropriate areas)
3. Comfortable seating for patients and family members
4. Visual access to the outside environment
5. Good visual cues and signage
6. Predictability
7. Reasonable sound levels
8. Good lighting
9. Access to rest rooms, water fountains
10. Parking access

Basketball at Sinai Wellbridge,
Pikesville, Maryland.

Everything in the environment of a wellness center must be designed to be clear. The path of the person moving through the spaces for a course of therapy or to examination, imaging, or treatment rooms should be rational, not full of surprises.

Predictability and the ability of the patient to feel psychologically and physically comfortable are keys to good wellness center design. These conditions are also important for the fitness participant. Not everyone who works out is in top condition. Therefore, it is important that a person who comes to the wellness center for fitness services can move easily from front desk check in, to locker room, to exercise area, and back again, especially if that person is pressed for time.

Fitness members will not be encouraged to keep up with their programs if the environment itself is a difficult hurdle. If it is a trying experience to find where everything is, if there is a sense of being rushed or crowded, these feelings will discourage a member from coming back with any regularity.

Architects must consider the nature of the fitness member. Is he or she at the center with a family? If so, and if marketing studies demonstrate the need, a family locker room may be required. Is the fitness member assisting a family member who is elderly or infirm ? If so, care giver locker areas are in order.

Basic needs should be addressed graciously. The ability to find a rest room or water fountain with ease is most necessary to a person's feeling of control and comfort in an environment.

Amenities such as computer connections and built-in computers in waiting rooms and lobby areas, as well as in health education classrooms, conference rooms, and employee lounge areas, should not be overlooked.

In order to address the future needs of the wellness center facility with two major business lines that have unpredictable futures—healthcare and fitness—flexibility is the only rational approach. Flexibility should be built into the design to accommodate any future requirements of the environment.

At the Springfield Healthplex, Crozer-Keystone Health System, the space below the floor is built with ductwork for future cabling, much like an office system floor. This allows the owner to change room functions if needed, for all but large ball court and swimming pool/spa spaces.

PROGRAMMING

The decision to add a wellness center to the full complement of healthcare buildings serving a hospital system is made by determining the market feasibility and acknowledging the mission of the hospital. Clinical departments that lend themselves to relocation within a wellness center are those that are allied functionally with rehabilitative medicine and with noninvasive diagnostic services. Healthcare education is also a likely function to be relocated.

This concept of clinical services that can appropriately be relocated is clearly reflective of what is true today only. As reimbursement strategies change in combination with technological advances, the entire fabric of the healthcare system is likely to be repatterned within the next 10 years.

As the shift to outpatient service continues, acute care facilities are serving increasingly ill patients. Emergency rooms, because of increased liability, are becoming larger, and additional space is being devoted to observation. Outpatient surgery areas are integrated with inpatient surgery areas in patient interchange areas. Cardiac catheterization rooms are designed so that expensive machines can physically swing between two dedicated rooms, serving one room and then the other, thus maximizing use of facilities and staff time. Increasing acuity levels demand more private rooms, private cubicles in emergency departments, transitional areas where families can gather with patients who are awaiting outpatient surgery.

The wellness center, as perhaps the least medical of all types of medical buildings, naturally assumes the functions that can be easily pulled out from the hospital chassis. Today these functions are primarily cardiac rehabilitation and physical therapy. We are seeing, however, an increasing trend toward the relocation of mammography and women's diagnostics, rheumatology, and family medicine. If a medical office building is adjacent to the wellness center, as is often the case, the medical offices tend to take up these functions and more.

In other areas of the world, fitness centers may or may not include clinical components, but almost always include spas. In Asia, fitness clubs are typically located in five-star hotels. Most hotels oversize their facilities to accommodate membership from the local community. As a result, Asian clubs differ in their design, layout, and function from typical clubs in, for instance, the United States. It is rare for Grade A city hotels to offer less than five-star standards in terms of interior finishes and fittings. In recent years, sports clubs have emerged, such as the Pacific Club Kowloon, the Hong Kong Football Club, the Europa Country Club (Singapore), the Capitol Club (Bangkok), Phillip Wain (female-only clubs) in Hong Kong (three), Thailand (two), Malaysia, and Singapore, Uraku (three in Japan and Hawaii), the Dynasty Club (Hong Kong, China, and Taiwan), and the Capital Club (Beijing). Designers tend to use high-end fixtures, furniture, and equipment for these fitness centers, taking their model entirely from the hospitality design industry.

Marble, crystal, brass, hardwood paneling, and glass are the selections of the day, which do not necessarily fare well in such environments. Maintenance and safety are issues of concern. Marble is porous, stains easily, and is slippery. In tropical countries there are problems with controlling solar gain. Condensation can eliminate the view that the glazing is supposed to provide. Tropical conditions also make timber finishes misbehave. Basketball/volleyball, racquetball, and squash court floors must be carefully laid with expansion joints to prevent buckling.

In Asian countries there is a cultural etiquette to be observed, which affects the design of locker room and wet areas. In countries such as Japan, Korea, and North China, it is customary to remove shoes at the threshold of the locker room. Here, the design calls for a raised threshold with an adjacent shoe storage room. This area is usually manned by a shoe-shine attendant. Particularly in Muslim countries, nakedness—even with a spouse or in same-sex groups—is taboo. Even within locker room and wet areas robes and slippers are used. The design must accommodate this requirement.

Laundry storage is particularly important, and its requirements are greater in Asian facilities than in most Western health clubs. According to John Chang of John Chang Design, Hong

Kong, today's club operator specifies functionality as the prime design criterion. With an unprecedented demand on monthly rental lockers, the locker room has been transformed from merely an amenity to a revenue generator. Changing cabanas are provided in the dry locker area, and individual shower cubicles include a private preshower disrobing and postshower toweling-off area. Common showers, even in male locker rooms, are never installed. Users change and shower in complete privacy if they so desire. The portion of space devoted to the locker and wet areas is quite disproportionate as compared with Western models. The most successful clubs cater to both Western and Asian demands. This involves blending the Asian-style health club, emphasizing relaxation, with the more active Western fitness center model. More space is allocated to massage rooms, the massage staff waiting area, and separate male and female rest lounges and bathing, which includes massage showers, deluge showers, cold showers, hot and cold gravel walks, hot and cold whirlpools, and sauna/steam rooms.

The main exercise activity area in the Asian fitness center tends to include high-tech equipment. Popular audiovisual systems include cardio theater and wireless headphones with user-selected audio and video channels.

The design of the fitness activity area is consistent with Western standards. Approximately 60 percent of the total space in a center is devoted to cardiovascular equipment. Certain proprietary fitness equipment manufacturers have gained market share in the Asian club market. The Nautilus Time Machine has gained popularity throughout Asia. Interactive heart rate control machines are very popular, as is the concept of heart-rate training. Free weights are generally limited to a rack of dumbbells, an Olympic bench, and one or two flat/adjustable benches. Most of the top Western trade name equipment is available here, such as Life Fitness, StarTrac, Nautilus, Body Master, Cybex, and Paramount.

A good example of a Western wellness center is in Springfield, Pennsylvania, at Crozer-Chester's Healthplex. The wellness center is part of a healthcare system of which Delaware County Memorial Hospital in Drexel Hill, Pennsylvania, is the flagship. This hospital has 313 beds, a regional cancer center, comprehensive obstetrics services, a neonatal intensive care nursery, a women'/s center, a women's and children's health resource center, an outpatient rehabilitation and sports medicine center, a surgicenter, and an adjoining medical office building with an apothecary and a conference center.

In addition to hospital-based programs for ambulatory care and 850 physicians' offices, Crozer-Keystone also has six ambulatory care facilities, four long-term care facilities, and two transitional care centers.

Within this complement of the full continuum of care is the wellness center, the Crozer-Keystone Healthplex. The Healthplex, located in Springfield, Pennsylvania, includes a small hospital with inpatient services, a surgery center, a center for occupational health, a cardiac and cancer center, rehabilitation and recovery, and an emergency room. A physicians' office building in the complex accommodates 30 physicians' practices, a health enhancement center, a women's health center, and a sports medicine center.

The fitness element in the Healthplex includes therapy and lap pools, racquetball and squash courts, tennis, basketball, a running track, weight training, cardiovascular exercise, whirlpools, saunas, steam rooms, a pro shop, a children's gymnasium, and child care.

In the Healthplex, as in most other wellness centers in the country today, the clinical functions are located along one hall and the fitness functions along another.

Design Tenets

The intricate design of well-ordered spaces for both major uses — the clinical and fitness functions — can be done well if some primary tenets are adhered to, as discussed in the following paragraphs.

1. *Signage.* Way-finding systems should be extremely clear. The rhythm of spaces should follow a clear logic, and the visitor, patient, or member should be cued accordingly.

2. *Professional appearance.* Clinical functions should be designed in such a way as to communicate professionalism, without appearing coldly clinical. A hospital-like, clinical design would be inappropriate for exam rooms, mammography suites, and similar rooms. Yet designing a cloyingly "homey" room is also inappropriate at the other extreme. The aim is to create a clinical function room that offers little confusion to the patient about the professional treatment he or she can expect. If a person arriving at a clinical area has the impression that he or she has come for a checkup by an exercise instructor, the design goal will have not been met.

3. *Engineering systems.* Engineering considerations should be taken into account early in the design process. Indoor relative humidity of 50 to 60 percent in a pool area is challenging to maintain and may require the design of a special air-handling unit or units to supply constant air volumes to various spaces. Humidity control in a building that houses both fitness and clinical functions may be difficult to achieve. Failure to address these issues at the outset, however, can result in creating an environment for medical technology that is not consistent with good engineering practice, as well as missing the mark in the design of fitness spaces, which are likely to be high-humidity areas because of the intense grouping of people who are all physically active at the same time.

   Another engineering issue is maintenance of air changes so as to refresh the environment, without allowing chlorine odors to invade common spaces. (Patients receiving medical treatment, especially cancer patients, are sensitive to such odors.)

4. *Acoustics and basic zoning considerations.* It is of critical importance to zone clinical functions away from fitness functions so as to maintain good acoustical control. Within the pool area, the design should include baffles or other devices to reduce the echo effect. Not only is sound reduction important from an aesthetic standpoint, it is also important from the standpoint of communication. Arthritis patients who are receiving aquatherapy must be able to hear the instructor. And because many arthritis sufferers are elderly, acoustics become even more important.

5. *Age separation and integration.* Wellness center patients and members represent a great cross section of ages and sexes. The idea of the wellness center as community center has great promise. At the same time, segregation of certain subfunctions should be considered. Care giver locker rooms can be a vital necessity. Similarly, family locker rooms can be necessary too. Men and women with young children should have space to change the children without interfering with adult patients and members. Areas zoned for adults and families, and a more private area for care givers, is the ideal arrangement.

6. *Other accommodations.* All areas of the wellness center should be handicapped accessible. Beyond the strict requirements of the Americans with Disabilities Act (ADA), the professional standard of care should include extra handrails worked sensitively into the design of cor-

ridors and large gathering spaces, along with the creation of frequent areas of rest. Envision a cardiac rehabilitation patient, entering an atrium lobby of a wellness center filled with natural light and other positive design elements, and not being able to sit down to catch her breath. There should be a natural rhythm of stopping points for patients and members throughout the facility, with water fountains available. Communication devices of some type are also important, such as telephones with a nurse call system. Wellness centers typically include telemetry in their designs, particulary around the running track. A patient/member monitoring system can be even more comprehensive.

7. *Site location, access, and design.* The wellness center should offer specially designated parking for members and patients, adequate handicapped parking, well-lighted spaces, and good signage. If at all possible, the drop-off area should be canopied, as should a pedestrian link to the parking area.

A wellness center should not be located close to magnetic fields generated by power plants and high-voltage electricity transmission lines. In *Alternative Medicine*, Robert Becker, M.D., John Zimmerman, Ph.D., and other scientists and researchers point out that we live in an environment that is filled with stress-producing magnetic fields generated by electrical devices. The book cites a large-scale study conducted in 1987 by the New York State Department of Health. This study confirmed an earlier study conducted in 1979 by Nancy Wertheimer, M.D., an epidemiologist at the University of Colorado, who found that there was a statistically significant increase in childhood cancers among children exposed to AC current from overhead power lines installed along their neighborhood streets. Zimmerman states, "Only a few farsighted individuals, such as Dr. Becker, have given much thought to the fact that the new electromagnetic environment created by twentieth-century technology may exert subtle, yet very important, effects upon biology."

Not to be overlooked in the programming of a wellness center is the inclusion of horticulture therapy. According to author Nancy Chambers in a recent magazine article, a horticulture instructor has been added to the staff of the Women's Occupational Therapy Department of Bloomingdale Hospital in White Plains, New York, and horticulture programs have been put in place in several hospitals in Illinois. The Veterans Administration also occupied returning soldiers with garden-related projects.

In 1981, Diane Relf, professor of horticulture, published an article in *Rehabilitation Literature* that discusses the benefits of horticulture therapy. Relf says that the New York University Institute of Rehabilitative Medicine has had success in using horticulture therapy to treat patients who are newly disabled. These patients frequently have problems with integration, the meshing of the personality into the new self-image evolving as a result of the disability. People who are treated with horticulture therapy benefit by seeing that "there is something they can do," completing a task that has concrete results.

At the John Deere Corporation, the employee wellness program requires that there be plants or flowers within 45 feet of every employee. Relf says that leaders of the company report that creativity was enhanced, productivity was increased, and employees voluntarily upgraded their standard of dress.

C. F. Menninger, founder of the Menninger Clinic, wrote of his peonies:

> There is gratification of the sense of sight in color and color combinations, of the sense of smell in the perfumes and odors, and to that inner aesthetic of beauty a charm that has, I believe, made a better physician of me. My whole nature has improved, my horizons wider and my appreciation increased in a way that has aided me in my vocation.

It is clear that including plants, flowers, and gardens in the wellness center is a wonderful concept. The interior, as well as the exterior, plantscape should be fully integrated into the design of the center. Color, form, shape, and scent should be considered for their appropriateness to the space.

A dedicated healing garden, outdoor atrium space, and the generous use of interior planting should highlight the center's design. A healing garden may be included for the exclusive purpose of taking a person through different levels of sensory communication. If space permits, a wellness center campus or wellness village may incorporate flower and vegetable gardens to be used for horticulture therapy. An herbalist may be engaged, as a part of a community education program, to lecture on the healing properties of plants and how best to grow herbs at home.

Green Design

Perhaps nowhere else in the design of buildings today is it more important to set an example for the way in which all buildings should be built than in the wellness center. Symbolically and practically, it is of primary importance that a wellness center be designed with materials that protect health and that it encourage, by example, this way of incorporating healthy design into the mainstream of the community.

In the past few years there have been sporadic gestures toward design of "healthy buildings." A great deal has been written about sick buildings and the syndromes that result when human beings are kept for long periods of time in environments that are less than desirable.

Sick buildings are those whose users complain of ailments ranging from chronic headache and fatigue to more serious asthmatic conditions. These buildings suffer from either bad design (sealing the building envelope so tightly as to allow no infiltration of air and so causing a series of problems that result from lack of air movement) or the specification of unhealthful materials or a combination of such factors. Additional ailments produced by exposure to the chemicals in these materials range from flulike symptoms to joint pain and brain dysfunction—dizziness, confusion, inability to concentrate.

Marshall Mandell, M.D., has discovered that even severe health conditions such as multiple sclerosis, cerebral palsy, and adult postpolio may be further complicated by superimposed allergic reactions; chemical sensitivities to the built environment.

Another expert points out several other syndromes that appear to be caused by environmental sensitivities or by allergies. These are vasculitis, thrombophlebitis, high blood pressure, angina, certain arrhythmias, edema, chronic pediatric disorders, abnormalities in the endocrine system, eye, ear, nose, and throat disorders, gastrointestinal disorders, and disorders of the skin.

Materials that are harmful range from the obviously dangerous and carcinogenic—urea foam formaldehyde, asbestos, lead paint—to furniture manufactured with chemicals that release unhealthful vapors, to certain paints that produce odors while drying (which precludes their application during business hours).

Natural light is best, of course, but for activities taking place in the wellness center after the sun has set, the next best lighting type is full-spectrum light. The incorporation of full-spectrum lighting, whenever possible, is encouraged for both ambient and task lighting. People suffering from seasonal affective disorder, attention deficit disorder, or attention deficit hyperactivity disorder are subtly disturbed by lack of light and by the glare of fluorescent light.

In his book, *Total Wellness*, Joseph Pizzorno, M.D., defines sick building syndrome as a special category of illness whereby people in a specific building suffer from ill-defined, but reproducible illness. What differentiates people suffering with sick building syndrome from those suffering with multiple chemical sensitivities is that the former get better when they change their exposure to the building and do not suffer from exposures elsewhere.

Approximately 15 percent of the population in the United States is chemically sensitive, according to a 1987 workshop at the National Academy of Science. Researchers postulate that this is due to the post–World War II petrochemical revolution.

Some chemicals are harmful to the body because the body cannot adequately break them down. The Environmental Protection Agency (EPA) tells us that more than 400 hundred toxic chemicals can be found in human tissue. Chemicals that typically cause trouble are toluene, xylene, benzene, trichloromethane, styrene, phthalates, and pesticides. For example, tolulene affects the central nervous system and slows the metabolism of benzene, which is released from furniture, carpeting, and paint.

A rapidly developing medical specialty in the United States concentrates on clinical ecology. Clinical ecologists treat people with chemical sensitivities that originate from a variety of sources. One significant source is the made environment.

People with environmental sensitivities should not go to a wellness center to have their conditions aggravated, and people who have no apparent sensitivities should not be exposed to dangerous chemicals in a place to which they have come for healing.

Water aerobics class, Sinai
Wellbridge, Pikesville, Maryland.

Of additional importance is designing the environment to avoid harming people who suffer from allergies. This is not to say that a wellness center should not have a garden area; in most cases, it should, but the built environment should always be composed of materials that are not only noncarcinogenic, but nonallergic.

Anyone suffering from an allergy to mold, mildew, or dust mites knows that an allergist's first recommendations are to seal off the offending allergen by encapsulating mattresses and pillows in allergy-free cases, to clean carpeting frequently, and condition the air with a HEPA filter. HEPA filters can be installed in the wellness center and maintenance policies should require frequent cleaning of surfaces with non-toxic products.

Tri-Cities Hospital in Dallas, Texas, has an Occupational and Environmental Unit, a clinic that specializes in detoxifying patients suffering with environmental sensitivities by using dry heat techniques, intravenous supplements, exercise, and massage.

Other Design Issues

In considering the basic design issues for a wellness center, the following may be helpful. Steve Robbins of Crozer's Springfield Healthplex offers the following suggestions:

1. Be sure there is enough space allotted for educational programs and for utilities and storage. (Clients tend not to think of educational space as revenue producing, but it can be; several of the centers developed by Robbins have generated revenue through rentals of conference room and entertainment room space to the general public.) In many communities, says Robbins, the wellness center is becoming the place to be.

2. The basic programming of a wellness center sometimes appears to be a counter-intuitive exercise. If you start small, for example, with a wellness center of 10,000 square feet, you are creating a very different thing from a center of 35,000 square feet. It is not just a smaller building, it is a different type of facility. The revenue produced, as well as every other aspect of doing business with the wellness center product line, will be vastly different. "If you decide to get into this business, either commit to a program fully, or don't bother."

3. Have a heart-to-heart talk with your architect, decide on the level of design you really want within the functional needs of the design you must meet—a Cadillac or a Chevrolet? Set down the basic guidelines regarding what is important to your project.

4. Worry a lot about pools. Be careful to get the experience of a knowledgeable consultant, a solid architect who has done it before and for whom this is not a learning experience. Include the operator/manager in the earliest meetings when the design is discussed. "You wouldn't design a surgical suite without consulting the surgeon," says Robbins. Similarly, operations people tend to have insights that others at the table might not have, and they have a special agenda; they have to make the facility work when it has been built.

5. Buy quality. As in any other building design, good quality materials included in the initial design quite often pay for themselves over time in longer wear and lower maintenance. Robbins advises the selection of tile for wet areas rather than concrete painted with a coating.

6. Remember that with hospital-based wellness centers, the reputation of the hospital is at stake. The design, operation, and maintenance of the wellness center reflects on the quality of care offered by the hospital system. Because the facility is part of a greater system, it is important to make sure that the design quality is consistent with the level of design within the system. Maintenance issues are critical. Even though no one will be practicing surgery in a locker room at the wellness center, the overall level of cleanliness should be excellent. Keep in mind that in addition to the need for a completely sanitary facility, members of wellness centers tend to be high-end consumers who are put off by poor conditions or service.

7. Pay attention to the strength of the engineering firm. Ideally, the engineering firm should be located within the architects' office and have worked with the designers on healthcare, sports, and wellness center projects.

8. Hospital-based wellness center architects and administrators should go back to the basics. What is the hospital's strategic plan ? What does the healthcare system want to be? What does that mean in terms of programs for the next few years? Which programs could be moved to the wellness center?

9. Think through the process. How will a patient move from area to area?

10. Think ahead. Both the fitness and the healthcare functions will change and grow in the next few years. Leave space for change, and build in flexibility.

Critical Adjacencies

As noted earlier, the primary zoning for functional areas at the wellness center fits into two major categories, clinical and fitness. The separation of these areas is a design response to the logic of the anticipated activities in each. Pool areas and garden areas should be visible, if possible, from other areas in the wellness complex in order to bring a sense of aliveness and fun, rest and respite from the hard work of everyday life. These areas often serve as magnets and focal points for people, lightening the often serious nature of the clinical experience and providing some visual relief. If pool areas are totally enclosed, with minimal exposure to the outdoors, less sunlight, and less able to suggest the natural environment beyond, then we are less enthusiastic about relating the building spaces to the pool as a focal point.

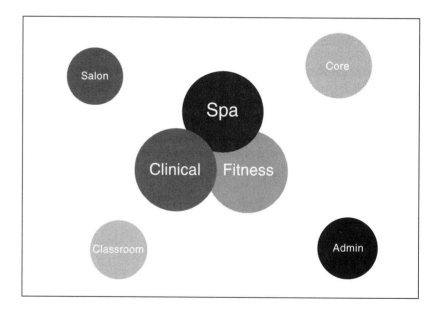

If the pool area is a focal point, it should be designed to project the image of a resort/spa environment rather than of a high school gym, even though it may indeed include lap spaces and areas specially designated for aquatherapy.

The more therapeutic areas, such as aquatherapy, should be located beyond the less utilitarian areas so that patients can realize the benefits of this therapy without being vulnerable to the gaze of every passing visitor. In all cases, where a rehabilitation patient is working under the guidance of a medical professional in a space adjacent to a fitness activity space, the goal is for the patient to have a view outward toward the fitness area while maintaining a measure of personal privacy. The design goal to be achieved here is a sense of balance and control for the patient, a sense of being special. The patient is indeed special and should not have to compete with fitness members for weight machine time. Likewise, a fitness member should have the sense that he or she is in a luxurious high-tech environment where the emphasis is on prevention and wellness, rather than in a rehabilitation facility.

Rehabilitation patients should share locker rooms with the fitness members, because a further delineation would border on social engineering. As previously mentioned, however, the option for care giver locker room spaces, spaces that include a handicapped-accessible water closet, sink, and lockers, should always be available.

Similarly, handicapped accessibility in all areas of a wellness center, including weight training areas, is of utmost importance. There are specially designed weight training machines for people with disabilities, and these should be included in the design of the weight training areas. The design must take care to work out the dimensional radius needed to maintain the proper angle of approach to these machines.

Weight machines and free weight areas are frequently located on special rubber flooring, which may present accessibility problems. The designer must give some thought to how a wheelchair-bound person can make the transition from one type of flooring, typically carpeting or conditioned wood flooring, to the dense rubber-tire-like flooring typically used in weight machine areas.

Aligned with this challenge is the need to find a way for a disabled person to access pool areas for general swimming or aquatherapy lessons. Wellness centers frequently include a handicapped ramp that brings swimmers down from deck level to pool level. Because the 1-to-12 slope required by ADA is typically used, this presents a special design challenge. Lifts are an expensive alternative, but their use can realize a tremendous gain in terms of pool space. More pool space can typically be devoted to the actual therapy itself instead of being used up by a cumbersome solution to access.

Another design challenge is whirlpool and hot tub design. The therapeutic effect of hot water has long been known, and arthritic as well as disabled people deserve to have this therapy. Unfortunately, most spa and hot tub designers have not considered how to make them available to everyone, but accessiblity should be of vital concern in the design of the wellness center pool and spa areas.

Decking materials in these wet areas can be a danger for everyone. The usual choice in most instances is either to leave raw concrete or to invest in ceramic tile. Certainly, in most cases ceramic tile is better aesthetically and can be installed with sufficient drainage to prevent ponding and potentially slick areas. Moisture-resistant grout will surely accompany a good tile installation and will increase durability and discourage the growth of mold. Efficient dehumidification systems and attentive mechanical engineering design can ensure a comfortable and safe environment.

Pool and spa areas should naturally be close to locker rooms and toilet rooms. A small transitional corridor is about the maximum amount of space desirable from the locker room area to the pool area. There are many reasons for this; chief among them is privacy. People using a pool dressed in bathing suits do not want to traipse across the lobby or waiting room area, nor do they want to be seen in the clinical corridor or, for that matter, to walk across a weight room area or past an aerobics or dance room. Locker rooms should always be located near pool areas.

Similarly, when the spa area includes more than the whirlpool and sauna spaces typically associated with pool areas, when the concept of the spa is broadened to include other therapies involving the use of water, such as Vichy rooms, eucalyptus steam rooms, constitutional hydrotherapy (an alternative medicine therapy that involves the application of hot and cold compresses in alternation), cold friction rubs (an alternative therapy that involves the application of ice water packs after preparing the patient with steam, sauna, immersion baths, and hot sprays), these wet areas should be collocated near the spa/sauna/pool/locker room functions.

As spa areas are broadened to include areas for self-care, they should also be located adjacent to one another. Self-care areas may include massage rooms, acupuncture therapy rooms, and the more cosmetic functions — hairdressing salon, facial rooms, manicure and pedicure rooms. In the more mature wellness center facilities around the country, these spa areas are being expanded and some of them are having difficulty in retrofitting administrative spaces to include expanded spa functions. Because administrative functions have almost never been located next to locker rooms or pool areas, there is some challenge in reengineering these spaces to perform reasonably well, to be appealing and functional for the user, without complicating the transition from the spa area back to the locker room. In a purely engineering sense, this reconfiguration becomes a challenge as well. If humidity controls and air conditioning

Whirlpool, Springfield Healthplex, Springfield, Pennsylvania.

schemes are serving a facility well, there should be no difficulty in conditioning the various spaces to meet the needs of users in the space.

If an administrative space does become a spa, however, the relative cost of this expansion is extremely high. Thus the basic design caveat for all medically related facilities is borne out once again: Designs should be flexible. If engineering systems are built with the potential for future change, the overall design of the facility will benefit.

Similarly, the structural grid should be built with the same logic, and plenum space should be adequate for the future reconfiguration of the various areas. There is always the possibility in a facility of this kind that more intense (an increase in equipment means larger space requirements) technological equipment for medical procedures may be located in the wellness center, given the potential for change in reimbursement patterns. If this trend continues, and more in depth medical functions are located in the wellness center complex, a margin for error in the design of the structural grid and floor-to-floor heights will be necessary and welcome.

The well-designed wellness center, with the anticipation of future change built in, will be the one likely to succeed financially, at least in regard to the facility itself. We are already seeing centers built only a year ago undergoing expansion, in most cases expansion that is more costly than it has to be because of the shortsightedness of a designer.

If trends reverse or take a different course, the nature of the wellness center may shift and, in doing so, its value in terms of real estate remains in its ability to convert to a smaller or different set of functions. Unduly large or overdesigned wellness centers are as much an absurdity as unduly small and underdesigned centers with little or no thought built into the program for future expansion.

The clinical function/examination rooms, diagnostic rooms, treatment rooms, and separate administration area within a wellness center should serve as the clinical component's own discrete environment, which can allow for the possibility of a separate lease from the fitness functions. (The inclusion of "demising walls" is to separate zones for purposes of separating the ownership and/or financing of different areas of the center.) Such flexibility is key to the financial success of a wellness center. Similarly, the retail and food service functions, services that are included in approximately half of all wellness centers built today, should be designed to be functionally discrete (although they should not project that image). The retail function may include an area for sales of sports clothing similar to that in a golf club pro shop, a limited range of sports equipment, sports drinks and food supplements, reading material, tapes and CDs, small electronic equipment items, a scaled-down version of drugstore inventory, basic necessities, some cosmetics, child care items (diapers), aspirin, and similar items.

Unless the wellness center is located close to a retail complex, there is almost always a need for a version of retail space, however small. People enjoy being able to pick up a newspaper or magazine to read on the treadmill or while lounging by the pool, or various other items that do not require a serious venture into merchandising.

Fitness clubs without medical/therapeutic functions have been successfully incorporating food service into their complexes for approximately the past 10 years, particularly on the West Coast. Very often these food service areas are limited to a coffee stand or juice bar, but some facilities have full-service restaurants or cafeterias. The Springfield Healthplex in Pennsylvania boasts a well-designed self-serve/cafeteria that offers simple, healthful food to members and their guests.

Today there is a growing trend toward expanding the food service element. Much like a golf club where the restaurant is also a place for members to gather, the wellness center restaurant/cafe may well evolve into a community entertainment and meeting place.

Some food service seating areas may well be partitioned off, with the use of movable walls like those found in hotel and classroom designs, into smaller areas to accommodate the ebb and flow of activity. This may be a way to incorporate health education classes into spaces used at times for dining, in order to maximize the potential of the space. This idea also lends itself well to holding cooking classes on healthful eating, designed to educate diabetes patients and their families, heart patients, patients actively involved in a weight loss program, and the general fitness membership population desiring to find new and inventive ways of healthful cooking.

These multipurpose spaces may also be used for group counseling sessions, lectures in smoking cessation or the management of certain illnesses, well baby care classes, maternity classes, or adult day-care classes. Adding the element of health education and learning brings another aspect of life to the wellness center as community center.

Beth Reitz, M.S., director of the Lifestyle Center at Chesapeake Hospital in Chesapeake, Virginia, has created a program in which community health education programs are important in the design of functional areas at each of her two wellness center facilities. Cooking classes for diabetes patients and their families are a favorite with patients and members alike. Reitz has uncannily captured the right marketing strategy as a result of her aim to better educate the public on matters of health. These cooking classes and other related health education activities bring people from the community into the wellness center and hospital environment and have helped Chesapeake Hospital increase its share of a growing and dynamic market.

Multipurpose spaces, then, can logically be located near administrative spaces. The ebb and flow of administrative spaces may be flexible enough to accommodate some future growth of health education space, and it may, indeed, also work the other way around. Multifunction spaces may be located near either the clinical corridor or the fitness corridor, considering that the nature of these functions lend themselves to both zones. Overlapping the food service function with the multipurpose room function may steer the adjacencies in the direction of core space, space near the front or retail/reception area of the building.

Ideally, upon entering and proceeding through a wellness center, a person should get a clear idea of where everything is. Spatially, this means drawing the user to a central location, a reception area where he or she will be able to check in, check appointment times, receive passes and locker keys for the locker areas, allow the clinical receptionist to know that the patient has arrived and direct that person to the appropriate area.

Perhaps a rehabilitation patient arriving at the center may check in with a central receptionist and be directed to a small fitness testing area office located next to the cardiac rehabilitation therapy area. Although he is a cardiac patient, there may be no need for a clinical examination that day, but the physician would need to track the therapy and so the patient would register, electronic records would be sent back to clinical reception, and the patient would meet the physical therapist at the fitness testing area rather back at an examination room. There may be no need for the patient to see the cardiologist that day or to check in with the nurse practitioner. Still, the patient is monitored, his records are kept up to date, and he does not have to travel unnecessarily.

Examples of Well-Programmed Facilities

Dow Chemical Employee Development Center

At Dow Chemical, the program developed by Ellerbe Becket Architects for Dow's Award-Winning Employee Development Center (EDC) in Midland, Michigan, included elements of what we would now consider the basics of a wellness center, along with a fully integrated state-of-the-art training center, an employee development center that was designed to provide training, informational presentations, and physical development capabilities to employees through computer-linked systems and technologies.

Seeking to develop its employees, the Dow EDC incorporated specialized Advanced Learning Classrooms, which included fully interactive media training capabilities designed so that the systems would be fully updatable with future technologies.

In the Dow facility the design centers on a vertical stacking concept, which accommodates the diverse program requirements while permitting flexibility on each building level. A fitness center and medical dispensary are located on the ground floor. The second level contains a 260-seat auditorium and several classrooms within the 30,000-square-foot training center. Raised flooring was used to provide easy installation and modification of electronic training equipment. Departmental offices are located on the third level. The 89,000-square-foot facility is located on the Dow corporate office campus, connected to the main buildings by a campuswide enclosed walkway system.

Although the Dow Learning Center was designed in 1989, it has retained its vitality because of the flexibility designed into the original building concept. Flexible architectural features include a free span structure; classroom sizes can easily be

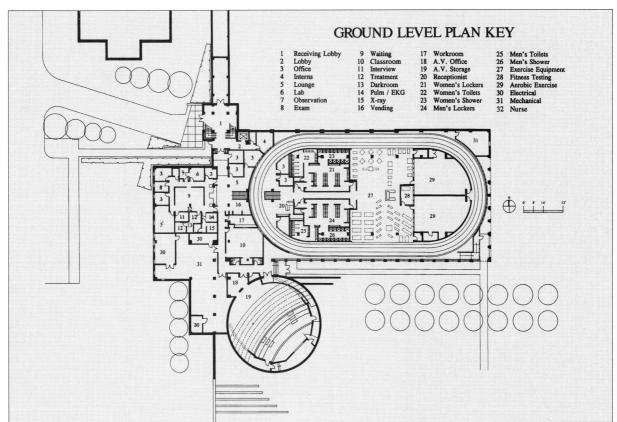

GROUND LEVEL PLAN KEY

1	Receiving Lobby	9	Waiting	17	Workroom	25	Men's Toilets
2	Lobby	10	Classroom	18	A.V. Office	26	Men's Shower
3	Office	11	Interview	19	A.V. Storage	27	Exercise Equipment
4	Interns	12	Treatment	20	Receptionist	28	Fitness Testing
5	Lounge	13	Darkroom	21	Women's Lockers	29	Aerobic Exercise
6	Lab	14	Pulm / EKG	22	Women's Toilets	30	Electrical
7	Observation	15	X-ray	23	Women's Shower	31	Mechanical
8	Exam	16	Vending	24	Men's Lockers	32	Nurse

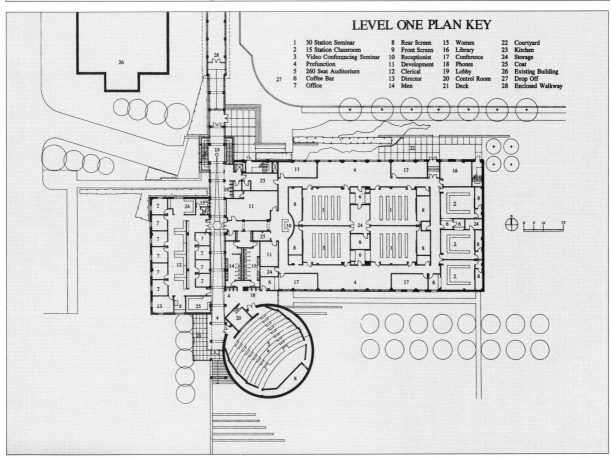

LEVEL ONE PLAN KEY

1	30 Station Seminar	8	Rear Screen	15	Women	22	Courtyard
2	15 Station Classroom	9	Front Screen	16	Library	23	Kitchen
3	Video Conferencing Seminar	10	Receptionist	17	Conference	24	Storage
4	Prefunction	11	Development	18	Phones	25	Coat
5	260 Seat Auditorium	12	Clerical	19	Lobby	26	Existing Building
6	Coffee Bar	13	Director	20	Control Room	27	Drop Off
7	Office	14	Men	21	Deck	28	Enclosed Walkway

Dow Center. *Ellerbe Becket Architects.*

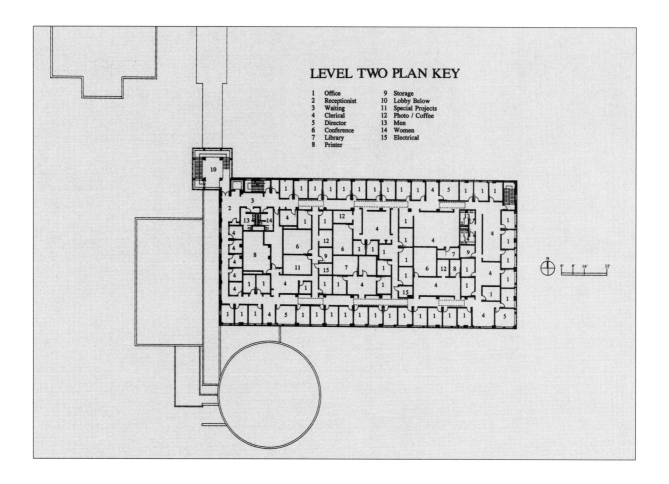

LEVEL TWO PLAN KEY

1 Office
2 Receptionist
3 Waiting
4 Clerical
5 Director
6 Conference
7 Library
8 Printer
9 Storage
10 Lobby Below
11 Special Projects
12 Photo / Coffee
13 Men
14 Women
15 Electrical

changed because the interior is free of load-bearing columns and walls; core elements, rest rooms, stairs, elevators, and other fixed elements are located at the edges of the training elements where they will not inhibit potential room changes. The site has designated areas for future expansion, and care has been taken to provide evenly distributed ambient light to illuminate any room configuration. In-room data outlets connect to cable trays in the ceiling for room-to-room cable connections.

The Dow Center, using vertical stacking, is a wonderful example of how a multipurpose facility should work. The Employee Development Center essentially includes three "buildings," with the architectural requirements of each merged into one. On the ground level the fitness center is configured around the length and width requirements of the running track, designed to be acoustically isolated from the rest of the building functions. Above the fitness center is the Learning Center, designed for flexibility and technological requirements. On the third level, directly above the Learning Center, are administrative offices designed around a structural module based on standard office sizes. Stacking the three dissimilar functional areas yielded the most cost-effective solution, but required careful integration of mechanical distribution, utility services, vertical circulation, structural and acoustical requirements.

Sound-absorbing materials and wall and door construction inhibit room-to-room and floor-to-floor sound transmission. Noisy rooms are physically separated from quiet rooms. The fitness center has a double ceiling that absorbs and reflects sound waves, which eliminates sounds from the Learning Center above. Here, an effort was made, which is suggested for the design of all wellness centers, to select heating and cooling equipment that has low noise transmission properties. Room shapes, combined with a balance of hard and soft surfaces in the auditoriums, yield environments where voice amplification is unnecessary.

The lessons learned from Dow's innovative approach can be applied directly to the guidelines for design of the wellness center.

The program for the medical component at the Dow Center comprises a total of 1,205 square feet. The patient waiting area, 220 square feet, includes seating for six to eight people, shelving for magazines and literature, and an outlet for a television monitor.

The receptionist area, 190 square feet, has a desk-height countertop with two computer workstations. The nurses station consists of a desk-height countertop with two workstations, and a 42-inch-high countertop for registration; it allows visual control of the entry and patient waiting area (120 square feet).

The treatment room, 100 square feet, contains an examination chair, 8-foot base and upper cabinets, a lavatory and an undercounter refrigerator with freezer.

The interview room, 100 square feet, includes an examination table, an eye examination chair, a portable examination light, 3-foot base and upper cabinets, a lavatory and a wall-mounted examination light.

The examination room itself is located adjacent to the treatment and observation rooms. EKG, pulmonary, and diagnostic imaging, 260 square feet, contains an examination table, a side chair, 3-foot base and upper cabinets, a lavatory, a wall-mounted examination light, physical therapy equipment, diagnostic imaging equipment, and a cubicle curtain.

Included in the medical component is a testing laboratory, 130 square feet, with 15 feet of base and upper cabinets and two lavatories, one workstation with knee space, and an audiology booth. The observation room is 100 square feet and contains a bed. There is one toilet, 40 square feet, which is handicapped accessible.

The assignable area of the Dow Center is 89,643 square feet, of which 18,807 square feet are devoted to fitness center space,

2,435 square feet to the medical component, 24,893 square feet to employee training, 1,810 square feet to audiovisual support, and 15,731 square feet to administration. Public lobby areas account for 1,162 square feet; mechanical and electrical, 6,104 square feet; and circulation, including exterior walls, 16,031 square feet.

Chesapeake Hospital Expansion

In 1982, in Chesapeake, Virginia, Chesapeake Hospital created a wellness center program. The small building adjacent to the 200-bed hospital was expanded in 1996, and a freestanding wellness center, the Western Branch Fitness and Wellness Center, was located on property bought by the hospital in the suburbs, considered a growth area.

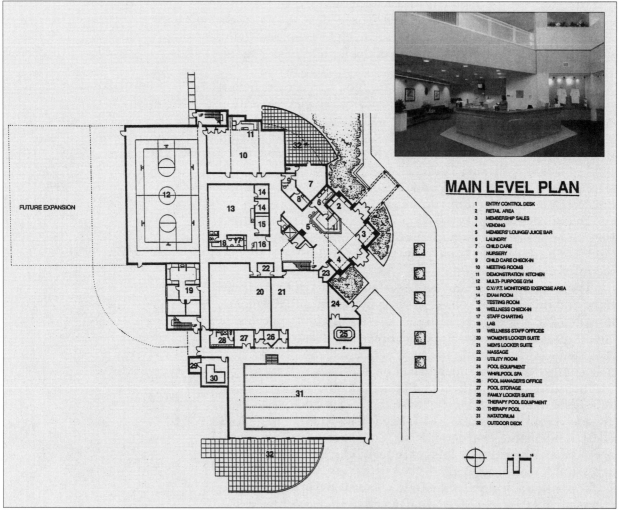

MAIN LEVEL PLAN

1. ENTRY CONTROL DESK
2. RETAIL AREA
3. MEMBERSHIP SALES
4. VENDING
5. MEMBERS' LOUNGE/ JUICE BAR
6. LAUNDRY
7. CHILD CARE
8. NURSERY
9. CHILD CARE CHECK-IN
10. MEETING ROOMS
11. DEMONSTRATION KITCHEN
12. MULTI- PURPOSE GYM
13. C.V./P.T. MONITORED EXERCISE AREA
14. EXAM ROOM
15. TESTING ROOM
16. WELLNESS CHECK-IN
17. STAFF CHARTING
18. LAB
19. WELLNESS STAFF OFFICES
20. WOMEN'S LOCKER SUITE
21. MEN'S LOCKER SUITE
22. MASSAGE
23. UTILITY ROOM
24. POOL EQUIPMENT
25. WHIRLPOOL SPA
26. POOL MANAGER'S OFFICE
27. POOL STORAGE
28. FAMILY LOCKER SUITE
29. THERAPY POOL EQUIPMENT
30. THERAPY POOL
31. NATATORIUM
32. OUTDOOR DECK

FUTURE EXPANSION

Western Branch, Chesapeake Fitness Center. *Robert Whorley, Architects.*

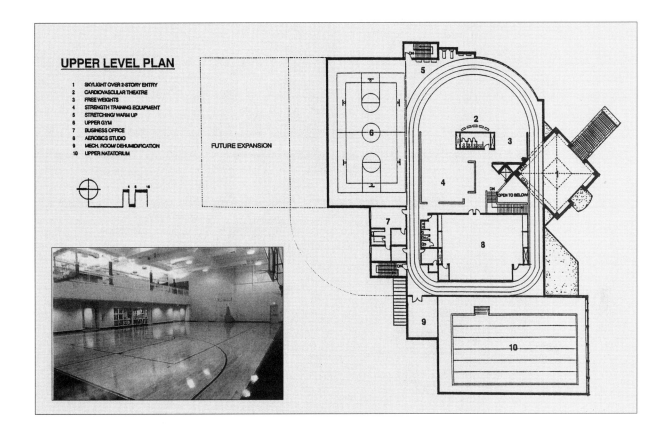

UPPER LEVEL PLAN

1   SKYLIGHT OVER 2-STORY ENTRY
2   CARDIOVASCULAR THEATRE
3   FREE WEIGHTS
4   STRENGTH TRAINING EQUIPMENT
5   STRETCHING/ WARM UP
6   UPPER GYM
7   BUSINESS OFFICE
8   AEROBICS STUDIO
9   MECH. ROOM/ DEHUMIDIFICATION
10 UPPER NATATORIUM

FUTURE EXPANSION

The original wellness center, the Lifestyle Fitness Center, underwent a $700,000 expansion project. With the expansion an effort was made to create a central entrance to the wellness center building, where there had been two secondary entrances that produced confusion. Added to the thriving program were two new aerobics rooms with the latest in aerobics flooring, a fitness testing room, an expanded free weight area, an expanded circuit weight area, additional cardiovascular equipment (treadmills, stationary bikes, rowers, and stair climbers), child care options, and a larger cardiopulmonary rehabilitation area. Staff offices were relocated into areas formerly used as classrooms. Future growth will include the addition of a pool.

Drawing on the experience gained from the original development of the on-campus wellness center, Chesapeake Hospital knew what programs it needed to include in the new Fitness and Wellness Center.

From the new Center's front atrium lobby, the visitor/patient is cued to the clinical elements located down a corridor to the right. Clinical elements include a large cardiopulmonary rehabilitation area and a physical therapy area. These areas have

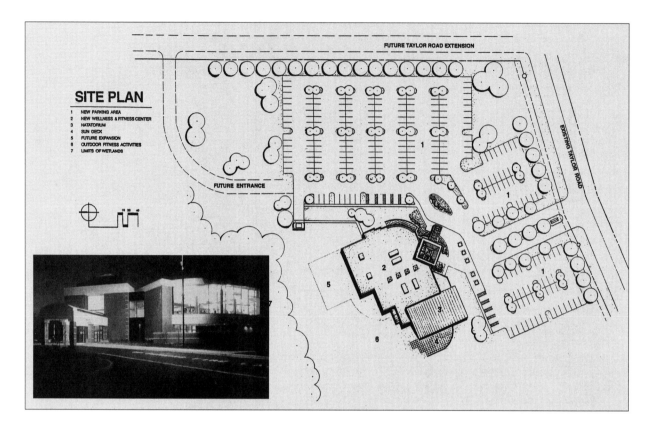

SITE PLAN
1 NEW PARKING AREA
2 NEW WELLNESS & FITNESS CENTER
3 NATATORIUM
4 SUN DECK
5 FUTURE EXPANSION
6 OUTDOOR FITNESS ACTIVITIES
7 LIMITS OF WETLANDS

some overlap and share a central clinical reception counter, as well as dedicated office space for medical professionals adjacent to the therapy areas. Just off this 400-square-foot room is a fitness testing area and rest rooms.

To the left of the atrium lobby is a corridor that leads to generously sized locker rooms that include a separately designated care giver suite with handicapped-accessible toilet facilities, a shower, lockers, and a changing area. The suite accommodates a small couch and coffee table and is large enough that two people can function comfortably.

Beyond the locker rooms with shower and the sauna areas is the pool area with a whirlpool and separately designed room for aquatherapy. This affords patients a great deal of privacy away from lap swimmers in the main pool.

The second floor houses a one-fifth-mile running track that encircles the weight machine and free weight areas and partially overlooks the pool below. Aerobics rooms are also on the second floor.

In this facility, laundry is handled at the main reception desk and actually processed in a laundry room behind the main desk. Towels are picked up and dropped off at the desk, where patients/members can also check in and obtain locker room keys. Membership passes are electronically scanned for access to the facility. In the 44,000 square feet available, there appears to be a generous use of space, and the possibility of future expansion is well designed.

Sinai Wellbridge

At Sinai Wellbridge Wellness Center, part of the Sinai Health System in Baltimore, Maryland, users enter the atrium lobby space and encounter the front desk staffed by several employees, who also manage the small retail area at the opposite side of the circular reception desk. Beyond the reception desk, adjacent to the visitor waiting area, is a laundry and key room, with a half-height partition, staffed by one employee who supplies towels and locker room keys in exchange for the members' photo I.D.s. The laundry, located behind the laundry/key reception area, is adjacent to the locker rooms and the wet areas of the building: pool, sauna, eucalyptus steam bath, and so on.

It is recommended that towel distribution be located away from the front desk so as to avoid creating the stereotypical image of a fitness club. There is also the obvious consideration of noise from the washing machines and dryers, as well as odors if ventilation is not well designed.

Springfield Healthplex

At Springfield, the organizing element is the entry-level basketball court that can be seen as one enters the wellness center. The Springfield Healthplex devotes a significant amount of space to indoor tennis facilities, which are located atop a parking facility. Because the Healthplex was designed on a site already owned and developed by the hospital, including a small ambulatory care/surgery center with a small number of inpatient beds, and a physicians office building, the footprint of the Healthplex was established by the existing buildings. The Healthplex inherited difficult parking accommodations and limited site access. But the Healthplex succeeds because it offers truly one-stop shopping for healthcare in Springfield, Pennsylvania.

Northwest Community Center

Northwest Community Center in Arlington Heights, Illinois is a good example of a well-thought-out design for a wellness center. This 85,000-square-foot center is three stories with a central corridor extending through each story. The first floor contains the reception/waiting area, men's and women's locker rooms, children's activity rooms, and a sports medicine clinic. The first floor is anchored by a basketball/volleyball court with an exercise equipment area at one end. The second floor contains community service/medical areas, including a library, conference rooms, a cardiac rehabilitation area, and a massage area. Warm water therapy, formerly offered at the hospital, is now offered at the wellness center.

The designers designed a curve in the corridor walls to deflect sound waves that would otherwise flow from the basketball court to the lobby. In order to reinforce the concept of "wellness," the designers used clerestory glass extensively to bring in natural light. Care was taken to provide vistas of greenery and landscaping, including those afforded by a nearby golf course. Masonry and other materials create visual and auditory barriers to unpleasant views of the parking lot.

WELLNESS CENTER DESIGN GUIDELINES

Clinical Space

In designing the clinical component of a wellness center project, there are certain rules of thumb that apply to the design of any clinical space. *The American Institute of Architects (AIA) Guidelines for Construction of Hospital and Medical Facilities* is an excellent guide to the design and development of all medical and medically related facilities. The section on "Rehabilitation Medicine," for example, describes the space necessary for this program as including :

1. Space for files, records, administrative activities
2. Hand washing facilities within the therapy unit
3. Space and equipment for carrying out therapy
4. Convenient facility access usable by disabled individuals
5. Lockers for storing patients' personal effects
6. Dressing facilities/ shower facilities
7. Storage for supplies and equipment

According to the National Fire Protection Agency (NPFA), "Where outpatient facilities are part of another facility separation and access must be maintained as per NFPA 101. Building entrances used to reach outpatient services shall be at grade level, clearly marked and located so as to not have patients have to go through other areas."

From the AIA Guidelines:

The waiting area for patients and escorts shall be under staff control. The seating area shall contain not less than two spaces for each examination and or treatment room. Toilets for public use must be immediately accessible from the waiting area. In smaller units the toilet room may be unisex and may be also used for specimen collection. A control counter shall have access to the patient files and records for the scheduling of services.

The *AIA Guidelines* clearly state that each outpatient facility must ensure patient dignity, as well as audible and visual privacy, during interviews, examinations, treatment, and recovery.

Clean storage and soiled utility spaces/soiled holding rooms must be included in the design of wellness center clinical spaces, and must also be addressed in complementary therapy and spa function spaces.

The Waiting Area

The reception area in the front, or central to the front desk, is often a place where people gather and meet. It should be generously sized so that conversations between members are not within hearing distance of the front desk. Family members may be meeting a loved one there to accompany the person to a doctor's appointment. Patients may be waiting to be greeted by a physical therapist or other healthcare professional. Persons at the front desk may be inquiring about a medical appointment or discussing a bill. The reception area and waiting area should be visually close, with sight lines enabling people at the front desk to have visual control of the front entrance and the lobby and to monitor the traffic to and from the facility. At the same time, privacy is needed for conversation in the waiting area.

The waiting area is often undersized. Because it is a public place and often a transitional space, there is generally little attention paid to it, and in some cases the overall design of the wellness center suffers. People like to meet one another. There is great social value in supplying an environment that encourages human interaction. A sense of isolation, which is daunting and inhibiting, and a sense of overcrowding and not being able to "hear oneself think" or communicate to others, are extremes to be avoided. The clever use of space, textures, and colors can provide just the right ambience needed to encourage stimulating human interaction.

There may be instances in which there are multiple gathering spaces, defined perhaps by the intersection of corridors. Like family waiting areas in acute care hospitals or living room clusters in hospitality areas, these smaller, more intimate spaces can be made aesthetically appealing as areas that have no other purpose than to allow people to rest, relax, and talk. With the busyness of fitness activity and the flow of patients vis-

Lobby and front desk, Sinai Wellbridge, Pikesville, Maryland.

iting clinical offices, it is refreshing to have places where one can gather one's thoughts, where there is no pressure to act, perform, buy something, or explain one's purpose in being there.

Outdoor waiting areas, especially in mild climates, perform the same function. Although the focal point may be a pool or garden, the purpose of such spaces is for people to rest and to relate to one another. It is tremendously beneficial to have these restorative places designed into facilities, especially in a wellness center building.

Spaces for Children

There is an increasing trend to include areas for children in wellness centers. The first wellness centers tended to have child care areas, which may or may not have involved some expert supervision, that provided children with activity and fitness programs. Primarily such spaces are drop-off day-care centers for parents who have come to work out. Although there is nothing wrong with this necessary function, some facilities are finding that parents are asking for expanded programs and the children themselves are excited about exercise.

At Disney's Celebration Health wellness center in Florida, developed in conjunction with the Adventist Health System, part of the second floor of the three-story center is devoted to children's fitness. Called "Kids Space," the children's area includes space for soft play, and an interactive technology area designed to help children build motor skills.

Kids Space is adjacent to an exercise studio and conference room designed for ballet and tumbling, as well as seminars and programs, physical therapy and sports medicine, cardio theater, and cardiovascular equipment. Child care is located on the first floor near the front desk, where there are also a life style counseling center, an administrative area, a retail area, a juice bar, locker rooms with lounges, family/senior changing areas, a warm water exercise pool, a lap pool, and a spa, with massage, herbal wraps, facials, sauna, and steam.

Children's fitness areas at Celebration Health are designated by activity areas relating to age groups. Children from ages 7 to 15 enjoy impulse technology, which is used to create interactive virtual reality games that employ physical activity, such as jumping, and motor skills to play laser games. Children are navigators in "a game of nonstop action, physical skill and fun."

Children from ages 3 to 6 use soft play equipment that encourages movement, exploration, and motor skill development. This is an inviting atmosphere with bright colors, and instruction by a counselor helps the children to move at their own pace. The infants-to-2-year-old age group have planned activities with an instructor.

Sinai Wellbridge in Pikesville, Maryland, has a day-care center, and will be expanding its allocation of space to children's fitness in the future. For now, Sinai Corporate Health is developing fitness programs for high school athletes between the ages of 12 and 18 in a series of small centers located throughout suburban Baltimore. Affiliated with Sinai Hospital, a 375-bed hospital, and Sinai Wellbridge, the primary medical center and wellness center, these satellite fitness facilities are highly specialized and centered on a patented proprietary training system that provides high school athletes with top-level training.

In an alliance formed with baseball player Cal Ripken Jr., these high-tech Cal Ripken Sports Acceleration Centers are keyed to reach out to an unserved market. Programs at the centers are scheduled to last between six and eight weeks, the goal being to improve the skill level of the athlete in a variety of sports.

The first center was built in Columbia, Maryland, the second will be in Fairfax, Virginia, and there are more planned. This is one of the first examples in the country of hospital-based wellness and fitness programs taking on a specific market with a specific product. Susan Heiser, business development director for Sinai Corporate Health, developed the concept, working closely with Darryl McKay, Sinai Wellbridge's executive director, under the visionary leadership of Sinai Health president Warren Green.

Within the Cal Ripkin Centers are activity spaces for specialized training equipment, which is part of the Acceleration Program package. These machines and methods have very different programmatic requirements than machines typically found on the open market. They require sliding mirrors for athletes to watch themselves while working out in certain positions and hard-surface walls for the areas that involve baseball and other ball sports training. Toilet facilities located at intervals throughout the training floor are also needed, because the intensity of the training requires that they be close by. A retail component and a family waiting area with Internet access and entertainment are included in the program.

These centers typically include a sports medicine clinic, staffed by medical professionals, with examination rooms, treatment rooms, and fitness testing rooms. Food service selections are usually confined to juice, coffee, and snack bar.

The allocation of more space to children's fitness areas appears to be a growing trend. Crozer-Keystone's Springfield, Pennsylvania, Healthplex has allocated space on the first floor of the three-story facility to a children's gymnasium, adjacent to the child care center, near the administrative offices, across from the basketball court.

Locker Rooms

Locker room design is driven by the number of lockers to be integrated into the design, the proposed relationship of locker room to the shower and toilet areas, and the relationship of these spaces to other wet areas—the pool, spa, and salon—of the wellness center.

Critical to the design of locker rooms in a wellness center facility is the primary decision that must be made, whether to include separate family locker rooms and/or care giver locker/dressing rooms in the overall design. The criteria for solving this design issue will be predicated on the market feasibility study and the market projections and demand analysis. The wellness center building committee has to decide at the outset what sort of facility it wants to develop, what people will use the center with what frequency, and at what times of day certain areas will be most active.

A rule of thumb suggested by locker manufacturers is to estimate the largest number of members who will use the facility at any given time and double that number. This allows for the swing factor, which means members coming and going before and after peak times.

Using the bay system of planning a locker room space is a good starting point. This involves the creation of a four-foot-wide circulation aisle at the end of each bay (a row of lockers with seats in between). Dry shoe traffic and wet shoe traffic should be separated at opposites of the locker room space. Fixed benches are typically used in the center of each bay configuration.

The distance between the face of the locker and the bench should be a minimum of three feet, more if this space is also used as a traffic aisle. Locker rooms may be carpeted with high-wear loop carpeting or tiled with vinyl or ceramic tile.

Shower areas adjacent to locker rooms should have built-in dressing areas, separated for privacy with a curtain for each area. Paying attention to the issue of privacy for members and patients alike is critical to the success of the wellness center design.

In both women's and men's locker rooms, if there are no separate family locker rooms, the center should provide an area to accommodate parents changing children, including infants. Although child care areas may or may not be provided, more than likely some parents will have occasion to take care of children while at the center.

Dressing, makeup, and grooming areas are also important design considerations. Spaces for these activities need not include a sink, but should contain generous counter space and good lighting. Additional ground fault interrupter (GFI) outlets should be included.

Lockers are available in metal, laminate, and wood. Wood is the most expensive and is often selected for use in high-end country clubs. Wood lockers provide visual warmth and a measure of elegance. Wood lockers are ventilated in much the same way as metal or laminated locker systems. All types of lockers can be ordered in full height, typically 60 inches high, or half height, 60 inches overall height, divided into an upper and lower locker. Many wellness centers, like commercial facilities, charge for locker rentals as a source of revenue. There are various locking systems available.

As in all areas of the wellness center, there should be adequate air exchange and airflow in a locker room.

Pools and Spas

Whirlpool spas are used for hydrotherapeutic massage, muscle relaxation, stress reduction, and pain relief. A whirlpool spa may be constructed of ceramic tile, concrete with a treated finish, or one of the many prefabricated systems available on the market today.

Decisions must be made regarding the size and configuration of the whirlpool bath itself, the shell (in the case of the prefabricated whirlpool), the type of water jets and their configuration, and the seating arrangement. Special foot wells can be selected that focus water jet pressure on the feet. Spas should be designed to be barrier free.

Swim spas are larger than relaxation spas and have no area for seating; combination units are available. Flotation therapy spas are also available on the market. These spas, designed to provide mental and physical relaxation through spa flotation, typically have 1,000 pounds of Epsom salts added to the water and are soundproof and lightproof.

Muscle stresses are relieved by the positioning of "cluster" jets toward the lower back. Other types of jets available are "power massage," "standard," and "mini." Each jet type has a different function; many can be used effectively in combination with others.

High-volume pumps power the jets, enabling them to produce the high pressure needed to create the intended effect. Larger jets produce a greater massage effect. The size of a whirlpool spa pump relates to the number of jets it can supply, not the degree of pressure it can maintain.

Bill Jaworski of Great Northern Engineering explained recently:

> Because there are so many different sizes of hydrotherapy jets, there is no hard-and-fast rule concerning pump size. In general, large jets require ¼ hp per jet. Some jets are so small you can have a 1 hp pump drive eight of them. At the other extreme, some small swim spa jets require 1 hp per jet.

Manufacturers often use two or more pumps to power individual groups of jets if the total jet area is extremely large. This practice generally saves money for everybody.

Whirlpool spas, like pools, must be well designed, with appropriate filtering and water purification systems. Dimension One spas offers spas specifically for hydrotherapy as well as purely for relaxation. Its Ultralounge spa-within-a-spa system massages neck, shoulders, back, thighs, and feet at the same time. These spas are prefabricated and insulated with polyurethane foam.

Pools

Many wellness center directors advise that no matter how big a pool a facility thinks it needs, it will always have to be bigger. Typically, wellness centers include in their initial design a 25-meter pool for laps. Larger centers separate aquatherapy areas from the lap pool by actually enclosing the therapy pool in a separate room.

Planning criteria for pools are a primary consideration for wellness center design. Lap pools generally follow standards requiring that the overall length be 25 yards as a minimum, in keeping with interscholastic and intercollegiate requirements. The next size is typically a 50-meter pool, included in some of the larger centers.

Lanes in lap pools are usually 7 feet wide, and the recommended pool deck area is 10 feet wide. Removable floating lane dividers are available. The depths of all pools vary, generally from 3 to 12 feet. Recreational pools in aquatic centers have adjustable floors that enable different depth configurations for different pool activities. Few lap pools include diving boards in their design, although there are aquatic centers that do include them.

Warm water therapy pools can vary in size, depending on the planning criteria of the center. Most warm water therapy pools are approximately 8 yards long and 5 yards wide. Handicapped accessibility is important in all pool areas. Perimeter gutter systems should be used for water and wave control.

Overhead floodlights for outdoor pools should be mounted at least 20 feet above the water line. Indoor pools should be lighted from above, and some variation of large pendant fixtures designed for this specific use are suggested. Fluorescent lights are to be avoided if possible. Anything reminiscent of a high school gymnasium/ pool environment is to be avoided. This is a special place. Design cues from the hospitality industry are more likely to be helpful as guides to designing these and other large activity spaces. Underwater lighting for outdoor pools can be achieved with the design of special niches around the inside of the pool, in keeping with National Electrical Code standards.

Amenity pools are for fun and can vary as to the design intent. Most wellness center administrators interviewed cautioned that one should err on the generous side when planning the size of an amenity pool for a wellness center. An amenity pool frequently becomes the drawing element for families and others wanting to relax.

Sufficient deck space should be included at poolside, first for reasons of safety, and second because these areas, like waiting areas and lounges, frequently become gathering places for groups of people. Poolside relaxation areas, both indoor and outdoor terraces, present a respite from the bustling activity areas and the serious clinical and therapeutic components of a wellness center. The introduction of nature at poolside is a wonderful way to provide visual relief from the hard edges of the swimming pool environment.

Filtering Systems

The oldest filtering systems for pools and spas use sand. Sand filters use a combination of sand and gravel to filter the water as it passes through. These systems must be backwashed occasionally to flush away trapped dirt, and sand has to be replaced every seven years.

Other filtering systems that involve the use of diatomaceous earth (DE) are called DE filter systems. The filters are made up of extremely fine-meshed grids coated with DE powder. The system acts as an adhesive, trapping small particles. Maintenance includes a backwash procedure.

Cartridge filter systems are made up of tightly folded or pleated mesh, designed to trap impurities. Cartridge filters are washed out periodically with a hose.

Pool and Spa Heaters

Pools and spas must be heated. There are several choices offered by manufacturers today. A heat pump, which transfers heat from the outside air to the pool water, is used mainly in outdoor applications. A gas heater heats water from the pool, which is then returned to the pool (gas heaters tend to heat pools rapidly.). There are also electric pool heaters, which have the advantage of being compact, and oil heaters, which use diesel fuel.

Saunas

Sauna rooms can be built from scratch or assembled from kits that offer precut parts in many standard sizes up to 12 by 12 feet with 7-foot ceilings, which is the maximum recommended height. Sauna rooms are typically built from western red cedar or spruce and include cedar benches with backrests and headrests, wall lights and thermometers, and heaters with guardrails.

Sauna heaters often include two-stage thermostats that provide consistent, comfortable heat. High air flow reduces the time it takes to bring the sauna room temperature to the desired level for bathing.

Steam

Steam baths are not always included in the design of a wellness centers, but appear to be typical in the design of the larger centers. Steam baths require generator units that are sized appropriately for the number of cubic feet of air that is being conditioned. Safety requires that the steam heads and controls do not heat in excess of 125 degrees, in order to reduce the risk of burning. Controls can be located both inside and outside the steam bath.

Because of the hot, moist environment, the growth of mold is difficult to control in steam bath areas. It is important to be aware of the threat to public health inherent in the creation and maintenance of any environment where people come in contact with standing water, humidity, and other people.

Not long ago an outbreak of Legionnaire's disease was discovered on ships traveling between the Caribbean and the United States. The *Healthline, Medical Data Exchange* reported that 50 passengers on nine cruises in a two-month period came down with Legionnaire's disease, which was isolated from the sand filter in the ship's whirlpool spa. The risk of acquiring Legionnaire's disease increased by 64 percent for every hour spent in the spa water. Passengers spending time around the spa, but not actually in it were significantly more likely to have acquired it than passengers in the water. The article called for new strategies in decontamination and testing of whirlpool spas.

Water Treatment Systems

The following table is a basic guide for the electrical requirements for saunas.

Typical Electrical Requirements for Sauna Heaters

Voltage	Phase	Amperes	KW	Minimum American Wire Gauge (AWG) Wire Gauge 90°C Copper Supply Wire	Floor Area (sq ft)	Ceiling Height
240	1	11.5	48.0	4–3 w/g	47	78 in.
	1	15.6	65.0			
208	3	8.6	24.0	8–4 w/g	28	
		11.7	32.5		47	
		15.0	41.7	6–4 w/g		
		7.5	20.8	10–4 w/g	28	
		8.8	24.3	8–4 w/g		

The Dimension One line of spas and others use ozone as an agent for water treatment. Ozone effectively kills bacteria, fungi, yeast, and molds on contact. Other water treatments include chlorine or bromine. The wellness center operator/manager should have experience in the selection of these systems and their advantages and disadvantages. Bromine, like chlorine, is a chemical used to sanitize and disinfect. Bromine will not oxidize the water or remove ammonia or nitrogen compounds. Bromine products are often sold in a two-part system that includes an oxidizing agent. An ozone generator can provide just this balance to bromine. Cautions in regard to specifying a bromine system include allergies in sensitive individuals and the compromising of plastic, vinyl, acrylic, aluminum, and other metals. Bromine can also bleach colored plaster in pools and spas and pool and spa areas.

Gardens

The wellness center design should take every opportunity to bring nature indoors. Using natural light, natural materials, and producing, through skilled design, a rhythm that encourages and uplifts people is the goal.

Interior gardens can be used to help heal the soul. As a design element, the inclusion of plants in a lobby or waiting area, in fact, in nearly all spaces in a wellness center, is highly encouraged. How can a center whose programs promote healing be designed without a reference to nature itself?

The rhythm of life should be replicated in the design of the wellness center. A glimpse to the outside environment, wherever possible, is in itself healing. The patient or member must feel that this is a special place, also subliminally cognizant of the relationship between indoors and outdoors, the time of day, the position of the sun, the weather.

Not every space has to have a view to the outside, which, of course, in a planning sense is difficult if not impossible. What is possible is for the architect to remember that the context of the environment in which the wellness center is located is highly important to a person's experience of the building.

How a person feels about the building has an effect on healing and an effect on the success of the project. If the community typically refers to the new wellness center as a special place, the architect will have succeeded.

If the wellness center manages by virtue of its design to become a site to which people are drawn, which has a sense of place, that too, is healing. "Knowing where you are" is important to the psyche, and the identification of a center within a community because of its well-created sense of context makes it an important inclusion in the fabric of the city or town in which it is located.

Garden terraces with small seating areas available for solitary meditation are also important. The varying of activity and quiet spaces creates a rhythm reflective of nature itself. The entire space becomes a series of light musical notes in the building symphony.

Meditation Room and Chapel

Nearly all wellness center owners surveyed for this book have considered allotting some space to a meditation room or chapel. The space allotted is typically not large, for the most part in the 120-square-foot range. What is important is that the meditation room is designed to be a place of quiet repose. Soft colors and substantial sound attenuation are suggested. A nondenominational design is required even if the sponsoring hospital has a religious affiliation. Meditation as a source of stress relief can be taught in group settings in health education classrooms or in aerobics/dance areas, as can other stress management techniques.

Meditation has been sanctioned by the National Institutes of Health (NIH) as being helpful in the control of stress. Although it can be practiced anywhere, dedicating a singular area in the heart of a wellness center to meditation may add to the patients' and members' well-being.

Laundry

Will towels be provided for members and patients? Most wellness center executives see this as a necessary amenity. This, then, implies that towel storage, laundering, and perhaps locker key distribution might all be located in the same space.

Will the towel area be staffed? Wellness centers often combine the front reception/control desk with locker key sales and distribution, as well as towel distribution. Sometimes, in an attempt to reduce the number of staff allocated for these functions, the laundry facility is adjacent to this area. The danger here is that such an arrangement may put off a sophisticated clientele made up of patients and members who do not want to feel as though they are in a commercial or high school gym.

The laundry function must be carefully considered and designed appropriately in regard to the needs of the user. A wellness center will require commercial laundry equipment. Laundry facilities are often operated by maintenance staff and located close to wet areas. Members and patients should have a clear idea of where to pick up towels before they venture to the pool, spa, salon area, or therapy area. The locker room is perhaps the most logical location for soiled towel receptacles.

A rule of thumb in designing laundry facilities for a wellness center is to calculate the total membership, ascertain the maximum number of members and patients coming through the center on a day when the center will have the most traffic, and designate two towels per member to develop a number to discuss with the manufacturer or distributor of the commercial washers and dryers.

The noise of these machines, even with the appropriate use of concrete pads and sound-dampening strategies is great. Thus, they should be located in an area that is not close to therapy, meditation rooms, food service, or offices.

The Lobby

The lobby and entrance area is the primary control area for a wellness center. All initial transactions—checking in, visiting, getting directions, meeting people—take place in this most important common area. Design logic dictates that this area, providing primary visual control of the main entrance and presiding over the wellness center functions, be an important and well-designed area.

The lobby desk should be large enough to accommodate two or more people working comfortably at the same time. It should also be large enough to allow each person to have private conversations with members, patients, and staff. The lobby desk is probably where communications functions will be centered.

If possible, the lobby should include a waiting area sufficient to allow for the gathering of small groups. Comfortable seating, good lighting, desktop telephones, and adequate sound

Dow Chemical Employee Wellness Center, Midland, Michigan. *Ellerbe Becket Architects.*

control should be the minimum design requirements. Clear signage, enough light, and good air circulation should set the stage in the lobby/waiting and main control desk area for a positive introduction to the space.

Near the lobby area should be a toilet room adjacent to the core areas. Stairways and elevators should be easily accessible and visible from the lobby. Quite often a space near the lobby area can be used for member testing. If such a space is located in this area, it should be private.

Administration

Adjacent to the lobby area should be a small administration area, with a reception desk/secretarial area and two or three offices, depending on the program and size of the facility. These areas should have good lighting and acoustical control. If possible, some visual contact with the lobby is suggested, but this is by no means a hard-and-fast rule. Too much visibility can give the impression to people in the waiting area that they are being observed, which does not foster the relaxed and uplifting atmosphere desirable in a wellness center.

Similarly, administrative staff members need a certain degree of privacy with which to conduct the efficient flow of business activity. Marketing or presale areas may also be located here.

Offices for the fitness manager, accountant, and center director, as well as a staff lounge, may also be included in this zone. Smaller centers, those with areas in the 35,000-square-foot range, will probably require two small administrative offices and a reception area. Another option is to design the employee lounge near other backhouse areas such as laundry, storage, janitor's closet, and staff rest room areas.

Clinical areas should be acoustically and visually separated from fitness areas and from the lobby. Visual cues in the design of the space should lead the user effortlessly to where he or she wants to go, but can be supplemented with well-designed signage. The clinical areaa should have its own receptionist, office, examination and treatment rooms, laboratory (if it is included in the program), cardiopulmonary testing, records, and physical therapy/occupational therapy area.

Combined-use areas, such as fitness areas used in rehabilitation, should be carefully thought out. If a wellness center is of modest size and the only area to be used for cardiopulmonary therapy is the main fitness area, planners will have to make decisions early in the program as to how this can gracefully be done. By no means should it appear that "patients" are hidden from "members"; on the other hand, the need for privacy during a rehabilitative procedure dictates that the design architect be sensitive to this need so as to avoid putting people on display.

If the wellness center is small, with an overall area in the 35,000-square-foot range, the weight training area should be close to the locker rooms and pool areas. Think of how the patient will move through various activities in the space. The design logic should follow the intent of the clinical program as well as the fitness program.

Typically, the health education/community program areas in wellness centers are located somewhere close to the front of the building, near the lobby/control desk and public rest rooms.

Salons

Many wellness centers throughout the country have included or are expanding to include beauty salons in their buildings. These spaces are good revenue producers and provide members and patients with one-stop shopping for personal care. Beauty salons must be ventilated properly and have sufficient air changes so as to not affect the adjacent spaces. Fumes from the processing chemicals used in permanent waves are strong and unpleasant and carry very quickly to nearby rooms.

Hair salon sizes vary with anticipated use. A basic guide suggests an area of approximately 900 square feet, which would contain approximately seven stations.

Hair salons typically include a front reception/ cash area, a display counter, customer seating, one rest room, a small stock room, and a laundry room containing a commercial washer/dryer. Stations include hairwashing stations, hair dryers, and hair styling chairs. Hair salons require a separate hot water tank.

Color

The use of color in environmental design is one of the most important considerations. The effect of color on human emotion is far more powerful than generally assumed. The emotional and physical effects of color are uniquely interwoven. Color heals. Color can be used to relax or excite, to stimulate conversation, or create a quieting effect. Color sends a message to the human psyche,which, through recent advances in science and technology, is becoming quantifiable.

A particular color is affected by the colors near it. This is why the selection of color is often a timely process. The size of the area in which the color will be used, the relationship of one color to another, the degree to which colored surfaces are textured, and the ambient light in the room in which they are displayed—all affect how we perceive the color itself.

In selecting colors, textures, and patterns, the largest samples possible should be viewed. Small sample patches do not reflect the true impact of the colors selected.

Color therapy, the therapeutic use of color, can be included successfully in all healthcare environments. The use of color as a communication tool in healthcare settings is only now, at the turn of the century, becoming credible.

We know that the human eye absorbs color. Age-related changes in regard to these perceptions are discussed in Elisabeth Brawley's book, *Designing For Alzheimer's Disease*. As we grow older, our ability to perceive and make sense of the environment changes, although these changes are very individualized.

Similarly, at the other end of the age spectrum, children are stimulated, some believe, to a greater degree than adults by the use of bright colors. This means that in environments where the user profile cuts across age barriers, the architect must take this range into account in selecting colors for the design of wellness center spaces.

As we age, we perceive colors that are brighter with more clarity. This suggests that the use of clear, bright colors in various areas of the wellness center would be beneficial, especially where the program includes a large number of cardiopulmonary rehabilitation patients of advancing years. Because today we are able to rehabilitate patients long into their golden years, and the baby boom generation is moving en masse in that direction, we must consider the influence of these factors in selection of color in the center's design.

As a general rule of thumb, one should avoid pastels that are at the muddy end of the range of hues. Brightness is encouraged in most spaces, as long as glare is prevented. Light affects color and color affects light. Light colors reflect light and dark colors absorb light. Light sources reinforce certain colors, and the type of light greatly affects this phenomenon. Warm light, such as incandescent, affects colors differently than cool light like that emitted by fluorescent lights.

The use of natural daylight and full-spectrum light should be encouraged in the design of wellness centers. Full-spectrum light mimics natural daylight. Artificial light lacks the complete balance of the natural spectrum, which is believed to interfere with the body's optimal absorption of nutrients, a condition known as "malillumination." John Ott, research scientist and author, believes that "the kind of light needed for adequate health must be…full-spectrum light and natural daylight."

The typical lighting level for an office space is 500 lumens per square meter. Natural daylight provides approximately 100 times more. Some happy medium should be realized in the design of the various wellness center spaces. The design should be keyed to the quality of the light (natural and full spectrum), applied with skill to the lighting level suggested by the anticipated use of a particular space.

Color and Light Healing

The effect of color on the well-being of human beings is well documented. Since formal studies in the 1950s suggested that correctional facilities be painted pink or blue to quiet the arousal levels of inmates, which had some effect on the design of those environments and some success in the implementation, architects have become increasingly aware of the effect of color in the environment on emotion, health, and behavior.

Color has a profound and long lasting effect on the wellness of individuals for a variety of reasons, some biological and some psychological. Suffice it to say that color selection is of absolute importance in the design of wellness centers. Here, however, we will note how specific color light therapy can and is being used to treat patients and how this treatment can be supported in the wellness center environment.

Postulates basic to the concept of color as a healing element are that human beings absorb color through the retina, color itself is made up of light waves of different frequencies, and different organs in the body have different characteristic frequencies.

Therefore, it may be logical to expect that different colors affect different organs in a variety of ways and that if disease means the altered functioning of different bodily systems, then this functioning may be altered, helped back to its natural state, by absorbing different colors for certain amounts of time each day.

The effect of color is both physiological and cultural. It has everything to do with association and memory. Complementary therapies that focus on treating patients with color therapy posit that red is a stimulating color; yellow is excellent for the nerves, brain, and motor stimulation; orange has an antispasmodic effect; green is soothing, cooling, and calming; and blue reduces nervous excitement and can be both calming and uplifting at the same time. Studies are continuing that investigate the effects of color and the possibilities for future uses in the healthcare environment.

Certain medical procedures, such as imaging (mammography, for example) suggest low lighting, as do areas designed to bring down blood pressure and the excitement and activity level. Certain areas may be designed for light therapy, specifically for the alleviation of seasonal affective disorder (SAD), a malady that requires the use of light for a certain amount of time each day in order to affect healing. Patients suffering from SAD exhibit symptoms of depression that can be tied to the change of seasons, typically becoming increasingly depressed with the onset of winter.

Currently available are a number of forms of light therapy that include full-spectrum light: bright light therapy, ultraviolet (UV) therapy, syntonic optometry, cold laser therapy, and colored light therapy. Full-spectrum lights are available commercially in 4-foot lengths and can replace fluorescent lights in ceiling fixtures for overall or ambient lighting purposes. These lights should be considered as appropriate throughout a wellness facility. Specific treatment lights for malillumination and other disorders require the use of a light box, which consist of two bright light tubes in a box that measures 2 feet by 2 feet and is set up in such a way that the patient is positioned about 18 inches away from the box. The patient is positioned so as to not look directly into the box while he or she is engaged in some small task. Sessions typically last from 30 minutes to two hours.

Bright light therapy, according to John Zimmerman, Ph.D., in *Alternative Medicine*, involves the use of a bright white light ranging in intensity from 2,000 to 5,000 l.ux. Bright white light of this type is light without ultraviolet rays, which may be harmful if stared into directly.

Hemoirradiation (photophoresis) involves the irradiation of blood with light after it is removed from the patient, followed by reintroducing it into the patient's bloodstream. Some of the benefits from hemoirradiation are improved calcium metabolism, increased systemic resistence, which results in the strengthening of the immune system, and increased oxygen absorption, William Clayton Douglass, M.D., of Clayton, Georgia, has successfully used this technique to treat cancer, rheumatoid arthritis, bronchial asthma, and symptoms of AIDS.

Color Light Therapy

Dr. Norman Shealy, M.D., Ph.D., of Springfield, Missouri, believes that colored lights and flashing lights can be used to treat pain and depression. He believes that because colors have certain frequencies, and flashing lights different frequencies, exposure to these different lights alters brain chemistry. Shealy's theories are being borne out by scientific research in the emerging field of pyschoneuroimmunology. It may be of some significance that at Florida Hospital's Celebration Health Complex, the wellness center has both a medical director and a noted psychoneuroimmunologist, Neil Hall, M.D., on its medical staff.

Monochromatic red light therapy is being used by Gerald Hall, D.C., of El Paso, Texas, to treat endocrine problems, gastrointestinal problems, and depression, and researcher Ray Fisch uses red light therapy to treat arthritis, allergies, and depression.

Light-activated chemotherapy is currently being used at UCLA Medical School and at Cedars-Sinai Medical Center in Los Angeles. The inclusion of light sources or the close proximity of light therapy rooms to chemotherapy treatment rooms makes sense.

Syntonic optometry, a form of colored light therapy using several patented devices, involves the specific application of pure light wave bands focused directly into the eyes.

Similar to the specific application of light directly into the eyes for purposes of healing is cold laser therapy, which focuses a beam of low laser light directly onto the area of the body that is showing a symptom of disease or, primarily, acute pain. The apparent effect is a change in the enzymatic functioning of the targeted cells, which reduces inflammation.

Cold laser therapy, color therapy, and bright light therapy all require fairly simple support in terms of room spaces. A room that is slightly larger than a typical examination room is best suited to these therapies, with room for an examination table for full-body therapy, and a desk/ chair arrangement for bright light therapy, which requires the patient to remain seated, performing a simple activity, while receiving the light therapy.

Artwork

The inclusion of artwork in the design of a wellness center is most welcome. Artwork has been incorporated in healthcare centers around the world. Art and music release the human spirit; the spirit freed lets the body heal. Art therapy is a bona fide therapy. People all over the world train as art therapists and receive certification from universities for their advanced work in the healthcare setting. Art therapists are skilled at diagnosis and treatment of patients with certain health problems. The freedom of expression that art affords the individual elicits previously untapped energy, which can be used for healing.

As a profession, art therapy utilizes art, media, images, and the creative process. Art therapy practice is based on knowledge of human psychology and development. This form of therapy is often used as a treatment for developmentally disabled people and is practiced in mental health, rehabilitation, educational, and other institutions. The American Art Therapy Association's Board certifies therapists and regulates educational, professional, and ethical standards.

Prinzhorn's *Artistry of the Mentally Ill*, published in 1922, focused the interest of the medical community on the value of art therapy in rehabilitation. Art was used as a tool in the 1940s by psychologist Margaret Naumburg, and, ten years later, Edith Kramer. The experience of art is thought to bring to the surface many subconscious issues, often in symbolic form. The field has grown since then to a viable rehabilitative program and has met with much success.

The value of art therapy to achieving wellness is substantial. Allied to art therapy and its benefits are the benefits of sound healing or music therapy, and of play therapy both for children and adults. Many acute care hospitals have pediatric playrooms where a play therapist works with children to elicit and discuss their feelings about themselves and their illnesses. There is also play therapy for adults. One group of actors/therapists visits hospital patients and involves them in spontaneous, interactive play in which everyone is a participant.

These therapies, particularly art therapy, are well worth considering in the wellness center program. An art therapy room should be approximately 12 by 15 feet as a minimum, but an employee-lounge-type area (with sinks and storage) might be used in the evenings for art therapy classes, as well as regular classroom space.

In a symposium held by the *Journal of Healthcare Design*, Michael Samuels, M.D., discussed the combining of art, music, and traditional medicine. Hospitals all over the world, Samuels says, are incorporating art and music into patient care.

> The most sophisticated medical centers are now using bedside artists and musicians to work with patients and change the hospital environment. Art and music can break the sterile space of fear and open it up to the human spirit.
>
> Art heals by changing a person's physiology from one of stress to one of deep relaxation...art and music put a person into a different brain wave pattern; they affect his or her autonomic nervous system, hormonal balance, and brain neurotransmitters. Art and music affect every cell in the body instantly to create a healing physiology that changes the immune system and blood flow to all organs.

Storage and Disposal

In any wellness center, storage as a component of the overall design must be addressed with singular focus. Wellness center executives have said that they never seem to have enough storage, and if they have a somewhat adequate amount, it is never the right type.

In Chesapeake, Virginia, Chesapeake Hospital's first wellness center, the Life Style Center, which is adjacent to the hospital on the main hospital campus, storage was a challenge. The staff at Chesapeake came up with some interesting and inventive solutions. Deep, wide closets adjacent to the aerobics room provided enough cubic footage, but not the right kind of space. The staff devised a customized stacking system to hold fitness balls and other exercise equipment such as steps, rubber tubes,

Women's locker room, Sinai Wellbridge, Pikesville, Maryland.

and free weights used in group exercise classes. Cubicles at the back of the aerobics room were installed to provide temporary storage for jackets, handbags, and other belongings of those attending class.

The design of the clinical component will have to address thoughtfully how soiled materials are to be disposed of. Quite often, a wellness center engages a service connected to the hospital to handle the matter, but this operational issue must be considered early in the design process so that adequate space is programmed into it.

Clean supplies will need their own space in the clinical area. This storage will be in addition to shelves and cabinets already included in the design of equipment storage and requires a separate closet or room. A sterilizing system must be included. In some cases a service that delivers presealed packs may be used, although this is typically done in regard to surgical procedures. An autoclave will certainly be required.

Details and Finishes

The clinical component of a wellness center, in compliance with all codes and regulations, particularly in using the *AIA Guidelines* as a standard, will require a minimum 5-foot corridor width.

Doors, sidelights, borrowed lights, and windows glazed to within 18 inches of the floor must be glazed with safety glass, wired glass, or plastic glazing that resists breaking. Similar materials should be used in wall openings of playrooms and exercise rooms unless otherwise required for fire safety.

Interior finish materials must have a flame-spread rating consistent with NFPA 101, as must building insulation materials unless sealed on all sides and edges.

Amenities

Unique amenities borrowed from the hospitality design industry may find their way, if appropriate, into the wellness center design. Gas fireplaces, often used as focal points in hotel lobbies in the Southwest, may find a home in a waiting, lounge, lobby, or library area. This simple element changes the atmosphere of the space. On cold winter days or rainy fall and spring days in most regions of the country, a fireplace in a waiting area can be a welcoming sight.

A bulletin/message board for members is also a welcoming addition. At Sinai Wellbridge in suburban Baltimore, Executive Director Darryl McKay has included, near the locker room area, a message board that serves as a communication tool for members to communicate with management in regard to suggestions and lets members leave messages for one another.

Another well-received amenity at Sinai Wellbridge is the lounge area designed into the locker room area. This relatively quiet space has couches, coffee tables, telephones, and a built-in large screen television, which enables those waiting for people to get dressed to make a telephone call, catch the news, or read a newspaper or magazine. Included in the locker room design are generous areas for grooming with adequate mirror and vanity space.

Therapy Rooms

Chelation Therapy

Robert Atkins, M.D., of New York has been instrumental in popularizing complementary medicine in the United States and is one of the first doctors of traditional medicine to encourage the use of supplemental vitamins and minerals. He is also a leader in the application of chelation therapy.

Chelation therapy, an FDA-approved therapy (at this writing only for the removal of toxic amounts of lead and mercury poisoning), involves the administration of the chelating substance EDTA (ethylenediaminetetracetic acid) through intravenous infusion. Simply put, the ionic makeup of EDTA acts like a magnet to remove substances, toxic metal ions, from the bloodstream, which reduces the internal inflammation caused by free radicals, destructive rogue molecules.

The benefit to the patient is largely in the area of degenerative, rather than simply chronic, diseases. Chelation therapy is considered a viable alternative to balloon angioplasty and is thought to have benefit in the reduction of atherosclerosis, by removing calcium plaques, relief from the chest pain associated with angina, healing of patients with gangrene, and slowing of macular degeneration in elderly patients.

Chelation therapy, it is theorized, can slow the aging process. This key complementary medical procedure is an essential clinical element to be included in the design of a complete wellness center. Protocols for the administration of chelation therapy include blood pressure and circulation testing, cholesterol and other blood component testing, pre- and post-vascular testing, blood sugar and other nutritional testing, kidney and organ function tests, and tissue mineral testing.

According to *Alternative Medicine*, chelation therapy takes about three and one half hours and is performed on an outpatient basis. Twenty to 30 treatments are given at an average rate of one to three per week, with patient evaluations performed at regular intervals. The American Board of Chelation Therapy in Chicago, Illinois, which established the medical protocol for chelation therapy in 1983, is an excellent resource for information regarding this form of therapy. As well, the American College of Advancement in Medicine in Laguna Hills, California, is seeking to establish board certification for physicians who are providing chelation therapy in their practices.

Because of the long duration of treatment, the physical space requirements for chelation therapy are potentially enormous. There may be some eventual comparison between dialysis environments and their space requirements, and those of chelation therapy. At some point in the future, as the benefits become more widely known and insurers take notice, chelation centers may be developed.

For the time being, at least some rooms should be devoted to this type of therapy in a wellness center. It would be cost-effective to combine these rooms with vitamin therapy rooms— the administration of intravenous vitamins and minerals for patients with abnormal absorption capabilities, or acute therapy such as vitamin C therapy for pain management for cancer patients.

What this means, in terms of room requirements, is a room with the minimum size of a typical clinical examination room or, at best, a large room with four reclining chairs adjacent to one another, with flexible wall partitions between them to allow a nurse or nurse practitioner to observe four patients simultaneously, thereby reducing the number of full time employees (FTEs.)

As in all other spaces in a wellness center, a view to the outdoors, especially to a garden with a water feature, is the optimum design option. Without the availability of such a view (and even with one), each reclining chair/IV station should include an individualized entertainment center with television, video, stereo, and Internet access.

Hyperthermia

Like many alternative and traditional medical therapies, the origin of hyperthermia can be traced back to an earlier time. The technique of hyperthermia as a curative therapy was first attributed to Parmenides, a Greek physician in the sixth century.

In many cultures, the concept of heat as a curative agent has been popularized through several centuries. We think of the development of the sauna in Finland, steam baths in eastern Europe, the ritual hot bath in Japan, hot springs in the United States, and the Roman baths of ancient times.

Cafe and basketball court, Springfield Healthplex, Springfield, Pennsylvania.

According to *Alternative Medicine*, high-tech methods of inducing a rise in body heat include diathermy, ultrasound, radiant heating, and extracorporeal heating. Diathermy involves raising of body temperature by the application of electromagnetic radio waves of a certain frequency; ultrasound raises body temperature by applying high-energy sound waves to create molecular friction as the waves hit body tissue; radiant heating, as the name implies, applies infrared heat to the body; the extracorporeal heating technique removes blood from the body, heats it, and returns it to the body. Diathermy and ultrasound are used for localized problems. Generalized infections, including viruses, HIV infections, and cancer, have been improved with the use of whole-body hyperthermia, in particular extracorporeal heating.

It is thought that hyperthermia treatment modifies cell membranes to enable chemotherapy and radiation to work better. In "The Effect of Whole Body Hyperthermia on the Immune Cell Activity of Cancer Patients," M. M. Park, et al. studied the application of hyperthermia to cancer patients and discovered a drop in white cell count immediately following treatment, and a rise within a few hours. The ability of white blood cells to destroy target cells appears to increase in certain circumstances.

There are no specific protocols developed, at this writing, for the application of hyperthermia treatments. In terms of use and function, a space the size of a clinical examination room is required, with an ultrasound machine, diathermy machines, infrared heating devices, and extracorporeal heating equipment.

The goal of wellness center design should be to maintain the best and highest standard of care, reflective of those clinical and fitness components that make up the basic elements of this new building type.

Clinical elements, which include all elements that may be found in an outpatient ambulatory care setting, are naturally subject to high standards such as those demanded by the Joint Commission on Accreditation of Healthcare Organizations (JCAHO), the body that represents a national consensus of what constitutes high-quality patient care. The Academy of Sports Medicine Guidelines are, for fitness elements, a starting point for good architectural design practice. Together these standards, along with the national building codes, the American Institute Guidelines for Healthcare Facilities, and others, form the basic framework for the design and development of quality environments to support the delivery of healthcare and the pursuit of wellness.

The JCAHO lists ambulatory care standards for a wide range of organizations, including the following:

- Ambulatory surgery centers
- Chiropractic clinics
- Endoscopy clinics
- Dental clinics
- Group medical practices
- Imaging centers
- Primary care centers
- Rehabilitation centers
- Women's health centers

The Joint Commission surveys healthcare organizations and gives ratings that reflect the degree of compliance to standards developed for particular types of facilities. To gain accreditation, a facility must gain overall compliance with the standards, not necessarily compliance with each standard.

Ambulatory care standards are published by JCAHO, and healthcare facilities quite often ready themselves for the JCAHO survey by conducting mock surveys, often led by architectural firm teams experienced in the design of healthcare facilities. Although JCAHO looks at procedures, operations, and record keeping, in assessing compliance it also looks at the manner in which a facility itself is designed. Architects should familiarize themselves with JCAHO standards for ambulatory care in addressing design issues for the development of wellness centers.

WELLNESS CENTER STANDARDS

Also important are the standards developed by the American Institute of Architects for the design of healthcare facilities. Any and all standards that relate to the design and functioning of ambulatory care facilities apply to those clinical areas that are included in the wellness center design. The following table provides space-planning guidelines for wellness centers. They are not intended to be authoritative, and it is unlikely that any single wellness center would include all the features listed in these guidelines. Nonetheless, they serve as a starting point for the programmer and designer.

Wellness Center Space Requirements by Room
— PART I: Clinical space —

Room	Area (Sq ft)	Remarks	Information systems					
			LAN	Phone	TV	Audio	Nurse call	Tele
Rehabilitation Medicine								
Treatment	100	Lavatory with gooseneck inlet and wristblades treatment table, medical air, oxygen, vacuum Nurse call Voice and data	x	x		x	x	x
Presurgical testing	130		x	x	x	x	x	x
General surgery operating room	447	Area is clear floor space; does not include built-in cabins. Minimum floor area is 400 sq ft in new work, 360 sq ft in renovation	x	x	x	x	x	x
Recovery	130		x	x	x	x	x	x
Nurses' station	120	2 desk-height workstations 42 in countertop Visual control of patient waiting	x	x	x	x	x	x
Patient waiting	260		x	x	x	x	x	x
Examination	100		x	x		x	x	x
EKG, pulmonary and diagnostic imaging	260		x	x	x	x	x	x
Laboratory	130		x	x	x	x		

— PART I: Clinical space cont.—								
Room	Area (Sq ft)	Remarks	Information systems					
			LAN	Phone	TV	Audio	Nurse call	Tele
Clerical	160	Voice and data files Visual control of patient waiting	x	x		x		
Exercise area	1200	3 mat tables parallel bars treadmill traction table training stairs	x	x	x	x	x	x
Rehabilitation medical office	120		x	x	x	x	x	
Wheelchair alcove	90	Accommodates 6 wheelchairs or 2 stretchers						
Clean linen	110							
Soiled linen	110	Accommodates 2 soiled utility carts, 2 linen carts						
Therapists' workroom	170	5 charting stations	x	x		x		x
Patient demonstration room	56	Provide 3-foot horizontal clearance for therapist assisting patient				x	x	x
Occupational therapy	450	Mat table Standing table Wheelchair table Sink w/gooseneck and wristblades	x	x	x	x	x	x
Activities of daily living, toilet/bath	85	Toilet, sink, tub Door locks	x	x		x	x	x
Activities of daily living, kitchen	150		x	x		x	x	x
Prosthetics/cast	150	Steel sink w/gooseneck inlet and wristblades Plaster trap	x	x		x	x	
Audiology office and examining	120	Audiology testing equipment Provide sound attenuation	x	x		x	x	
Conference room	1150	4-panel film illuminator	x	x	x	x		x
Telemedicine	160		x	x	x	x	x	x
Apothecary	250		x	x		x		x

Continued on next page

— PART I: Clinical space cont.—								
Room	Area (Sq ft)	Remarks	Information systems					
			LAN	Phone	TV	Audio	Nurse call	Tele
Cardiopulmonary Therapy								
Soiled workroom	150	Hot water and drain for pasteurizer and washer Floor drain Respirator Stainless steel counter w/double integral sink, drainboards, backsplash, and marine edge		x		x		
Clean workroom/ equipment storage	375			x		x		
Respiratory therapy/ patient waiting	210			x	x	x	x	
Respiratory waiting/ reception	150		x	x		x	x	x
Respiratory therapy/ stress testing	120	Cardiopulmonary exercise testing system Exercise bike Sink Gas tanks and gasses	x	x		x	x	x
Pulmonary function	140	Whole-body plesmograph Sink Gas tank and gasses	x	x		x	x	x
Mammography								
Mammography	156	Interlock between X-ray equipment and entrance doors Emergency power for X-ray equipment	x	x		x	x	x
Toilet	38						x	
Dressing	56					x	x	
Waiting	104	Room-in-use light over door to Mammography		x	x	x	x	
Endoscopy with Imaging								
Endoscopy/surgery	180		x	x		x	x	x
Endoscopic imaging	360		x	x		x	x	x

— PART I: Clinical space cont.—								
Room	**Area (Sq ft)**	**Remarks**	**Information systems**					
			LAN	Phone	TV	Audio	Nurse call	Tele
Integrative Medicine								
Hydrotherapy	108	2 sinks, refrigerator				x	x	
Whirlpool room	108	2 sinks				x	x	
Chelation therapy	108	May share space with H_2O_2 therapy 2 sinks				x	x	
Artificial sun therapy	160	UVA lamps, control room (50 sq ft)				x	x	
Oxygen therapy	225	Medical gasses 2 sinks				x	x	
Hydrogen peroxide therapy	108	May share space with O_2 therapy 2 sinks				x	x	
Hyperthermia	224	Includes diathermy, ultrasound, radiant heating, extracorporeal heating 2 sinks, hot tub Ultrasound equipment				x	x	
Nutritional counseling	108		x	x	x	x	x	x
Meditation room/ chapel	108							
Acupuncture	150	1 sink	x			x	x	
Massage	150	1 sink				x	x	
Naturopathic exam room	108	1 sink	x	x		x	x	
Osteopathic physician exam room	108	1 sink	x	x		x	x	
Environmental medicine physician's room	108	1 sink	x	x		x	x	
Chiropractic exam room	150	1 sink	x	x		x	x	
General Clinical Functions								
Conference room	150		x	x	x	x		
Staff lounge	182		x	x	x	x		
Staff locker room	93			x		x		
Staff toilet	46					x		
Office	100		x	x	x	x		x

Continued on next page

— PART II: Fitness —

Room	Area (Sq ft)	Remarks	Information systems					
			LAN	Phone	TV	Audio	Nurse call	Tele
Aerobic Exercise								
Exercise rooms	2 @ 1335	Operable partition between rooms		x	x	x	x	
Storage	80							
Fencing	742	2 pistes at 2 m × 14 m ea, plus 1 m at each end		x	x	x	x	
Fitness								
Track	4,840	1/12 mile, resilient surface, continuous banked corners Windows and access to exterior running area		x	x	x	x	x
Equipment exercise	3,410		x	x	x	x	x	x
Fitness testing	175	Office area for monitoring	x	x		x	x	x
Weight training	400		x	x	x	x	x	x
Resistance training	250		x	x	x	x	x	x
Mens' Lockers/Showers								
Locker room	840	120 lockers 1 private cubicle 2 soiled towel carts 100 in. coat rod			x	x	x	x
Lavatories/grooming	122	4 lavatories Continuous countertop w/mirror above Outlets @ 3 ft. on center		x		x	x	x
Shower	275	1 handicapped stall w/curtains				x	x	
Toilets	275						x	
Storage	35							
Womens' Lockers/Showers								
Locker room	840	120 lockers 1 private cubicle 2 soiled towel carts 100 in. coat rod		x		x	x	x

— PART II: Fitness cont.—								
Room	**Area (Sq ft)**	**Remarks**	**Information systems**					
			LAN	Phone	TV	Audio	Nurse call	Tele
Aerobic Exercise								
Lavatories/grooming	122	12 lavatories Continuous countertop w/mirror above Outlets @ 3 ft. on center				x	x	
Shower	275	1 handicapped stall w/curtains				x	x	
Toilets	240					x	x	
Storage	35							
Fitness Administration								
Coffee bar	160		x	x			x	
Offices	120		x	x	x	x	x	
Pools								
Pool	3,375	25-yd 6-lane pool		x		x	x	
Pool deck	1,680	7 ft around pool						
Basketball Court								

	4,700	Collegiate size.
		Add 3 ft (min) to 10 ft
		  (preferred) unobstructed
		  space on all sides
				x		x	x	

Racquetball/Handball								
	800	20 ft ceiling				x	x	
Tennis Courts								
	2,808	12 ft clearance on sides, 21 ft clearance at ends		x		x	x	
Climbing Wall								
	180	2 climbing stations @ 9 ft × 10 ft each				x	x	

Continued on next page

— PART III: Spa—

Room	Area (Sq ft)	Remarks	Information systems					
			LAN	Phone	TV	Audio	Nurse call	Tele
Aerobic Exercise								
Massage	120 (min)	Include 2 sinks 30 in. × 72 in. massage table		x		x	x	
Sauna	80	8 ft ceiling						
Steam room	80	8 ft ceiling						
Whirlpool	40	500-gallon recommended						
Salon								
Facial room	80	1 sink		x				
Manicure/pedicure	80	1 sink		x				
Hair salon	200	2 sinks for hair washing		x				
Vichy shower	100	Multiple spray heads		x				

— PART IV: Common Areas —

Room	Area (Sq ft)	Remarks	Information systems					
			LAN	Phone	TV	Audio	Nurse call	Tele
Offices	600	5 @ 120 sq ft each	x	x		x		
Secretary	140		x	x		x		
Waiting	140	3 chairs and table	x	x	x	x	x	
Classroom	720	Multipurpose seating for 25	x	x	x	x	x	
Workroom	120	Photocopy, storage, work table	x	x		x		
Coatroom	12							
Storage	55							
Toilets	80					x	x	
Entry/reception	240	Reception desk, sign-in, key storage for locker room	x	x	x	x	x	
Child care	400		x	x	x	x	x	
Retail	150		x	x	x	x		
Lounge	280	Casual seating for 6 3 vending machines		x	x	x	x	

— PART IV: Common Areas cont.—								
Room	Area (Sq ft)	Remarks	Information systems					
			LAN	Phone	TV	Audio	Nurse call	Tele
Mens' Lockers/Showers								
Locker room	600	50 lockers 1 private cubicle 2 soiled towel cart		x		x	x	
Lavatories/grooming	122	4 lavatories						
		Continuous countertop w/mirror above Outlets @ 3 ft on center				x	x	
Shower	275	1 handicapped stall w/curtain				x		
Toilets	275					x	x	
Storage	35							
Womens' Lockers/Showers								
Locker room	600	50 lockers 1 private cubicle 2 soiled towel carts		x		x	x	
Lavatories/grooming	200	12 lavatories Continuous countertop w/mirror above Outlets @ 3 ft on center				x	x	
Shower	275	1 handicapped stall w/curtains			x	x		
Toilets	240					x	x	
Storage	35							
Family lockers/showers								
Locker room	200	25 lockers 1 private cubicle 2 soiled towel carts		x		x	x	
Lavatories/grooming	122	4 lavatories Continuous countertop w/mirror above Outlets @ 3 ft on center				x	x	
Shower	275	1 handicapped stall w/curtains				x		
Toilets	275					x	x	
Storage	35							
Laundry	200							

Air Handling

The AIA Guidelines require the design of facilities that comprise a clinical component to include consideration of recognized requisites such as variable air volume systems, load shedding, programmed controls for unoccupied periods (nights and weekends), and the use of natural ventilation, site and climatic conditions permitting.

The guidelines also suggest that controls for air-handling equipment be designed with an economizer cycle in order to use outside air for heating and cooling. Ventilation standards permit maximum use of simplified systems, including those for VAV (variable air volume) supply. Care must be taken to avoid the possibility of large temperature differentials, high velocity supply, excessive noise, and air stagnation. To maintain asepsis control, airflow supply and exhaust should generally be controlled to ensure movement from clean to less clean areas.

Lighting

Lighting is a key component in the design of any building and is especially important in a wellness center. Light, particularly natural light, can draw people to focal spaces and can enhance the perception of an environment. Proper lighting can increase a sense of well-being, and people entering and being active in a wellness center deserve the most positive environment possible. This environment should take a person one step beyond the ordinary in terms of color, interest, luxury, and activity.

If the wellness center makes every effort to offer an upbeat atmosphere without being cloyingly artful or cute, it will be a success. Because every color in the spectrum is created by the number of light waves it absorbs and reflects, we must take care to select colors for every aspect of the center that work well with the lighting sources selected.

Natural daylight is the most desirable light, because it includes the full spectrum of available light on the planet. The next desirable types of light are artificial full-spectrum light, which mimics natural light and is often used in light therapy treatments, and low-voltage halogen light. Low-voltage halogen light is often used in retail facilities to call attention to jewelry, artwork, clothing, or fine collectibles. Halogen and other incandescent lights produce a warm light that respects skin color and color rendition in furnishings, fixtures, and materials. If possible, fluorescent light should be avoided. The economy achieved with fluorescent lighting is usually not worthwhile, inasmuch as it can wash out the carefully selected colors of a specially designed environment.

Lighting level requirements, measured in footcandles (FC), range from 100 FC for an office environment, to 30 to 50 FC for general sports, basketball, volleyball, tennis, squash, and racquetball, to 25 to 45 FC for waiting areas, to 5 to 10 FC for common areas such as corridors.

Spa areas should have lighting that is controlled by a dimmer switch. Areas for massage and certain other body therapies, facial rooms, and rooms for other beauty treatments, herbal wraps, and so forth, demand a quiet environment. Aerobics and group fitness rooms, too, require that the lighting be adjustable. Quite often, at the end of aerobics activities the instructor concludes the session with a quiet period of relaxation exercises; for this the lighting level needs to be adjusted downward. One solution seen in a wellness center was the selection of banks of suspended porcelain enamel reflectors with incandescent lights on a dimmer switch. This provided an even, warm light to an aerobics/dance room which could be adjusted to meet the needs of aerobics, dance, and yoga classes.

Lighting levels in the waiting areas in clinical offices should be low and warm. Mammography waiting and dressing rooms are often designed with high-quality fixtures and low lighting. We would like to see this carried through to other examination waiting areas. The proper lighting level can calm or excite a person, and these are surely areas where peaceful, low lighting will enhance the experience of the user.

Weight training areas should have good general lighting, in the 30 to 50 FC range. The rubberlike floors of weight rooms are often made of recycled tires and are, therefore, black. This area acts as a color drain in the weight room space. Care must be taken to counteract the intense darkness of the floor and the predictable gleaming chrome of exercise machines in order to balance out the colors in the space and make it appealing.

Mirrors, often included in weight rooms so that members can gauge their form as they work with machines and free weights, add other reflective surfaces to contend with. The spacing of weight machines is determined by the activity on the machines, and the predicted time of use each machine.

Recommended lighting sources for indoor running tracks are metal halide, mercury vapor, and fluorescent lights with illumination levels of at least 50 FC at the surface of the track. This lighting level will enable the runner or walker to comfortably see the lane markings on the track. The colors used for the textured surface of the track itself tend to be those in the gray to earth-tone range, often light clay brick color or grayed greens with lane markings in white.

Racquetball, tennis, and other court sports require even lighting, again at the 50 FC level. This measurement is taken at 36 inches above the court surface. The Illuminating Engineering Society charts the level of lighting for indoor tennis for different levels of play from 125 FC for professional tournament play to 75 FC for college tournaments, 50 FC for high school and 40 FC for recreational or social play. Racquetball and tennis have playing surfaces that also tend to be in the earth-tone family. It is recommended that wall surfaces in sports court areas be painted in light colors to improve reflectivity and that lighting, from whatever source selected, be even so as to avoid hot spots and glare.

High-intensity lights should be mounted no closer than 6 feet from the ceiling surface to prevent glare. If fluorescent lights are used, they should be mounted along the length of the court no closer than 16 to 22 feet over or outside the alleys.

Basketball and volleyball courts should have hard surface walls, typically concrete masonry units with a painted wainscot to 8 feet above the floor surface. The painted wainscot should be a darker color than the area of wall above the wainscot. Lighting levels for basketball and volleyball are about 50 FC.

Pool areas require emergency lighting systems. Regular lighting systems are typically metal halide, mercury vapor, or fluorescent at about 60 FC. Shatterproof light fixtures are necessary. It is important for the architect and/or electrical engineer to take maintenance into consideration. A beautiful lighting plan in a pool area must be thought out in terms of how a facility will replace the bulbs at a future date without having to rent expensive equipment to do so.

Underwater lighting is generally 1 watt per square foot of underwater area. All of the preceding recommendations should be consistently followed throughout pool areas, including the therapy pool area, which is often in a separate room.

Fencing and martial arts can be practiced in an aerobics/group fitness room or in a basketball/volleyball court if class size so requires. The lighting levels that exist in either space are sufficient for the practice of these sports/arts, and in the case of martial arts, the addition of padded mats is all that is required to alter the use of the space. Fencing requires a strip that can easily be marked with temporary markers on the floor of a basketball court or aerobics room. Other group fitness activities, such as spinning, require a room to be outfitted with stationary bicycles. Spinning classes often have a visualization component that requires a lower lighting level. It would be helpful to have dimmer switches in these rooms.

Corridors can have relatively low lighting levels, between 5 and 10 FC. We recommend that artwork used in corridors with low lighting levels be highlighted with wall washer lamps.

Some recommendations suggest that locker rooms have lighting levels at 50 FC, but we suggest that the level can be lower. Other than the adjacent toilet rooms and shower areas requiring a 50 FC level for reasons of safety, so as not to produce shadows that may allow people to slip and fall, locker room areas are generally carpeted, and, because of the importance of privacy, a level of 40 to 45 FC is adequate.

Well-designed wellness centers generally include lower lighting levels in locker rooms. Grooming areas, in both men's and women's locker rooms, should have task lighting over or over and around the mirror areas. Baby changing areas require higher lighting levels, and these areas should be included in both men's and women's locker rooms as well as in family/care giver locker rooms. If there is an option to design into the program a separate single-room care giver locker/changing/toilet/shower area, this room will require 50 FC, as such areas are typically used by elderly patients and members.

The use of color in the locker room area can set a mood of quiet and luxury or bright and lively activity. We recommend a lower lighting level and subdued color selections for these areas, to add quiet and privacy to the dressing experience. Locker rooms are often transition spaces into which exercisers come from the outside world to embrace the fun, activity, camaraderie or solitary efforts available at the wellness center. The symbolic changing of clothes is meaningful to some people, as is the reentry process: dressing back into street clothes to face the world. These transitional times in locker rooms occur mostly before and after the workday, when locker rooms tend to be most crowded. Lower lighting levels and good design can prevent people from bumping into one another at peak times.

Troffered lighting, which is a recessed lighting unit typically installed flush with the ceiling, must be handled with care. Troffered lighting can produce visually uncomfortable brightness in the contrast between the ceiling plane and the fixture. Troffered lighting is generally not recommended for hallways, but is suggested for open office areas.

The positioning of the troffered fixture and the design of the fixture itself affects the quality of light in the room. Certain troffered lights have a "wall washer" option, which can effectively direct light around the room. Troffers using T8 lamps can be specified.

The "Litewave" by Lite Control is a recessed indirect luminaire with a shallow housing, curved upper reflector system with low glare, high reflectance matte white finish, and perforated metal lamp shield backed with an opal acrylic diffuser. Hanging from the troffer is an inverted acrylic shield that covers the lamps themselves and produces a diffuse light on the ceiling and walls. This type of light is recommended for healthcare environments as well as small offices. The fixture uses high-lumen compact fluorescent and T5 lamps.

Combinations of direct and indirect lighting can be used to create a wonderful environment. Indirect lighting requires that more attention be paid to ceiling brightness. The reflectivity characteristics of the finishes of a space, as well as its size and configuration, will greatly affect the perception of brightness, no matter what the actual footcandle measurement is.

In general, wellness centers require a wide variety of lighting. Indirect ceiling fixtures may be suspended as much as 24 inches below the ceiling plane and spaced accordingly. Peerless Lighting manufactures two small-size indirect light fixtures that maximize the effect of high-output T5 fluorescent lamps, like those offered by Ostram Sylvania. T5 lamps are 40 percent smaller than T8 lamps. The wider spacing allowed by this smaller, brighter lamp and fixture means lower initial cost and produces good uniformity of light, which is helpful in eliminating glare from video display monitors.

A 12-inch-square recessed downlight, such as Neoray's "Fancy Free" downlight, can eliminate the harsh visual contrast between fixture aperture and ceiling. This downlight uses two compact fluorescent lamps with a transparent/translucent louver cell assembly, which softens its appearance and diffuses the light produced. White or aluminum louver cells are used with a colored panel or perforated metal diffusers. The fixture can be selected in a variety of combinations and can therefore be adapted to produce a number of lighting conditions.

Adjustable cove lighting is available that can be set at a variety of angles to produce a number of different lighting effects. Low-voltage lighting, particularly appealing in retail applications, can be found in a number of different fixture configurations, the most common being track lighting. Low-voltage lighting in combination with a few suspended fixtures can produce a nicely balanced light.

Downlights are now available in incandescent, low-voltage, and high intensity (HID) fixtures with high-performance characteristics. Some, such as "Portfolio" by Halo lighting, have equal cutoff to the lamp and lamp image, which provides glare-free illumination in all optical distributions.

Specialty lighting for fitness areas includes tennis, basketball/volleyball, and indoor pool lighting. Whenever possible, daylight should be used in the design of these areas of the wellness center, carefully modified with artificial lighting so as not to produce glare. Glare is not only unpleasant and dangerous in fitness areas, but is psychologically and physically wearing to the individual.

Tennis lighting should be in the area of 80 to 83 footcandles for wellness centers, even though suggested standards would have them lower. Experienced wellness center executives and operators concur that the higher the number of footcandles, the less likely the chance that shadows falling on the court will inhibit play and cause unnecessary stress to members.

Circular luminaires can be used in a ceiling space to mimic skylights. Where daylight is unavailable, this alternative can be a positive one in corridors, lobby, and other spaces in the wellness center.

Acoustics

In addition to the inclusion of suspended acoustical tile in the ceiling of certain areas of the wellness center, it will most likely be necessary to take measures to ameliorate the noise produced by high-activity centers—pools, basketball/volleyball courts, and aerobic areas. Electronic sound-masking systems are one means; another is the inclusion of acoustic panels that reduce background noise and reverberation. Although large activity spaces in a wellness center can be modified by clever use of sound-dampening baffles and panels, other sound-dampening methods can be employed in other areas of the building.

Basketball court, Sinai Wellbridge, Pikesville, Maryland.

Sound attenuation can be achieved by running the interior wall partition all the way to the underside of the floor or roof deck. Sound attenuation can also be achieved by using sound-absorbing material within the cavity of the partition wall. This material is frequently composed of fabric-wrapped glass fiber or mineral wool. Noise reduction varies with the thickness of the material and the consistency of the fabric facing.

Spray-on acoustical material is also available. This is made up of cellulose fibers applied to a substrate including gypsum wallboard.

Hard surfaces reflect sound, soft surfaces absorb it. Carpeting, furniture, well-designed HVAC (heat, ventilation, and air conditioning) systems, and the proper juxtaposition of spaces (i.e., not locating the laundry room next to a clinical space) will all contribute to a well-designed acoustical environment in the wellness center.

Sound dampening can be achieved by the use of sound-absorbing materials, carpeting, and the like, and can also be achieved by planning spaces so that sound waves are deflected off wall surfaces through altering their configuration, possibly by introducing curves and angles.

Active noise technology (a system utilized for dampening sound) uses computers to generate sound waves in a certain sequence that meets or counters the sound waves being generated from a particular source. As this technique is becoming more widely available, it will be an option in the design of the wellness center. A quick cost-benefit analysis by the architect can compare the relative costs of the active noise system against the inclusion of baffles in the ceilings of indoor pool areas, basketball and volleyball courts, and aerobics rooms. It may well be more economical to select the electronic system.

Traditionally, sound baffles used for pool areas have been successful in improving the acoustical environment. Excessive reverberation is common in these large areas with hard surfaces. At times it makes communication difficult, especially for older people. Lack of speech intelligibility and poor acoustics make for an uncomfortable atmosphere and pose potential safety problems. Acoustic panels have the potential to alter the reverberation time from 9.6 seconds at 500 Hz in a 160,000 cubic foot space to 1.84 seconds at 500 Hz. A general rule of thumb is that reverberation time should be less than 2 seconds for 1,000 cubic feet of space for a person to hear speech comfortably.

These panels, typically 30 inches × 10 feet are made of 2-inch fiberglass attached to aluminum framing members. In pool area applications the panels are generally sealed with a flame-guard polyethylene.

Similarly, the basketball/volleyball court area can benefit from the application of sound baffles of this kind. Aerobics rooms may benefit from wall-mounted baffles worked into the design of the room or ceiling baffles applied contiguously along the plane of the ceiling.

A full-size basketball court is 50 × 84 feet, with a recommended 6 to 10 feet of unobstructed area around the perimeter of the court and a minimum of 23 feet of unobstructed height to the lowest point in the ceiling. These dimensions should be considered in designing baffles, lighting, and exposed ceiling ducts in a basketball court area. An ideal height to the underside of any obstruction would be 30 feet. The Sound Transmission Class (STC) rating for a gymnasium is 45 to 55.

Racquetball and squash courts require the same STC rating, and in these areas it is also achieved with the introduction of materials like baffles or sound attenuation in the common walls. An added challenge is that at least one racquetball court wall is typically made of glass. Racquetball courts are typically 20 × 40 × 20 feet high and have cushioned hardwood floors.

Indoor tennis courts are typically grouped together. A general rule of thumb is that for every 50 to 100 users, there should be one indoor court. If more than one court is designed, the courts should be designed side by side. Each tennis court requires approximately 7,200 square feet of area. If an indoor court has a bubble ceiling (air-supported fabric roof) acoustics will be less a consideration than if it is totally enclosed within a building envelope. In such a case, it will be subject to the same acoustical challenges as racquetball and basketball/volleyball courts.

Aerobics or group fitness areas also have a sound transmission requirement of 45 to 55. Aerobics areas can be designed to have either a cushioned wood aerobics floor made of composite wood with spacers beneath to provide a cushioning effect, or aerobics flooring composed of carpeting with a specially designed cushioning/padding system. Both systems provide some acoustic benefit.

The hard surface of walls and the relatively low ceiling height (10 feet, minimum), however, allow very little opportunity for sound baffling. Instructors generally use microphones for groups of 30 exercisers or more, depending on the room size and configuration.

Suspended acoustical tiles (SAT) can be used in aerobics/group fitness areas and are recommended throughout the facility for their sound-dampening effect. It is often difficult to find SAT with interesting designs, and integrating tiles with lighting systems and diffusers is always a challenge; however, they offer an easy and practical solution. We recommend them for areas other than those that are open to the structure for design reasons. SAT is certainly the product of choice for clinical areas, and with the easy access they provide to plenum spaces, they are critically important in clinical areas where power, lighting, and telecommunications requirements may change or be updated.

Well-selected doors, especially for examination rooms, diagnostic rooms, and treatment rooms, will help control sound, and well-selected windows can ensure that outside noise does not inhibit the free flow of conversation between patient and doctor or nurse.

Physical therapy, occupational therapy, and cardiopulmonary therapy generally take place in large rooms, with several people receiving treatment at the same time, often with weight machines, bicycles, and treadmills running simultaneously. These rooms call for an STC in the 45 to 50 range. This level can be achieved by all the means mentioned, with the particular inclusion of padded carpeting. These acoustical requirements also apply to areas where integrative clinical therapies take place.

The acoustical guidelines for spa areas are the same as those that apply to rooms where private conversations will take place. STC ratings of 50 to 55 are required in most massage treatment rooms, manicure and pedicure and hairdressing salons, and rooms that serve other beauty service purposes (herbal wraps, paraffin treatments, waxing).

A general effort to group certain sports/ fitness functions—aerobics, basketball/volleyball, and racquet—together, distancing this active zone from the quieter zones, would be a logical step.

Laundry areas are noisy and should be located away from the central registration and reception area. A 6- to 8-inch concrete pad on top of the floor surface for the washer extractor should be a requirement.

Weight room areas require special flooring to absorb the sound of free weights as they are lowered and the sound of machines in use. Sound transmission requirements for a weight room area ranges from 40 to 50 STC. Sound dampening in this area can be achieved by using heavy rubber floor tiles, which also act to level out the sounds transmitted from nearby activities or from instructors/personal trainers who are working one-on-one with clients/patients.

Acoustical challenges in the clinical areas range from masking the sounds of conversation in the waiting areas and ensuring patient privacy in examination rooms, to masking the hum of certain machines. Any space requiring privacy for conversations should have an STC rating of 50 to 55 as a minimum.

Mechanical equipment rooms, as in any building type, require that the STC be 55 to 60. Certain steps can be taken to design quieter HVAC systems also, and this is highly recommended.

General office areas and lobby/waiting/reception areas should have STC levels of 40 to 45. Classrooms, libraries, and laboratories should have a minimum STC of 50. For any area of a wellness center, the quieter the better.

Sound systems are recommended throughout the wellness center and have specific use in aerobics areas, where tape and digital music systems are needed to support class instruction. Many wellness centers have cardio theater systems in the treadmill area, where an exerciser can plug headphones into a connection for either music or television. Some wellness centers sell headphones at their retail facility. Newer technology will improve this entertainment aspect of wellness center design.

Outdoors, the sound-absorptive qualities of trees, dense plantings, and masonry garden walls will help to control and deflect sound. Clever landscape design can make the best of a site that is less than ideal, masking both the views and the sounds of parking lots or nearby streets. Any potential threat to a peaceful environment should be challenged early in the design process, with the initial consideration of site selection and, following the selection, a view to creating an entrance, as well as areas that may grow toward the outdoors, that makes sense.

Music can be introduced in the outdoor setting, as background to conversation or rest. This, of course, must not be intrusive in level or in selection, but can enhance the overall experience of the environment if well chosen.

The following table provides general guidelines for acoustical, lighting, and mechanical design in wellness centers, based on the space requirements listed in the previous table.

Wellness Center Environmental Requirements by Room
— PART I: Clinical Space —

Room	Light Level (footcandles)	Temperature (degrees F)	Acoustic Guidelines		Humidity (%)	Air Exchanges per Hour (per AIA guidelines*)
			STC Rating	Measured Reverberation Time (s)		
Treatment	50 to 100	68 to 72	60	0.8 to 1.4	60 or less	6
Pre-surgery testing	50 to 100	68 to 72	60	0.8 to 1.4	60 or less	6
Operating room	50 to 100	68 to 72	60	0.8 to 1.4	60 or less	15
Recovery	50	68 to 72	60	0.8 to 1.4	60 or less	15

Continued on next page

*AIA guidelines for traditional medical spaces only

— PART I: Clinical Space cont. —

Room	Light Level (footcandles)	Temperature (degrees F)	Acoustic Guidelines		Humidity (%)	Air Exchanges per Hour (per AIA guidelines)
			STC Rating	Measured Reverberation Time (s)		
Nurses' station	40 to 60	68 to 72	60	0.8 to 1.4	60 or less	2
Patient waiting	40 to 60	68 to 72	60	0.8 to 1.4	60 or less	2
Examination	50 to 100	68 to 72	60	0.8 to 1.4	60 or less	—
EKG, pulmonary and diagnostic imaging	40 to 60	68 to 72	60	0.8 to 1.4	60 or less	15
Laboratory	50 to 100	68 to 72	60	0.8 to 1.4	60 or less	6
Clerical	40 to 60	68 to 72	50 to 55	0.8 to 1.4	60 or less	2
Exercise area	50	68 to 72	45 to 55	0.8 to 1.4	60 or less	2
Rehabilitaion medicine office	40 to 60	68 to 72	50 to 50	0.8 to 1.4	60 or less	2
Wheelchair alcove	40	68 to 72	40 to 45	0.8 to 1.4	60 or less	—
Clean linen	40	68 to 72	40 to 45	0.8 to 1.4	60 or less	—
Soiled linen	40	68 to 72	40 to 45	0.8 to 1.4	60 or less	—
Therapists' workroom	50	68 to 72	60	0.8 to 1.4	60 or less	2
Patient demonstration	50	68 to 72	60	0.8 to 1.4	60 or less	2
Occupational therapy	50	68 to 72	60	0.8 to 1.4	60 or less	2
Activities of daily living, toilet/bath	50	68 to 72	50 to 55	0.8 to 1.4	60 or less	2
Activities of daily living, kitchen	50	68 to 72	50 to 55	0.8 to 1.4	60 or less	2
Prosthetics/cast	50	68 to 72	60	0.8 to 1.4	60 or less	2
Audiology office and examining	50 to 100	68 to 72	70	0.8 to 1.4	60 or less	—
Conference room	40 to 60	68 to 72	50 to 55	0.8 to 1.4	60 or less	—
Telemedicine	50 to 100	68 to 72	50 to 55	0.8 to 1.4	60 or less	6
Apothecary	50 to 100	68 to 72	50 to 55	0.8 to 1.4	60 or less	6

Cardiopulmonary Therapy

Room	Light Level (footcandles)	Temperature (degrees F)	STC Rating	Measured Reverberation Time (s)	Humidity (%)	Air Exchanges per Hour
Soiled workroom	40	68 to 72	40 to 45	0.8 to 1.4	60 or less	—
Clean workroom/ equipment storage	40	68 to 72	40 to 45	0.8 to 1.4	60 or less	2
Respiratory therapy/ patient waiting	40 to 60	68 to 72	50 to 55	0.8 to 1.4	60 or less	6
Respiratory waiting/ reception	40 to 60	68 to 72	50 to 55	0.8 to 1.4	60 or less	2
Respiratory therapy/ stress testing	50 to 100	68 to 72	60	0.8 to 1.4	60 or less	6
Pulmonary function	50 to 100	68 to 72	60	0.8 to 1.4	60 or less	6

			Acoustic Guidelines			Air
Room	Light Level (footcandles)	Temperature (degrees F)	STC Rating	Measured Reverberation Time (s)	Humidity (%)	Exchanges per Hour (per AIA guidelines)

— PART I: Clinical Space cont. —

Mammography

Room	Light Level	Temperature	STC Rating	Measured Reverberation Time	Humidity	Air Exchanges
Mammography	50 to 100	68 to 72	60	0.8 to 1.4	60 or less	15
Toilet	50	68 to 72	45 to 50	0.8 to 1.4	60 or less	—
Dressing	50	68 to 72	45 to 50	0.8 to 1.4	60 or less	—
Waiting	50	68 to 72	50 to 55	0.8 to 1.4	60 or less	—

Endoscopy with Imaging

Room	Light Level	Temperature	STC Rating	Measured Reverberation Time	Humidity	Air Exchanges
Endoscopy/surgery	50 to 100	68 to 72	60	0.8 to 1.4	60 or less	15
Endoscopic imaging	50 to 100	68 to 72	60	0.8 to 1.4	60 or less	15

Integrative Medicine

Room	Light Level	Temperature	STC Rating	Measured Reverberation Time	Humidity	Air Exchanges
Hydrotherapy	40 to 60	102 to 105	45 to 55	0.8 to 1.4	60 or less	3
Whirlpool	50	102 to 105	45 to 55	0.8 to 1.4	60 or less	3
Chelation therapy	40 to 60	68 to 72	45 to 55	0.8 to 1.4	60 or less	3
Artificial sun therapy	40 to 60	68 to 72	60	0.8 to 1.4	60 or less	2
Oxygen therapy	40 to 60	68 to 72	60	0.8 to 1.4	60 or less	2
Hydrogen peroxide therapy	40 to 60	68 to 72	60	0.8 to 1.4	60 or less	2
Hyperthermia	40 to 60	68 to 72	60	0.8 to 1.4	60 or less	3
Nutritional counseling	40 to 60	68 to 72	50 to 55	0.8 to 1.4	60 or less	—
Meditation room/chapel	50	68 to 72	50 to 55	0.8 to 1.4	60 or less	—
Acupuncture	40 to 60	68 to 72	60	0.8 to 1.4	60 or less	6
Massage	50	72-78	45 to 55	0.8 to 1.4	60 or less	3
Naturopathic exam room	50 to 100	68 to 72	60	0.8 to 1.4	60 or less	—
Osteopathic physician exam room	50 to 100	68 to 72	60	0.8 to 1.4	60 or less	—
Environmental medicine physician's room	50 to 100	68 to 72	60	0.8 to 1.4	60 or less	3
Chiropractic exam room	50 to 100	68 to 72	60	0.8 to 1.4	60 or less	—

General Clinical Functions

Room	Light Level	Temperature	STC Rating	Measured Reverberation Time	Humidity	Air Exchanges
Conference room	50	68 to 72	50 to 55	0.8 to 1.4	60 or less	—
Staff lounge	50	68 to 72	50 to 55	0.8 to 1.4	60 or less	—
Staff locker room	50	68 to 72	45 to 50	0.8 to 1.4	60 or less	—
Staff toilet	50	68 to 72	45 to 50	0.8 to 1.4	60 or less	3
Office	40 to 60	68 to 72	50 to 50	0.8 to 1.4	60 or less	—

Continued on next page

			Acoustic Guidelines			Air Exchanges per Hour (per AIA guidelines)
Room	Light Level (footcandles)	Temperature (degrees F)	STC Rating	Measured Reverberation Time (s)	Humidity (%)	
Aerobic Exercise						
Exercise	50	68 to 72	45 to 55	0.8 to 1.4	60 or less	3
Storage	50	68 to 72	40 to 45	0.8 to 1.4	60 or less	—
Fencing	50	68 to 72	45 to 55	0.8 to 1.4	60 or less	3
Fitness						
Track	50	68 to 72	45 to 55	0.8 to 1.4	60 or less	2
Equipment exercise	50	68 to 72	45 to 55	0.8 to 1.4	60 or less	2
Fitness testing	50	68 to 72	45 to 55	0.8 to 1.4	60 or less	2
Weight training	50	68 to 72	45 to 55	0.8 to 1.4	60 or less	2
Resistance training	50	68 to 72	45 to 55	0.8 to 1.4	60 or less	2
Mens'Lockers/Shower						
Locker room	50	72 to 78	45 to 50	0.8 to 1.4	60 or less	3
Lavatories/grooming	50	72 to 78	45 to 50	0.8 to 1.4	60 or less	3
Shower	50	72 to 78	45 to 50	0.8 to 1.4	60 or less	3
Toilets	50	72 to 78	45 to 50	0.8 to 1.4	60 or less	3
Storage	50	72 to 78	40 to 45	0.8 to 1.4	60 or less	—
Womens'Lockers/Shower						
Locker room	50	72 to 78	45 to 50	0.8 to 1.4	60 or less	3
Lavatories/grooming	50	72 to 78	45 to 50	0.8 to 1.4	60 or less	3
Shower	50	72 to 78	45 to 50	0.8 to 1.4	60 or less	3
Toilets	50	72 to 78	45 to 50	0.8 to 1.4	60 or less	3
Storage	50	72 to 78	40 to 45	0.8 to 1.4	60 or less	—
Fitness Administration						
Coffee bar	40 to 60		50 to 55	0.8 to 1.4	60 or less	2
Offices	40 to 60		50 to 55	0.8 to 1.4	60 or less	—
Pools						
Pool	60	80 (min.)	45 to 55	0.8 to 1.4	60 or less	4 to 6
Pool deck	60	80 (min.)	45 to 55	0.8 to 1.4	60 or less	4 to 6
Basketball Court	30 to 50	68 to 72	45 to 55	0.8 to 1.4	60 or less	2
Racquetball/Handball	30 to 50	68 to 72	45 to 55	0.8 to 1.4	60 or less	2
Tennis Courts	30 to 50	68 to 72	45 to 55	0.8 to 1.4	60 or less	2
Climbing Wall Area	30 to 50	68 to 72	45 to 55	0.8 to 1.4	60 or less	2

— PART II: Fitness —

— PART III: Spa —

Room	Light Level (footcandles)	Temperature (degrees F)	Acoustic Guidelines		Humidity (%)	Air Exchanges per Hour (per AIA guidelines)
			STC Rating	Measured Reverberation Time (s)		
Massage	50	72 to 78	45 to 55	0.8 to 1.4	60	6
Sauna	50	170 to 180	45 to 55	0.8 to 1.4	5	—
Steam room	50	100 to 110	45 to 55	0.8 to 1.4	100	—
Whirlpool	50	102 to 105	45 to 55	0.8 to 1.4	60	3

Salon

Room	Light Level (footcandles)	Temperature (degrees F)	STC Rating	Measured Reverberation Time (s)	Humidity (%)	Air Exchanges per Hour
Facial room	30 to 50	68 to 72	45 to 55	0.8 to 1.4	60	3
Manicure/pedicure	30 to 50	68 to 72	45 to 55	0.8 to 1.4	60	3
Hair salon	30 to 50	68 to 72	45 to 55	0.8 to 1.4	60	3
Vichy shower	30 to 50	80	45 to 55	0.8 to 1.4	60	—

— PART IV: Common Areas —

Room	Light Level (footcandles)	Temperature (degrees F)	Acoustic Guidelines		Humidity (%)	Air Exchanges per Hour (per ACSM)
			STC Rating	Measured Reverberation Time (s)		
Offices	40 to 60	72 to 78	50 to 55	0.8 to 1.4	60 or less	—
Secretary	40 to 60	72 to 78	50 to 55	0.8 to 1.4	60 or less	2
Waiting	40 to 60	72 to 78	50 to 55	0.8 to 1.4	60 or less	
Classroom	40 to 60	66 to 70	50 to 55	0.8 to 1.4	60 or less	
Workroom	40 to 60	66 to 70	50 to 55	0.8 to 1.4	60 or less	
Coatroom	40 to 60	72 to 78	40 to 45	0.8 to 1.4	60 or less	
Storage	50	72 to 78	40 to 45	0.8 to 1.4	60 or less	
Toilets	40 to 60	72 to 78	45 to 50	0.8 to 1.4	60 or less	3
Entry/reception	40 to 60	72 to 78	50 to 55	0.8 to 1.4	60 or less	
Child care	50	72 to 78	50 to 55	0.8 to 1.4	60 or less	4 to 6
Retail	40 to 60	72 to 78	60 (min.)	0.8 to 1.4	60 or less	3
Lounge	40 to 60	72 to 78	50 to 55	0.8 to 1.4	60 or less	3

Mens' Lockers/Showers

Room	Light Level (footcandles)	Temperature (degrees F)	STC Rating	Measured Reverberation Time (s)	Humidity (%)	Air Exchanges per Hour
Locker room	50	72 to 78	45 to 50	0.8 to 1.4	60 or less	3
Lavatories/grooming	50	72 to 78	45 to 50	0.8 to 1.4	60 or less	3
Shower	50	72 to 78	45 to 50	0.8 to 1.4	60 or less	3
Toilets	50	72 to 78	45 to 50	0.8 to 1.4	60 or less	3
Storage	50	72 to 78	40 to 45	0.8 to 1.4	60 or less	—

Continued on next page

— PART IV: Common Areas cont. —						
Room	Light Level (footcandles)	Temperature (degrees F)	Acoustic Guidelines		Humidity (%)	Air Exchanges per Hour (per AIA guidelines)
			STC Rating	Measured Reverberation Time (s)		
Womens' Lockers/Showers						
Locker room	50	72 to 78	45 to 50	0.8 to 1.4	60 or less	3
Lavatories/grooming	50	72 to 78	45 to 50	0.8 to 1.4	60 or less	3
Shower	50	72 to 78	45 to 50	0.8 to 1.4	60 or less	3
Toilets	50	72 to 78	45 to 50	0.8 to 1.4	60 or less	3
Storage	50	72 to 78	40 to 45	0.8 to 1.4	60 or less	—
Family Lockers/Showers						
Locker room	50	72 to 78	45 to 50	0.8 to 1.4	60 or less	3
Offices	40 to 60	72 to 78	50 to 55	0.8 to 1.4	60 or less	—
Lavatories/grooming	50	72 to 78	45 to 50	0.8 to 1.4	60 or less	3
Shower	50	72 to 78	45 to 50	0.8 to 1.4	60 or less	
Storage	50	72 to 78	40 to 45	0.8 to 1.4	60 or less	—
Laundry	50	72 to 78	50 to 60	0.8 to 1.4	60 or less	3
Toilets	50	72 to 78	45 to 50	0.8 to 1.4	60 or less	3

Interior Finishes and Materials

The best available materials to be specified for a wellness center may well be those designed for general healthcare facilities. Certainly clinical and clinical/integrative areas will benefit from the inclusion of chemical-resistant laminates where appropriate, bacteria-resistant carpeting, durable vinyl flooring, and ceramic tile with mold-resistant grout. Inert materials should be selected when possible, for the simple reason that they tend to be less likely to trigger allergic reactions in sensitive individuals.

Special devices are now available for inclusion in healthcare designs, such as the Windowsill Electronic Window from Art Research Institute. This 3 by 4 foot transparency of a scene from nature is illuminated by a central processing unit (CPU)-controlled light box that replicates the entire cycle of night and day. This device may be useful in a light treatment room or in a waiting area that has no natural light available.

Thirty percent of all Americans suffer from some sort of allergy or sensitivity to building materials or commercial or

Lobby of Arlington Heights Wellness Center. *OWP&P Architects.*

household cleaning agents. As mentioned earlier, "sick building syndrome" is any illness brought on by exposure to buildings with little or no infiltration of air, containing noxious materials, furniture and maintained with dangerous cleaning agents. People suffering from this malady exhibit a variety of symptoms: headache, fatigue, rash, asthma, depression, and aching joints, among others. It is critical that people avoid environmental substances that include arsenic, formaldehyde, pesticides, fungicides, and volatile petroleum distillates as well as particulates: mold, mildew, pollen, dust, bacteria, airborne viruses.

Interior finishes should be of the same quality as those selected generally for healthcare facilities. Special flooring for fitness areas, including suspended flooring for aerobics, basketball flooring, running track materials, and weight room flooring should be considered for durability and wear, as in the design of the best fitness facility. Wellness center design demands that all materials be considered in terms of their health-maintaining characteristics. The potential for toxic out-gassing from synthetic resigns, enamel paints, composite furniture materials, allergy-inducing wallpaper pastes, and other unpleasant characteristics of some popular materials should be severely limited.

Wall Coverings

Wall coverings are an alternative to paint in wellness center buildings. Antimicrobial backing should always be specified. Vinyl wall coverings selected should be nonglare types.

Many companies specialize in the manufacture of wall coverings, as well as other materials, furniture, and equipment, specifically for use in healthcare applications. Because a wellness center is truly a hybrid facility with multiple simultaneous uses, the design criteria for each distinct function, clinical, fitness, spa and retail, should be respected. High-performance wall coverings, generally of vinyl, are typically specified for healthcare use. Design Tex, Maharan, and other manufacturers produce high-performance wall coverings. JM Lynne is a leading supplier of wall coverings for healthcare facilities. Design Tex also has a line of fabrics for healthcare use, featuring a special finish that offers a combination of stain and abrasion resistance, is flame retardant and antimicrobial. These fabrics maintain their ability to stretch, unlike other vinyl-impregnated fabrics.

Examination room walls can be designed with millwork and accent panel designs that have the look of wood grain. Although these surfaces are not authentic wood, the warm look of wood is achieved.

Carpeting

When properly selected, installed, and maintained, carpeting can perform well in a wellness center. Carpeting should be selected with care. It should meet the standards set for healthcare settings. This consideration is important for several reasons, chiefly the materials' durability and their ability to reject the growth of mold and bacteria, which is especially beneficial in clinical areas.

Carpet has an advantage in healthcare settings because it attracts airborne particles that can be removed by a vacuum with a HEPA filter. Vacuum cleaning in healthcare environments should make use of high-efficiency particulate air filter HEPA bags. Bacteria that are picked up in these bags are not blown back into the atmosphere.

Health-care-grade carpeting is typically made up of nylon fibers, polypropylene, and wool. Polypropylene does not perform well in high-traffic areas. Nylon is less expensive than wool and has the properties needed: strength, color, and so on. Good backing materials for carpeting are critical to its integrity. Solution-dyed carpeting, which is colored through the extrusion process, is more resistant to bleach than yarn-dyed carpeting. Chlorinated bleaching products will impair the integrity of carpeting and are not recommended for use in areas that are close to wet areas of the fitness or spa functions that use a chlorine-based water purification system.

Exercise machine area, Springfield Healthplex, Springfield, Pennsylvania.

Carpeting may be an option in areas that are appropriate, particularly lobbies, waiting areas, libraries, some locker room areas, offices, some examination and treatment rooms, certain core areas, and retail and food service/restaurant areas. Carpeting for healthcare uses, as well as synthetic or vinyl backing and adhesives, can be specified to be antimicrobial. Certain chemicals involved in the installation of different types of flooring have been found to cause contact dermatitis in workers performing the installation. Manufacturers should be contacted early to make sure that their materials are safe for installers.

The best carpets available today incorporate the backing as part of a permanent bond to the yarn itself. This arrangement creates a moisture barrier that makes the carpet impenetrable to stains. Stains cannot become embedded in the backing, as so often happens in areas of heavy use.

Carpets are, by their nature, glare resistant, and today they are static resistant as well. The reduction in noise level and in potential slipping should be considered when making this important material selection. In a recent magazine article Mary Wells Gorman, a registered nurse and certified interior designer with Ellerbe Becket Healthcare in Minneapolis, Minnesota, said that families now expect to see carpeting in a patient care setting. "Carpet can be helpful. It's a softer finish in a hard industry where patients are having hard experiences." Gorman suggests carpet tiles as a good solution because they allow for easy access to a subfloor that may have been installed in a particular area.

Resilient Flooring

Resilient flooring is made of sheet vinyl, vinyl tile, rubber tile, or sheet rubber. Homogeneous sheet vinyl is second only to rubber flooring and solid vinyl tile in its ability to withstand traffic in high-use areas. Inlaid vinyl tile and vinyl composition tile can be used for healthcare as well as fitness area uses and can be customized to reinforce a design theme throughout the wellness facility.

Armstrong, Tarket, and Amtico make vinyl flooring products keyed to healthcare use. Amtico, for example, promotes its vinyl flooring products as being highly resistant to a wide range of chemical agents, mildew and odor resistant, and easy to install and maintain. Laboratory areas in particular require special vinyl flooring to resist the spills of chemicals. Marmoleum™ is a linseed oil–based floor material successfully used in hospitals and other healthcare settings. Chemically related to linoleum, it has some very positive characteristics that make it a reasonable choice in appropriate areas in a wellness center.

Many vinyl floors are glare resistant, which helps the comfort level and mobility of patients, particularly older patients. Vinyl can be chemically bonded or heat welded to seal out bacteria and moisture that cause the growth of mold and mildew, which is especially important in the healthcare environment.

Aerobics Flooring

Aerobics flooring can be either vinyl, wood flooring with spacers, or carpeting over a thick layer of other aerobics flooring. Polyethylene aerobics padding is made of closed cell foam and engineered for aerobics use. Aerobics padding underlayers are typically a half-inch thick.

Wood aerobics flooring generally consists of prefinished oak or maple parquet panels installed over pneumatic pads and spacers, which creates a floating floor with an approximate one-eighth inch of air space that absorbs shock and offers resiliency. There are modular systems available that offer easy installation, although lifetime use has not been satisfactorily demonstrated.

Hard surfaces, such as existing hardwood floors, can be turned into temporary aerobics floors with the use of aerobics mats composed of EVA foam. These mats are designed to fit together (panels are $40 \times 40 \times \frac{7}{8}$ inches) and have textured surfaces designed to insure against slipping.

Solid maple floors for basketball/volleyball courts and aerobics/dance use must be installed on a level slab over a vapor barrier and an underlayment system (underlayment systems vary). Care must be taken to ensure that the wood floor material is stored properly before installation—at the correct temperature and humidity—or the installation will be compromised.

Northern maple hardwood flooring material is available in competition grade, standard grade, and multipurpose grade. The painting of logos is generally not included in the manufacturer's installation responsibilities. In a normal gymnasium floor installation, a minimum of $1\frac{1}{2}$ inches of wood should be installed at the perimeter walls and at all vertical obstructions.

There are a variety of methods used to sand and seal gymnasium floors. The two main applications are oil- and water-based sealants.

Tile

Ceramic tile flooring is the selection of choice of owners and operators of many wellness centers today, especially for wet areas. The cost savings of using painted concrete can be effectively compared with the superior wear and maintenance of ceramic tile over time. Ceramic tile is almost always the better choice. The aesthetic "high end" appeal of ceramic tile is also a consideration. The designer must remember, however, that a tile floor means a depressed slab, and the selection of thin-set over thick-set tile will affect the cost.

Court Wall Systems

Racquetball, handball, and squash courts are composed of hardwood court floors, three wall sides — one back court wall and two side court walls — and one glass wall that houses the entrance door. Because these games are dependent on bouncing a ball off the side and back walls, special systems have been created to fulfill this need. Package systems are available that include the flooring system, made of hard maple tongue-and-groove-flooring set on resilient rubber pads and sleepers (the underlayment). The back wall and side wall systems integrated into this package are made of high-density particleboard with balanced high-pressure laminates on the front and back. This balanced laminate ensures unmatched dimensional stability and resilience to warping. The tongue-and-groove wall panels attach to 6-inch, 18-gauge galvanized metal "C" studs or wood studs, or to wood furring supported by existing structural walls. International squash and racquetball courts are slightly wider than their North American counterparts.

Tennis courts are classically designed using clay or grass. For most wellness center applications a concrete substrate is covered with a surface material such as Plexacushion, Novacushion, or Decort. These integrated systems are expensive but have favorable maintenance value. A more elaborate tennis court system design may involve the structural system itself. Post-tensioned concrete tennis court systems are seen around the country. Because of the way they are engineered, there is no need for expansion joints, which can be hazardous and are always unsightly. These systems also resist cracking.

Tennis courts currently tend to be a solid green color, especially for outdoor applications. Tan, gray, and blue have not fared well as color selections in outdoor courts, particularly where there is a greater likelihood of glare.

Textiles

Textiles included in the design of wellness centers are those fabrics used in lobbies, waiting areas, libraries, restaurants, retail areas, and other areas when they are appropriate to the design intent. Flame-resistant fabrics, such as Trevira, are designed to have great longevity and to not break down chemically in the cleaning process, which can produce allergic reactions. These fabrics, like many of the better materials on the market, are manufactured to be safe in the event of fire. Besides being flame-resistant, they will not give off noxious gases.

Ceilings

In large activity areas, such as pool areas and basketball/volley-ball courts, a painted, exposed roof structure with an accompanying array of HVAC ducts, sometimes brightly painted, seems the prudent choice. In aerobics areas, depending on the situation, exposed, painted steel joists (if they are actual structural components) can make a nice foil for track lighting and other special theatrical lighting used in these spaces for various types of group fitness classes. An aerobics area is also a natural for suspended acoustic tile, because it absorbs sound well and allows easy access to the plenum.

Recently, SAT has come a long way in terms of options offered by manufacturers to the design community. SAT lends itself to the use of fluorescent lighting but for a wellness center other lighting alternatives should be investigated.

Clinical areas will most likely use suspended acoustical tile for similar reasons. Again, selection should not be perfunctory,

Devil's Reach Sport and Health Club, Woodbridge, Virginia. *WA Brown & Associates, Architects.*

but based on aesthetic as well as practical considerations in choosing the best tile available.

In wet areas, the ceiling tile selected should fit the specifics of such use, including locker rooms, toilet rooms, and whirlpool areas. Saunas and steam rooms have their own particular requirements, SAT treated for use in wet areas should be specified.

Paint

Wall coverings in different areas of the wellness center are selected according to the nature of the space and the design intent. Within a healthcare setting, it is recommended that the safest materials be selected. In choosing paint, we recommend the selection of a nontoxic paint—certainly, at the least, a latex, water-based paint. The plant-based paints on the market today, such as those manufactured by AFM, are highly recommended. The Safecoat line of paints, base coats, and sealants are a good alternative to other paint selections. Nontoxic paints, including Safecoat, reduce toxic emissions, have a low odor level, which permits drying time to be accelerated, and are recommended for use in hospital ICUs (intensive care units) and pediatric intensive care areas. Sherwin Williams' Healthspec is another safe alternative.

4

Project Portfolio

Wellness center designs vary widely across the nation and around the world. From the smallest hospital-based centers created on the hospital campus itself as an adjunct to a physical therapy program (a few exercise machines dedicated to employees), to freestanding centers designed with dedicated clinical programs and the commitment of cardiologists, orthopedists, physical and occupational therapists, and radiologists, to wellness villages such as that developed by Disney as its Celebration Health Project, to large hospital projects that include fitness, retail, and complementary therapy components (such as Hospital 31 in Moscow), all have one thing in common: a dedication to the pursuit of health. The current wave of interest in the wellness center building type develops from a deep human need to search for the positive in life.

The programming and design of wellness centers vary regionally in this country and are as interesting as the diverse programs and designs of wellness centers in other parts of the world. Cultural differences are clearly illustrated, yet there are common themes. All designers and owners desire to select programs that reflect the market demand for clinical, fitness, and educational components as well as the ancillary spa, salon, and retail components.

Because market feasibility studies are not hard science, the demand for each program must be interpreted by the owner with guidance from the architect and other specialist-consultants. Market feasibility studies can only predict trends, and although they are very necessary to the process, the inherent experience and wisdom of healthcare executives and architects should also inform the decision-making process.

In the United States we are seeing large centers being built in suburban areas and succeeding. Similarly, we see wellness center programs grow up within hospital campuses, using whatever facilities are available at the time—a failing health club, an empty office, industrial or retail space—and succeed as well.

It is easier, in many ways, to begin a building project on a new site with adequate parking, pleasant views, access from main roads, great signage, a fair budget, and a good mix of programs. What is more difficult is having to select clinical and/or fitness programs to fit into existing space and make them work.

Programming decisions, what to include in the wellness center design, are about what will work, financially; what will fit, physically; and what will fly, politically.

Yet in the healthcare design industry programming is contingent on power. Programs can make sense on paper, but will be sifted through a screen of political variables, a process that is always necessary in the design of a healthcare building. Hospital boards, administrators, committees, and department heads will all have a say as to which programs are to be included in a wellness center.

Whoever has the greatest investment—the hospital system, physicians group, or developer/investor group—will have the greatest influence in deciding the program mix.

The excitement rises when all parties sit down at the table, committed to the project, and work out their agendas. A facilitator is often engaged to achieve consensus, to help the various parties "buy into" the basic project goals, and to help work out the detailed schedule and program.

Even when a hospital system is fully committed to the creation of a wellness center program, which may or may not include the development of a new freestanding building, the system will have to be educated in the fitness/retail programming area. The hospital system may have to be informed on the alternative, complementary, and/or integrative therapies the market is beginning to demand and managed care companies are beginning to support.

In some cases, fitness club owners will be addressing the inclusion of clinical programs in their facilities, as well as the possibility of integrative programs and spa/salon programs. In such instances, it is advisable to engage the services of a specialist consultant, along with an architecture firm that has a healthcare and sports club background.

The following are examples of successful wellness center projects from around the world.

BUFFALO GROVE PARK DISTRICT
NORTHWEST COMMUNITY HOSPITAL-COMMUNITY
RECREATION AND WELLNESS CENTER
BUFFALO GROVE, ILLINOIS

North of Chicago, Highland Park Hospital, a 250-bed community hospital, operates an ambitious wellness program. This hospital, part of the Northwestern Healthcare System, has a healthy philosophy in regard to prevention and wellness.

Exterior view, Buffalo Grove Wellness Center, Buffalo Grove, Illinois. *Philips Swager Associates.*

Buffalo Grove Wellness Center, Buffalo Grove, Illinois. *Philips Swager Associates.*

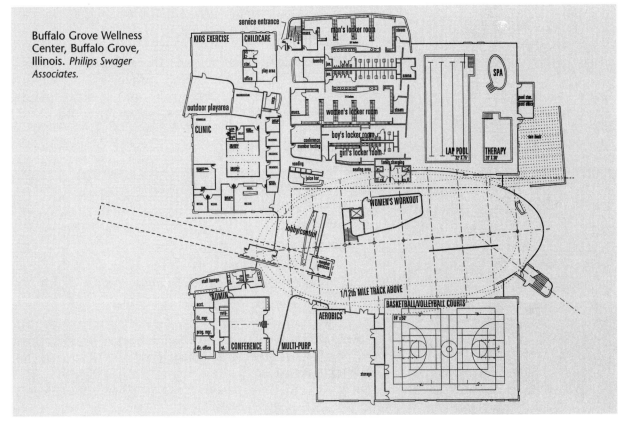

Our medically based approach reflects changing attitudes about healthcare delivery and individual fitness. Instead of reacting to medical conditions as they emerge, individuals are learning that maintaining a proper level of fitness can help prevent medical conditions in the first place. Proper exercise, nutrition and lifestyle choices all help control debilitating conditions like heart disease, osteoporosis, obesity and diabetes, while also boosting an individual's natural immunity to common infections. A balanced wellness program delivers a longer and more fulfilled life to anyone willing to embrace certain positive lifestyle changes.

Expert medical advice is offered at the Highland Park Hospital Health and Fitness Center. New members undergo health assessments, including tests for cardiovascular endurance and flexibility, blood pressure, pulse and cholesterol level, and assessment of body fat.

The facility includes the following components:

CLINICAL PROGRAMS
Cardiopulmonary Therapy
Physical Therapy
Occupational Therapy
Osteoporosis Screening

(The clinical area includes three treatment rooms, hydro-therapy room, cardiac office, speech therapy room, occupational therapy room, physical therapy area, receptionist, two offices, one business office, etc.)

FITNESS PROGRAMS
Aerobics
$\frac{1}{12}$-mile running/walking track
Women's workout area
Lap pool
Therapy pool
Basketball/ volleyball
Kid's exercise with outdoor play area
Child care area with office

SPA/ Men's, Women's, and Family Locker Rooms, Boys' and Girls' Locker Rooms
JUICE BAR

ADMINISTRATIVE AREA (director's office, program manager's office, fitness manager's office, accounting office, receptionist's area, future office area, etc.)

CONFERENCE ROOM

DECK

MULTIPURPOSE ROOM

THREE RIVERS AREA HOSPITAL
FITNESS AND WELLNESS CENTER
THREE RIVERS, MICHIGAN

In 1889, Borgess Hospital in Kalamazoo, Michigan, opened its doors, with 20 beds, as the first medical facility in that city. A parish priest, Father Francis A. O'Brien, started the new hospital assisted by 11 Sisters of St. Joseph, who came from Watertown, New York, to provide staffing. Eventually, a 100-bed facility was built, which in 1927 was expanded to 350 beds.

Wellness center floor plan, Three Rivers Area Hospital, Michigan. *Philips Swager Associates.*

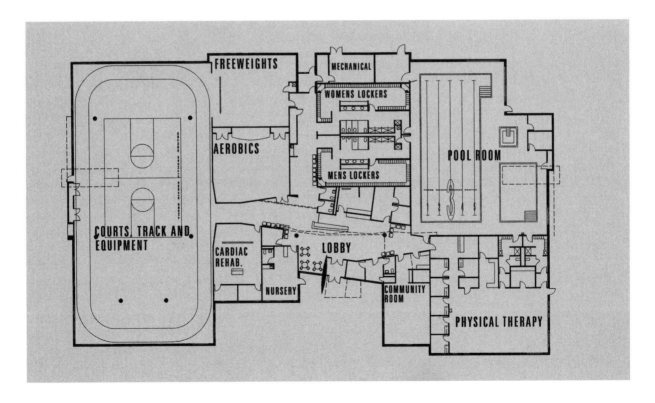

Borgess Medical grew in its ability to attract specialists and is today a leader in the region in open heart surgery and the area's only spinal injury center. It has the region's only organ transplantation program, a state-of-the-art emergency medicine program that serves the entire area, the region's only neurological intensive care unit, and psychiatric mental wellness and treatment programs.

The Borgess Health Alliance, as it is known today, offers extensive programs in the area of prevention and wellness. The system's CorpFit program offers work site wellness services that draw on the resources of the Alliance, communicating a company's commitment to employee health. Occupational health screenings are also offered, which help employers to identify employees who may be at risk for future health problems. Employers often contract with health systems for employee health education programs.

Employee preplacement and Department of Transportation physicals are performed at this facility, and the need for workplace modification is assessed. Through functional tolerance evaluations that assess performance levels, the Back to Work Center helps determine an individual's ability to work. A clinical specialist visits the work site to analyze the employee's job and identify any modifications needed to ensure a smoother return-to-work process.

The Borgess Health Alliance is networked with a small community hospital, Three Rivers Area Hospital, which has 60 beds. A recent addition to the system has been the Three Rivers Area Hospital Wellness Center. Built for approximately $3.9 million, this one-level, 33,800-square-foot facility includes the following programs:

CLINICAL PROGRAMS
  Physical therapy

CARDIAC REHABILITATION

OCCUPATIONAL THERAPY (including occupational medicine screenings, assessments, and evaluations)

EDWARD HOSPITAL HEALTH AND FITNESS CENTER SEVEN BRIDGES RECREATION COMPLEX WOODRIDGE, ILLINOIS

Edward Hospital is a full-service, not-for-profit hospital located in Naperville, Illinois, 25 miles west of Chicago. Its parent corporation is the Edward Health Services Corporation.

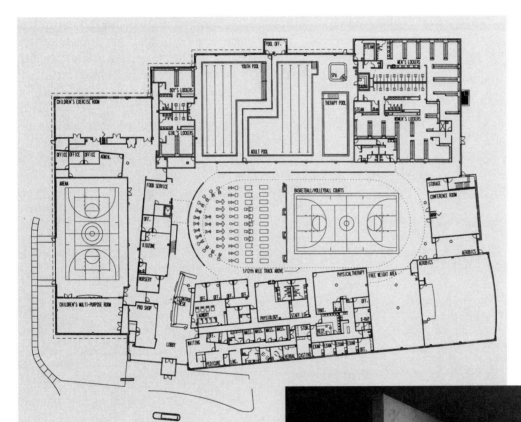

Floor plan, Edward Hospital Health and Fitness Center at Seven Bridges, Woodbridge, Illinois. *Philips Swager Associates.*

Exterior view, Edward Hospital Health and Fitness Center at Seven Bridges, Woodbridge, Illinois. *Philips Swager Associates.*

The hospital began as a tuberculosis sanatorium in the early 1900s. Today it provides a broad range of medical services to the community. In addition to the main hospital, which has 150 beds, the system includes 10 facilities in the area, among which are the Edward Cardiovascular Institute, the Cancer Center, Linden Oaks Hospital, the Edward Women's Center for Health, the Edward Healthcare Center, and the Center for Surgery.

Edward Hospital has two wellness center facilities, the Edward Health and Fitness Center located on the Edward Hospital Healthcare Campus, and the Edward Hospital Health and Fitness Center-Seven Bridges in Woodridge, Illinois.

The first center, built as an extension of the main hospital, is a not-for-profit, full-service facility. The wellness center includes 64,000 square feet of space, housing a six-lane lap pool, basketball/volleyball courts, racquetball and handball courts, a 4,000-square-foot aerobics room, a six-lane indoor cushioned track, exercise machines (including ski training machines), an Olympic free weight area, a spa whirlpool, sauna, and private steam room area, a nutrition analysis program and counseling services, massage therapy, a pro shop, a supervised nursery, and a juice/snack bar with lounge.

The Edward Hospital Health and Fitness Center-Seven Bridges, Woodridge, facility includes the following components:

CLINICAL PROGRAMS
Physical therapy/treatment
Imaging
Examination rooms (4)
Offices (2)

Reception area
Physiology
Casting
Staff lounge

FITNESS PROGRAMS
Youth lap pool
Adult lap pool
Therapy pool
Aerobics (primary and secondary rooms)
Basketball/volleyball courts

Arena (for soccer)
Children's exercise room
Children's multipurpose room
Weights
Exercise machines
Indoor running/ walking track

SPA PROGRAM
Whirlpool
Sauna
Steam
Massage rooms (4)
Herbal wrap room
Waiting area
Lounge
Office

ADMINISTRATION
Offices (4)

RETAIL
Pro shop

NURSERY

KIDZONE (child care)

FOOD SERVICE

LAUNDRY

CONFERENCE ROOM

This satellite health and wellness center is a full-service, state-of-the-art athletic facility of approximately 104,524 square feet and cost approximately $11 million to build. It is one of the first in the nation to pay particular attention to children's fitness.

NORTHERN ILLINOIS MEDICAL CENTER
HEALTH BRIDGE FITNESS CENTER
CRYSTAL LAKE, ILLINOIS

Northern Illinois Medical Center in McHenry, Illinois, a city northwest of Chicago, is a community hospital with 150 beds. Recently, the hospital built a wellness center in nearby Crystal Lake, Illinois. The Health Bridge Fitness Center, a facility of 57,205 square feet, was built at a cost of $5.6 million in 1994. Its fitness and clinical programs include the following:

Entrance to Northern Illinois Medical Center, Crystal Lake, Illinois. *Philips Swager Associates.*

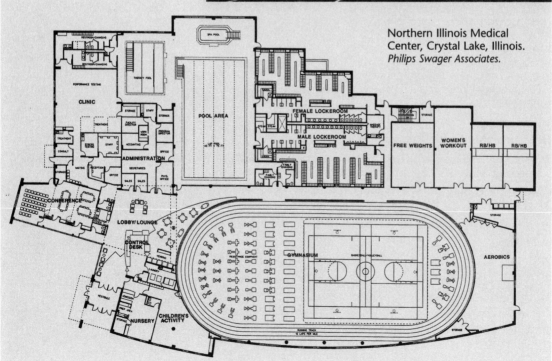

Northern Illinois Medical Center, Crystal Lake, Illinois. *Philips Swager Associates.*

CLINICAL PROGRAMS
- Physical therapy
- Occupational therapy
- Performance testing
- Examination/treatment rooms (4)
- Rest room/changing area
- Stress testing
- Consultation room
- Waiting area
- Office
- Staff lounge
- Therapy pool

FITNESS PROGRAMS
- Aerobics
- Exercise machines
- Free weights
- Basketball/volleyball court
- Racquetball/handball courts
- Lap pool
- Indoor running/walking track
- Men's and women's locker rooms/family changing area (2)

SPA PROGRAMS
- Spa pool
- Sauna
- Steam room

ADMINISTRATION
- Offices (4, including program director's office, facility director, accounting, program director, 2 sales offices)

CONFERENCE/Community Meeting Rooms

LOBBY/WAITING AREA

NURSERY

CHILDREN'S ACTIVITY AREA

PEORIA PARK DISTRICT/ST. FRANCIS MEDICAL CENTER
RIVERFRONT REC-PLEX
PEORIA, ILLINOIS

One of the largest medical centers in the country is St. Francis Medical Center in Peoria, Illinois. The Sisters of the Third Order of St. Francis, whose order was founded in 1877, began with a two-story frame house that served as their first hospital. Land overlooking Peoria's East Bluff was purchased for a new hospital building, with the capacity of 30 beds.

The largest medical center in downstate Illinois, St. Francis Medical Center now has built 730 licensed beds. In 1986, the Gerlach Building, named for the hospital's Administrator, Sister M. Canisa Gerlach, O.S.F., brought to 1.2 million square feet the total size of the medical center complex.

Main level, Peoria Park District/St. Francis plan.
Philips Swager Associates.

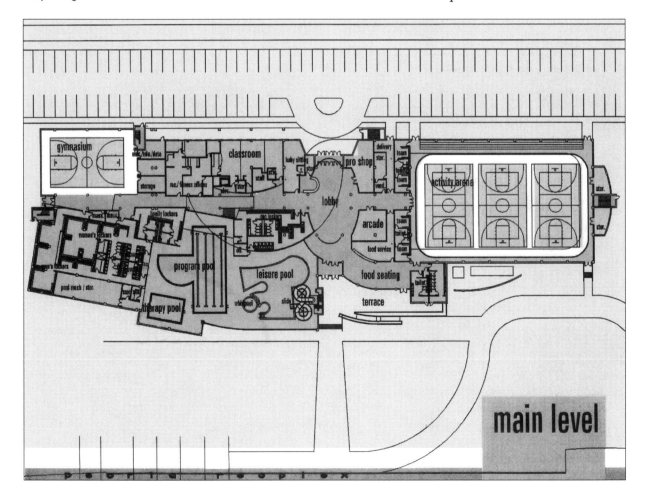

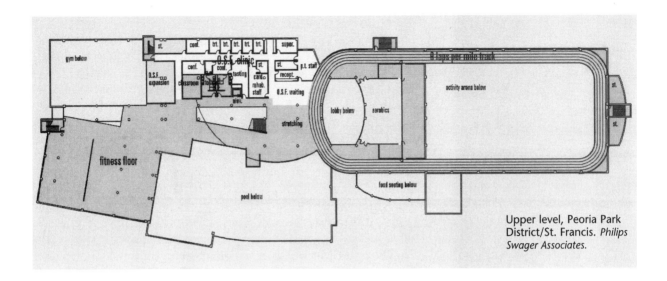

Upper level, Peoria Park District/St. Francis. *Philips Swager Associates.*

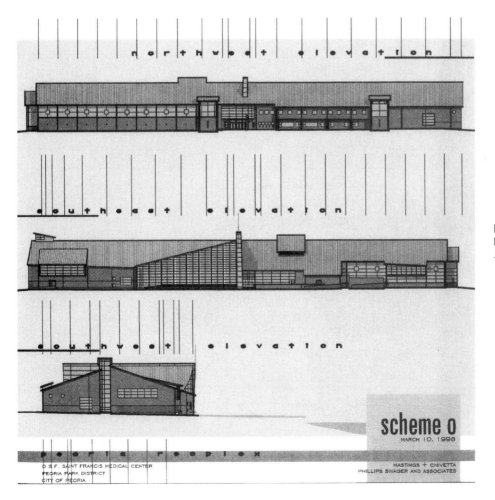

Elevations, Peoria Park District/St. Francis. *Philips Swager Associates.*

Outpatient facilities include the Glen Avenue Outpatient Center, which shares a building with the Susan B. Komen Breast Center; PromptCare North, which treats minor medical emergencies; and two other outpatient centers in the Peoria area.

The St. Francis Medical Center is an academic medical center, affiliated with the University of Illinois College of Medicine. It has a distinguished program in pediatrics; the Children's Hospital of Illinois is located within the hospital campus.

A unique project is just now being built with an interesting group of partners. St. Francis Medical Center has an existing health and fitness center located in the Pioneer Industrial Park. This center is home to fitness programs, youth programs, cardiac rehabilitation, outpatient rehabilitation, and day treatment.

St. Francis Medical Center has partnered with the Peoria Park District to jointly develop the Peoria Park District/St. Francis Medical Center Riverfront Rec Plex. This facility includes the following (note the unique feature, a Family Aquatics Center):

CLINICAL PROGRAMS
Cardiac testing
Physical therapy
Rehabilitation
Treatment rooms (5)
Conference rooms (3)
Rehabilitation staff area
Physical therapy staff area
Clinical expansion area

FITNESS PROGRAMS
Activity arenas (3)
Gymnasium
Fitness floor
Stretching area
Program pool
Therapy pool

AQUATIC CENTER (for families)
Leisure pool
Arcade
Food service (including seating)
Terrace

EDUCATION
  Classrooms (3)

ADMINISTRATION
  Staff office
  Recreation/fitness offices (5)

RETAIL

PRO SHOP

WOMEN'S LOCKERS, MEN'S LOCKERS, FAMILY LOCKERS, RECREATION LOCKERS

BABY SITTING

PITT COUNTY MEMORIAL HOSPITAL- WELLNESS CENTER GREENVILLE, NORTH CAROLINA

The University Health System of Eastern Carolina is one of the largest health systems in North Carolina, serving 29 counties. Its members include Pitt County Memorial Hospital, the East Carolina University School of Medicine, physicians groups, and regional affiliates. The system owns, manages, and leases hospitals, home healthcare agencies, and physicians' practices.

Entrance to Pitt County, North Carolina, Memorial Hospital Wellness Center. *Philips Swager Associates.*

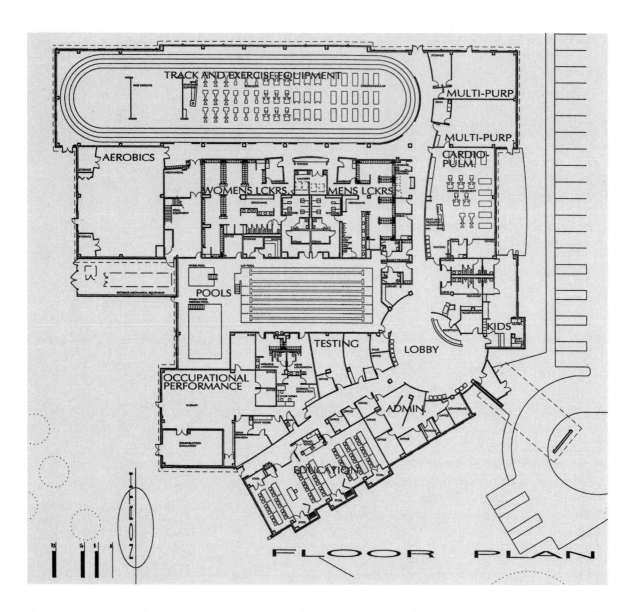

Pitt County, North Carolina, Memorial Hospital Wellness Center plan. *Philips Swager Associates.*

East Carolina University School of Medicine in Greenville, North Carolina, became affiliated with Pitt County Memorial Hospital almost 25 years ago. The University Health System has developed a comprehensive wellness program, HealthQuest Horizons, based on the concept that prevention and maintenance are key components of a healthful life-style. HealthQuest was launched in 1985 at Pitt County Memorial Hospital and has grown from an in-house hospital program involving 300 employees to become an incorporated wellness provider with training activities that serve several states and include 15,000 participants.

This healthcare system decided a few years ago to develop a freestanding wellness center. Today the Pitt County Memorial Hospital Wellness Center in Greenville, North Carolina, is a 50,000-square-foot facility, built at a cost of $6 million. The wellness center features the following components:

CLINICAL PROGRAMS
Cardiopulmonary
Physical therapy
Occupational therapy/performance testing
Offices (2)
Men's and women's lockers
Staff work area

FITNESS PROGRAMS
Aerobics
Indoor jogging/walking track
Exercise machines
Weight training area
Lap pool
Warm water exercise pool
Whirlpool
Fitness testing
Multipurpose rooms (2)
Men's and women's lockers/family changing
Library
Children's area
Pro shop

ADMINISTRATION

OFFICES (7)
Conference room
Registration area

EDUCATION
Classrooms (3, with removable partitions)

CLUB INDUSTRIAL

Ellerbe Becket International is developing a wellness center project in Istanbul. Elements of a 1998 feasibility study completed by Ellerbe's Michael D. Jones, A.I.A., and David Rova, A.I.A., are provided following this introduction.

The interesting variation on the wellness center model illustrated by the study is the inclusion of spa therapy areas that, on the whole, reflect European requirements and are rapidly finding popularity in the United States. Remarkable, culturally, is the separation of the "Executive Fitness Area" from the common fitness area.

This project, Club Industrial, is also interesting because it is an excellent example of adaptive reuse; in this case, an industrial building was converted to a wellness center with a heavy retail component.

Exterior of Club Industrial, Istanbul. *Ellerbe Becket Architects.*

Several wellness center projects are on the board now in this country, which will include heavier retail components than the wellness centers previously noted. We see this as a positive trend, as the ability of the wellness center to succeed and flourish will not lie purely in the clinical and fitness income stream but will, in certain areas of the country, benefit from an expanded retail component.

The following, then, is presented as an example of high-end design for an Asian client, from which lessons can be drawn.

Club Industrial Feasibility Study 1998

Club Industrial is the proposed expansion and adaptive reuse of an existing heavy machinery manufacturing factory of approximately 9,600 square meters in size. It is programmed to be developed into a sports-health club, retail, and entertainment complex of 12,000 square meters with emphases on life-style and living trends of the new millennium.

With the site being located in the suburbs of Istanbul and priced accordingly, establishing a sense of place for the wellness center was important.

Istanbul experienced a population boom from two to three million people in the 1950s and is currently approaching fourteen million. This population increase has dramatically changed the demographics of the city. The surrounding developments entail office, retail, and residential structures, within two square miles. Following the current life-style and trends in Istanbul, and comparing them to other major cities in the world, it was felt that a facility such as Club Industrial would be in high demand.

The following is a summary of the initial program for the project.

Site Modifications and Improvements

Landscaping for the project includes both hardscape (paving, barrier walls) and plantings (trees, ground cover, green areas, and water features), an outdoor recreation area (recreational swimming pool, pool deck, and café terrace), road improvements, surface parking, and a security gate. Site additions are to include a new service area, complete with loading dock and site storage.

Exterior Improvements

Exterior changes include replacement and upgrade of exterior glazing, roofing, and some wall systems. The exterior concrete and stucco facade is to be replaced and resurfaced with a new stucco finish system of varying architectural textures and colors. Both the existing Guardhouse and Storage Building will remain, but will have renovated interiors to upgrade their functions, and new exterior stucco finishes which correspond to the main building. Major demolition is limited to removal of the separate Toilet Shed, and of the southernmost section in the first bay of the main building, to open up the site and improve the overall appearance. Building Additions to the main structure include a three-story glass enclosure for the new Executive Entry on the north side of the building, a similar glass system to fill in the outer bays surrounding the Interior Pool area, a covered Main Entry Bridge at the second level on the south side, a new Loading Dock and canopy located at the northwest corner of the building, and a new solid wall and flat roof system at the northwest corner of the main building, clad in metal panels, used to enclose the courts and Executive Gymnasium at the Third Level.

Interior development is to consist of finished partition walls, glass storefront wall systems, doors and frames, railings, fixtures and equipment which provide the appropriate materials and finishes corresponding to the room or space type. The building is to provide the framework for a fully functional Health Club facility including Fitness and Weight Training Areas, Gymnasiums, Lap and Recreation Swimming Pools, Squash and Racquetball Courts, Golf Range, Boxing and Workout Room, Climbing Wall, an Elevated Running Track, with the required service and support areas. Also included in the interior development is the shell space for numerous Shops and Salons and Bar and Restaurant Facilities including Sports Shops, General Retail (Travel, Gifts, News, etc.), Beauty and Hair Salon, Chiropractor's Office, Premier Bar and Restaurant, Indoor and Outdoor Cafeteria, and a Snack and Juice Bar. Interior demolition is to include the selected removal of partition walls, doors, fixtures and miscellaneous equipment. The existing Building Structure appears to be adequate, but some limited work may need to be provided after a more extensive study is made. In general, the site MEP provisions appear to be adequate, but internally, full Mechanical, Electrical, Plumbing services are to be replaced and upgraded to fit the requirements of this type of facility.

Executive Area

The Executive Area is a specific area within the building which provides club amenities and services for Executive Level Members. It is located on the Third Level and connects to all three levels of the complex at the northern end of the building.

The Ground Level contains the Main Executive Entry, which is an enclosed three-level space within a new glass vestibule. It is adjacent to the Executive Administration area and is connected to the upper levels by open staircases or a private executive lift.

The Second Level provides both Men's and Women's Executive Locker areas each consisting of Changing Rooms, Toilet and Shower areas, with amenities including a Concierge Station, Lounge, and individual, full-height lockers. Access to the upper and lower areas is from an interconnected Lobby/Balcony located between the two spaces. The Third Level holds the Executive Club facilities including active, therapy, and lounge areas. Active spaces include the Executive Gymnasium (basketball, aerobics, dance, etc.), three (3) Squash Courts and a Fitness Deck (treadmills, stationary bicycles, stair climbers, rowing machines, weight training, free weights, boxing bags, etc.).

An Executive Salon provides therapy, with private rooms and stations for massage, tanning, hair styling, first aid, and an oxygen room. Lounge and Gallery spaces complete the Executive Level, providing business, bar, and theater areas centrally located within the floor. The Executive Area is additionally supported with an Executive Suite/Conference Room located at its south end. This, along with the Executive Lounge and Fitness Deck, is stationed at the edge of the Third Level, providing overall visibility of the entire complex below. Architecturally, the Executive Areas are to be designed with high-quality materials and finishes.

Public Spaces

The Main Entry to the complex is located at the south end of the building through a covered bridge that leads from an off-site parking area. It is positioned between the Information Area and the Premier Bar and Restaurant, overlooking the ground-level facility, and leads directly to the Locker Rooms via a Gallery Bridge.

The Information Areas include counters and support offices and are positioned at both entry points to the complex, one at the Main Entry on the Second Level and the other between the Administration and Fitness Areas on the Ground Level, adjacent to the glass public lift and main open stair. Public services (toilets, phones, drinking fountains, etc.) are provided throughout the complex, adjacent to the above zones. Architecturally, the Public Spaces are to have a combination of raw (existing) and finished elements, using medium-quality materials and finishes.

Retail Area

The complex provides an area of shelled lease space for Retail. Located in the northeastern portion of the Ground Level, it opens onto the main Training and Fitness areas. This area provides for Sporting Goods Shops (equipment, clothing, golf, tennis, skiing, etc.), General Retail (news, books, travel, etc.), and a Therapy Salon (massage, tanning, hair styling, first aid, oxygen room) with a separate Chiropractor's Office. Architecturally, a glass storefront system will be provided around its perimeter and the spaces will be unfinished for future tenant fit-up.

Bar/Restaurant

The complex provides areas of shelled lease space for Bar and Restaurant facilities. A Premier Bar and Restaurant space is located adjacent to the Main Entry on the Second Level, and overlooks the entire complex above and below. The Ground Level provides space for both an Open Cafeteria and Snack and Juice Bar. The Cafeteria is located directly below the Premier Bar and Restaurant and opens into the Main Fitness area to its north and the outdoor Café Terrace to its south. The Snack and Juice Bar is situated in a small area adjacent to the Outdoor Pool Deck, Retail Shops, and the Weight Training areas. Architecturally, these spaces will be unfinished for future tenant fit-up.

Outdoor Recreation

The Outdoor Recreation zone wraps around the southeastern corner of the building, providing an outdoor pool and deck area that relates directly to the adjacent interior functions. An Indoor and Outdoor Recreational Pool is centered in this area and is surrounded by a Pool Deck with cabana changing rooms, whirlpool, and kids play pool. A Café Terrace is located in the southern portion of this area, next to the Open Cafeteria inside the building. Architecturally, this area is to be treated with quality deck paving, designed in a variety of colorful mosaic patterns.

Indoor Recreation

Located at the Ground Level in the southeastern part of the building, the indoor pool area includes a spacious deck with whirlpool, kids play pool, and a five (5)-lane lap pool. The lap pool is fully integrated with the indoor-outdoor recreation pool. The Pool area is completely enclosed within an exterior glass wall system on all four sides up to the clerestory roof above, designed to take advantage of the natural light and keep the spaces visually connected.

The Main Sports Court is located at ground level on the west side of the building. This court area is large and flexible enough to support a variety of activities, including full-court basketball, indoor football (soccer), volleyball, badminton, and aerobic-dance classes. Directly above the sports court is a suspended Running Track of approximately fifteen (15) laps per kilometer. It is accessed either via open stairs located at the far ends or from the second-level Gallery Bridge area. The north end of the sports court faces three (3) squash courts, with the glass back wall facing the open gym.

Additionally, two racquetball and one squash court and associated lobby are located on the Third Level. These are accessed from the glass pedestrian lift located at the ground-level Information Area or second-level Gallery Bridge. These courts overlook the sports court and running track from above at the Court Lobby. Architecturally, all of these spaces are to be finished with the appropriate wood court flooring and wall systems, and are to be designed with these specific activities taken into consideration.

Locker Areas

The Locker Areas are located on the Second Level of the complex, providing facilities for the goal of 15,000 members (14,000 Standard, 1,000 Executive). The Standard Locker Room area is split in half, with equal facilities and services for men and women members. Provisions for 20–25% locker space are programmed for these areas (approximately 1,400–1,750 lockers each). These lockers are to be double stacked with benches. Services for these areas also include staff stations, changing rooms, toilets, showers, and sauna and steam rooms.

Executive Locker areas are currently designed to split 25% women and 75% men but are flexible to future change. Provisions are made for 100% full-height locker capacity (1,000 lockers) along with executive facilities and services, which are explained in the earlier Executive Area section.

Fitness Center

The main activity area is on the Ground Level centered in the complex, containing Open Fitness, Weight Training, Free Weights, and Stretching areas. These are supplemented by a large Training Station area that anchors them at the northern end. The Open Fitness area has the most variety and flexibility in activities, ranging from gymnastics, trampoline, to step and rowing machines. Just north of this are the Weight Training and Free Weight areas, providing a range of high-tech training equipment along with low-tech weights and barbells. Directly above this area is the open Fitness Bridge which provides equipment, including stationary bicycles, stair climbers, and treadmills. This bridge is not only a workout area, but also acts as a secondary path of access connecting the Second Level to the Ground Level via open stairs.

Specialty areas are also provided within the Fitness Center category, including a simulated Golf Range, Climbing Wall, and separate Workout Gym. The Golf Range is located in the southwest corner of the building and simulates virtual golf course scenarios within a controlled environment. The Climbing Wall is located outside the Golf Range area at the southwest corner of the Sports Court. Faux walls are designed to create a rock climbing wall that runs vertically through the suspended Running Track on the Second Level and terminates above at the third-level Climbing Deck. Finally, a separate Workout Gym is provided for boxing, martial arts, and their associated instructions. Architecturally, all of these spaces are to be finished with the appropriate fitness court floor and wall systems, and are to be designed with these specific activities taken into consideration.

Services

The Service areas of the project include Kitchens, Housekeeping and Laundry, Receiving, Engineering, Administration, and MEP Equipment Spaces. These are distributed in minor areas throughout the complex, but are primarily located on the Ground Level at the north end of the building. Kitchens are located directly within the related Bar and Restaurant area. Receiving, Engineering, MEP, and Housekeeping and Laundry areas are situated in the northwest corner of the complex, directly relating to the outside service and loading dock areas. Internally, they are located to have direct access to the service lift and vestibule. The Administration area is centralized within this area, housing both Corporate and Health Club Offices (management, sales, accounting, etc.) and their individual service requirements (lobbies, toilets, kitchens, storage, copy and workroom, etc.). Architecturally, these areas remain fairly minimal, with standard levels of materials and finishes relating to the office fit-out spaces.

Club Industrial Program

	Quantity	M²	Total M²	Total SF
GROSS BUILDING AREA (3 STORIES)			12,419	133,628
Parking				
Surface parking	68	28	1,904	20,487
Off-Site Parking	250	28	7,000	75,320
	103 Stalls		8,904	95,807
BUILDING AREA SUMMARY BY DEPARTMENT				
Elevators			132	1,420
Executive Area			1,023	11,005
Public Spaces			894	9,619
Retail Area			788	8,479
Bar/Restaurant			944	10,155
Outdoor Recreation Areas			2,245	0
Indoor Recreation Areas			3,007	32,352
Locker Areas			2,336	25,140
Fitness Center			1,802	19,387
Kitchen			254	2,733
Housekeeping & Laundry			145	1,560
Receiving			152	1,636
Engineering			75	807
Administration			460	4,944
MEP Equipment Space			408	4,390
Total			12,419	133,628

TABA RIVIERA HEALTHCARE CAMPUS

This new healthcare campus is being designed by Frank Nemeth, a senior designer, Joe Ellis hospitality specialist-architect for Ellerbe Beckett, with program consultation by Joan Whaley Gallup. It will encompass a wide range of building types supporting the concept of a wellness community for the mature adult on a spectacular site. The wellness village will include residential, entertainment, hotel, educational, recreational, clinical, and fitness components, designed to be fully integrated into an environment that supports these activities in a graceful and exciting design.

The centerpiece of this design is the International Center for Wellness and Mature Life, a complex within the village that will encompass all aspects of fitness, spa and preventive medicine elements, including a health appraisal center, fitness cen-

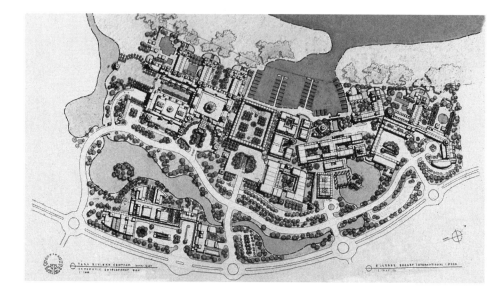

Taba Riviera site plan, Cairo, Egypt. *Ellerbe Becket Architects.*

Inpatient wing courtyard, International Center for Wellness and Mature Life, Centrum, Taba Riviera, Cairo, Egypt. *Ellerbe Becket Architects.*

ter and day spa, sports medicine clinic, health resource center, dental center, community education center, and a healthcare–related retail center.

Adjacent to the wellness center is a 100-bed hospital with the following departments: intensive care, cardiac care, respiratory medicine, oncology, orthopedics, dermatology, psychiatry, surgery/outpatient surgery, and diagnostic imaging. Recreational components to the village include a marina and a luxury inn, a five-star hotel, and an aquarium.

The following is a preliminary draft of the building program for this complex.

Program for Initial Construction Phases, Taba Riviera Healthcare Campus

	area (SF)
CENTRUM	
Village square	80,000
Retail	91,400
Urban entertainment	130,200
FIVE-STAR HOTEL	
350 rooms at 750 SF ea	225,00
Wedding hall	30,000
HOTELS/INNS	
Marina inn, 25 rooms at 600 SF ea	15,000
Luxury inn, 45 rooms at 750 SF ea	48,750
Spa	10,000
MARINA/MARINE BIOLOGY INSTITUTE	
Institute	10,000
Aquarium	7,500
Marina (150 slips)	
Marina buildings	600
INTERNATIONAL CENTER FOR WELLNESS AND MATURE LIFE	
Health Appraisal Center	6,000
Nutritional Guidance and Fitness Center	20,000
Women's Center	1,350
Day spa	6,000
Sports medicine and rehabilitation	10,000
Dental Center	1,920
Behavioral Health Center	3,600
Community Education Center	18,800
Health-related retail	9,320
MEDICAL CENTER HOUSING	
Independent living, 250 units	300,000
Assisted living, 75 units	75,000
Skilled care, 50 units	40,000
RECREATION	
18- and 9-hole golf courses	
Golf club	20,000
Tennis club	7,500
Equestrian center	6,500
HOSPITAL COMPONENT (100 BEDS)	193,860
Affiliated Study Institute	57,500
Total Area, Taba Riviera Healthcare Campus	1,425,800

HOSPITAL 31

Moscow Hospital 31 is the mixed-use development designed by Ellerbe Becket International's Frank Nemeth, A.I.A., David Rova, A.I.A., Emmett Ahearn, A.I.A., Michael D. Jones, A.I.A., Michael Newland, Rodney Nygaard, and Oleg Gregoret.

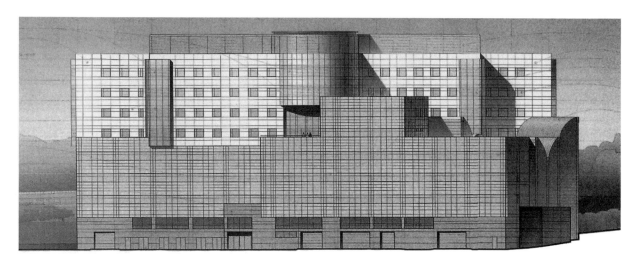

Southwest facade, Moscow City Hospital 31. *Ellerbe Becket Architects.*

Hydrotherapy area, Moscow City Hospital 31. *Ellerbe Becket Architects.*

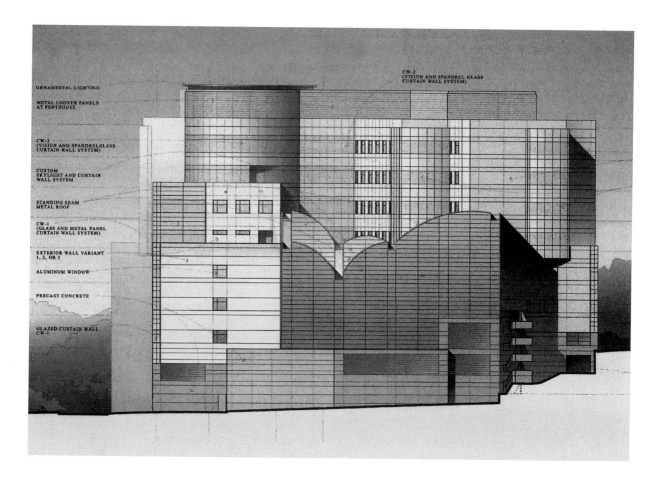

ORNAMENTAL LIGHTING

METAL LOUVER PANELS
AT PENTHOUSE

CW-2
(VISION AND SPANDERLGLASS
CURTAIN WALL SYSTEM)

CUSTOM
SKYLIGHT AND CURTAIN
WALL SYSTEM

STANDING SEAM
METAL ROOF

CW-1
(GLASS AND METAL PANEL
CURTAIN WALL SYSTEM)

EXTERIOR WALL VARIANT
1, 2, OR 3

ALUMINUM WINDOW

PRECAST CONCRETE

GLAZED CURTAIN WALL
CW-1

CW-2
(VISION AND SPANDREL GLASS
CURTAIN WALL SYSTEM)

Southeast facade, Moscow City Hospital 31. *Ellerbe Becket Architects*

Phase One will include the design and construction of a new medical rehabilitation hospital with infrastructure, parking, and a tunnel connecting the new building with the existing Moscow City Hospital. Phase Two will include a hotel and medical complex with the required infrastructure. The fitness center component of Phase Two includes an extensive spa therapy program. Although this enormous medical complex is at the very extreme end of what could be considered a wellness center, many of the programmed elements are those usually included in a typical wellness center. The extent to which the client has demanded a fully integrated clinical and fitness program is visionary. We predict this project will become a model of a new way of thinking about healthcare delivery. Many of the discrete clinical and spa therapy programs, like those in the Istanbul example, are becoming popular in the United States. (We are now seeing the inclusion of "Vichy showers" in many new wellness center programs in the United States.)

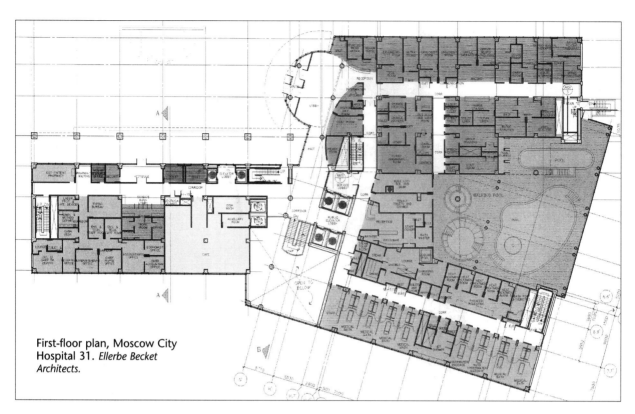

First-floor plan, Moscow City
Hospital 31. *Ellerbe Becket
Architects.*

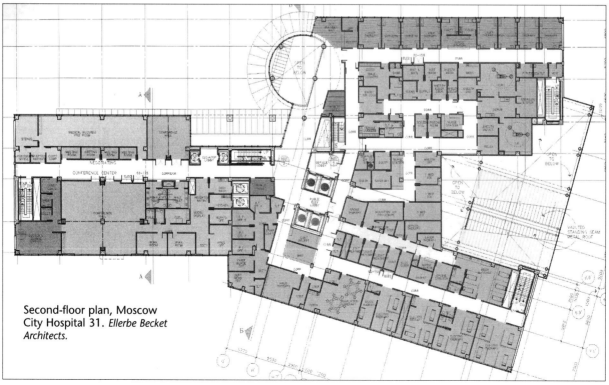

Second-floor plan, Moscow
City Hospital 31. *Ellerbe Becket
Architects.*

Third-floor plan, Moscow City
Hospital 31. *Ellerbe Becket
Architects.*

Fourth-floor plan, Moscow
City Hospital 31. *Ellerbe Becket
Architects.*

Fifth-floor plan, Moscow City Hospital 31. *Ellerbe Becket Architects.*

The following is the Master Plan submission for Moscow Hospital 31.

The design organization of this project, known as the Rehabilitation Hospital and Hotel Complex for Moscow City Hospital No. 31, is a mixed-use development. It is located on a 3.45-hectare site within a plot of land situated on the crossing of Leninskiy Prospekt and Lobachevskovo Street, across from City Hospital No. 31.

This project is a collaborative effort by Ellerbe Becket International (EBI) and the Moscow Government Moscomarchitectura (MNIIP), the Moscow Research & Design Institute for Culture, Leisure, Sports & Public Health Construction, for Moscow City Hospital No. 31 (Client).

Ellerbe Becket International is the Head Design Organization, specializing in architecture, engineering, and construction. The Project Leaders of the EBI team include Michael Newland and Rodney Nygaard of the Moscow office, and Emmett Ahearn and Oleg Gregoret of the U.S. offices. Frank Nemeth and David Rova are the Design Architects.

The Russian Consultant for assembling the submittal and conducting the design and code review is Moscomarchitectura (MNIIP). The leader of the MNIIP team is Michael Berklaid. Architects Audrey Bokov and Vyacheslav Zaziyants support the design process.

The client, Moscow City Hospital No. 31, has determined that the Master Plan development shall be constructed in a phased sequence. The Master Plan is designed as two (2) phases of construction. The client determined that Phase I is fully funded to proceed with construction. The Hospital has obtained financial resources to initiate the design of a full property Master Plan and has secured funds to construct a Rehabilitation Hospital on-site. A subsequent phase, or Phase II, will develop future sites within the property. Specifically, the phasing of the project will consist of the following:

Phase 1

Design and construction of a new medical Rehabilitation Hospital with infrastructure, parking, and a tunnel connecting the Rehabilitation Hospital complex with the existing Moscow City Hospital buildings.

Rehabilitation Hospital

A 200-bed, 24,400-SM facility built for short- and long-range patient rehabilitation care is planned. This will be a six-story structure with two levels of below-grade parking. Two (2) lower occupied levels of the hospital serve the treatment, administrative, and service functions of the hospital. Four (4) upper floors will house patient rooms. Two patient wings are planned for immediate construction, and a third expansion wing is designed for future growth. The hospital rehabilitation functions include therapy pools, surgery rooms, outpatient care, kitchen and cafeteria, laundry, pharmacy, and medical offices.

The program for the Hospital Center consists of two major components:

Component A
Medical Rehabilitation Unit (inpatient) (Physical Medicine Department) to serve 200 inpatients. Component A shall have the following facilities and services:

1. Two restaurants, one for everyday menu and one for dietetic menu
2. Conference Hall (Auditorium), this to be dividable by movable partitions into two or three conference rooms
3. Training Room—with workout equipment
4. Gym

5. Psychotherapy Room
6. Electrotherapy Room
7. Hypothermic Chambers with all necessary equipment including pools, hydrotherapy tanks, massage showers, modality booth for manual massage, thermal procedures (mud and paraffin), special rooms for infrared radiation, solariums, rooms with ionized air, etc.
8. Post Office
9. Savings Bank
10. Beauty Salon/Barber Shop
11. Underground Garage
12. Swimming Pool (25 × 14 meters with depths of 1.4 meters to 2.5 meters)
13. Consultation and Exam Rooms
14. Physician's Office (8 offices)
15. Procedure Rooms such as EKG, Stress Testing, Ultrasound, and Phlebotomy

The project should contain a Laundry, Dry Cleaning, Trash Incinerator and Vacuum Trash Removal System, Materials and Management Storage for consumable goods.

The Inpatient Facility allows an occupancy level of 150 patients and shall be designed to international standards.

Component B

A Preventive and Rehabilitation Ambulatory Center for 50 patient visits per day. Component B shall function as the Outpatient Department for Preventive and Rehabilitation Ambulatory Services for City Hospital No. 31, with an anticipated load of 50 patients per day. The following facilities shall be provided:

1. Hydrotherapy (including a pool of 16 × 8 meters with depth ranging from 1.4 meters to 2.4 meters). At the shallow end of the pool there should be an observation gallery for the staff to facilitate observation and assistance to the patients. Also at this end, a patient lift should be provided. This pool shall be provided with all necessary equipment for hydrotherapy, and a storage room shall be provided to store such equipment.
2. The Physical Medicine portion of this department shall contain modality cubicles, mud application, saunas, solariums, and infrared and ultraviolet radiation rooms. In addition, there should be a group inhalation therapy room, a room for suntanning, and others.

3. A pedestrian and transportation link should be established between City Hospital No. 31 and this department.

4. The infrastructure of this department should be tied in with the hydrotherapy department with all utilities, including water supply, heating, power, and ventilation, as well as air conditioning.

Structured Parking

A two- or three-level parking structure for 170 cars is planned for the hospital staff, patients, and visitors. This below-grade structure is also seen as a future building pad for long-range Hospital growth. A helipad is under consideration for emergency transportation of patients, and this function could be located atop the structured parking area. If a helipad is not used, then the grade level would be landscaped as a pedestrian/patient park.

Phase 2

"Apart-Hotel"

This mid-rise building of 28,482 SM will have 120 furnished suites designated for long-term residence of out-of-town families and individuals, including patients' relatives. The hotel suites shall have floor plans similar to 1-, 2-, and 3-bedroom apartments with a kitchen, toilet, bathroom, and auxiliary spaces. This building shall have all supporting facilities, including a child care and preschool facility, laundry and cleaners, commercial services for food stores, post office, bank, canteen, cafes, hair salon, and movie cinema. Two (2) levels of below-grade parking are included for 120 cars.

Fitness Center

This full-service fitness facility, comprising 12,042 SM, expands upon the rehabilitation effort of outpatient care, as well as serving the sport and recreation needs of the community. Therapeutic care includes massage, balneotherapy and fitness, strength and aerobic training. Various swimming pools provide training, diving, and leisure activities. Full-service indoor and outdoor facilities for tennis, basketball, and volleyball will be housed in this four-level building, as well as a specialized golf training area. Restaurants and outdoor play and park areas, as well as support services, will be provided. Two levels of below-grade parking are included, for 50 cars.

Medical Office Building

This 24,000-SM mid-rise commercial tenant office building provides an accessible medical office location for the complex, as well as tenant space for people living in the Apart-Hotel and the surrounding neighborhood. In addition to leased offices, the building will have conference room and dining facilities, limited retail space, and site amenities. Visitor parking will be on grade, and all other parking will be located below-grade, totaling 600 cars.

Hotel

At 41,205 SM, this three-star-quality, 500-room, high-rise hotel offers single and double suites for short-term out-of-town visitors and guests of the hospital and surrounding area. Located at the corner intersection of the site, this building will become a very prominent landmark for the entire hospital complex. The hotel will include a typical business-class environment with support services, including underground parking for 300 cars, several restaurants, a full-service business center, conference facility, retail shops, and hotel administration.

Number of Employees

The estimated occupancy level for this project is based on the individual program of the building types and sizes. These occupancy numbers account for the number of employees and visitors. Although some building functions will operate on a normal weekday business schedule, other building functions will operate for extended hours or a full 24-hour/7-day-a-week operation. Peak occupancy is foreseen as occurring on weekday mornings and evenings.

Building Type	Employees		Visitors		Hours
Rehabilitation Hospital	800	staff	200	patients	24 hours
Apart-Hotel	399	staff	1,255	residents	24 hours
Fitness Center	222	staff	967	users	0600–2200
Medical Office	2,580	occupants			0800–1900
Hotel	1,148	staff	1,495	guests	24 hours
TOTAL	9,066	maximum occupancy			

INDIVIDUAL BUILDING PROGRAM

Rehabilitation Hospital

DIAGNOSTIC AND TREATMENT

Room Name	Net m^2
Ambulatory Clinics	
Standard Modules	
Exam Rooms	9.0
Doctor's Office	11.5
Subtotal	20.5
Total Standard Module × 4	**82.0**
Specialty Modules	
Exam Rooms, 2 @ 9	18.0
Doctor's Office	11.5
Subtotal	29.5
Total Specialty Module × 2	**59.0**
Cardiology	
Stress Test	20.0
CCG Office	12.0
Subtotal	33.0
Dental	
Dental Exam	8.0
Dental Lab	7.0
Subtotal	15.0
Nurses' Station	16.0
Clean Utility	11.0
Soiled Utility	4.5
Medications	4.5
Patient Toilets, 2 @ 7.5	15.0
Staff Lounge	13.0
Staff Toilets, 2 @ 6	12.0
Subtotal	76.0
Reception/Control	8.0
Waiting (20 seats)	30.0
Office	12.0
Subtotal	50.0
Total Gross Area (net area × 1.20)	**378.0**
Total Ambulatory Clinics Net Area	**315.0**

Physiotherapy

Inhalation Block

Medical Inhalation, 12 @ 4.5	54.0
Specialty Inhalation	
Salt Room	10.0
Mountain Air Room	10.0
Special	10.0
Kitchen	6.0
Aromatherapy	18.0
Subtotal	108.0
Total Gross Area (net area × 1.25)	**135.0**

Electrotherapy Block

Procedure Rooms, 10 @ 10	100.0
Kitchen	5.0
Patient Toilets, 2 @ 5	10.0
Subtotal	115.0
Total Gross Area (net area × 1.25)	**145.0**

Massage Block

Mechanical Massage 5 @ 6	30.0
Nurses' Station	6.0
Utility Room	7.0
Manual Therapy	16.0
Horizontal Spine Stretching	16.0
Laser Room	14.0
Storage	18.0
Classic Massage, 5 @ 14	70.0
Storage	8.0
Subtotal	185.0
Total Gross Area (net area × 1.25)	**231.0**

Psycho and Emotional Rest Block

Music Therapy	20.0
Light Therapy, 3 @ 10	30.0
Artificial Sun Therapy	20.0
Control Room	5.0
Vichy Shower (Dry), 2 @ 10	20.0
Sleep Therapy	12.0
Control Room	8.0

Rest Area	50.0
Subtotal	165.0
Total Gross Area (net area × 1.25)	**206.0**

Support Block (2nd Floor)

Reception/Control	10.0
Patient Waiting	15.0
Doctors' Offices, 2 @ 10	20.0
Staff Room	8.0
Patient Toilets, 2 @ 15	30.0
Subtotal	83.0
Total Gross Area (net area × 1.25)	**104.0**

Water Treatment Block

Tub Rooms

Medical Bath with Dressing, 4 @ 28	112.0
Automatic Underwater Massage with Dressing, 2 @ 28	56.0
Jet Showers	28.0
Patient Toilets, 2 @ 5	10.0
Changing Room	5.0
Storage Room	19.0
Foot, Arm Bath	14.0

Sauna

Changing Room w/Toilet	16.5
Sauna	11.5
Steam Bath	8.0
Generator	3.0
Lounge w/Showers, Plunge Pool	48.0
Recovery	18.0
Subtotal	405.0
Total Gross Area (net area × 1.25)	**506.0**

Pools w/Decks/Storage

Motional Pool	
Exercise Pool	
Amenity Pool	
Walking Pool	
Subtotal	
Total Gross Area (no factor)	**715.0**

Health Bar

Prep/Patient Area	24.0
Toilets	5.0
Subtotal	29.0
Total Gross Area (net area × 1.2)	**35.0**

Support Block (1st Floor)

Reception/Control	10.0
Patient Waiting	15.0
Doctors' Offices	26.0
Bathmaster Control Staff	10.0
Toilet	3.0
Patient Dressing, Lockers, Toilets, Showers, 2 @ 42	84.0
Subtotal	148.0
Total Gross Area (net area × 1.25)	**185.0**

Exercise Therapy Block

Group Exercise	180.0
Individual Exercise	8.0
"Bobath"	21.0
Lockers and Toilet	17.0
Storage	13.0
Subtotal	239.0
Total Gross Area (net area × 1.2)	**286.0**
Total Physiotherapy	**2,548.0**

Surgery Suite

Inpatient

Operating Rooms, 2 @ 34	68.0
Scrub, 2 @ 10	20.0
Sterilizer Room	14.0
Induction Room	20.0
Reception/Control	12.0
Male Changing Room/Toilet, Shower	22.0
Female Changing Room/Toilet, Shower	22.0
Staff Lounge, Female	20.0

Staff Lounge, Male	16.0
Doctors' Dictation	6.0
Anesthesia Workroom	12.0
Medication Room	6.0
Clean Utility, Supply	32.0
Soiled Utility, Collection	16.0
Equipment Storage	16.0
Intensive Care	
One-Bed Room	32.0
Three-Bed Room	38.0
Subtotal	372.0

Outpatient	
Reception/Control	7.0
Supervisor's Office	8.0
Waiting (18 seats)	25.0
Procedure Rooms, 6 @ 18	108.0
Laser Rooms, 2 @ 19	38.0
Nurses' Station	15.0
Clean Utility and Meds	10.0
Soiled Utility	8.0
Patient Toilets, 2 @ 6	12.0
Subtotal	231.0
Surgery Suite Gross Area **(net area $\times$ 1.6)**	**965.0**

X-Ray	
Diagnostic Room	48.0
Ultrasound Room	15.0
Dark Room	6.0
Light Room (Reading)	12.0
Patient Dressing and Toilet, 2 @ 4	8.0
Subtotal	89.0
Total X-Ray Gross Area **(net area $\times$ 1.35)**	**120.0**

Laboratory Satellite	
Blood Bank	15.0
Urinalysis	16.0

Blood Draw	10.0
Specimen Toilet	8.0
Sub-Wait	4.0
Subtotal	53.0
Total Laboratory Satellite Gross Area (net area × 1.2)	**64.0**
Pharmacy Satellite	
Outpatient Dispensing	24.0
Inpatient Storage and Dispensing	37.0
Subtotal	61.0
Total Pharmacy Satellite Gross Area (net area 3 1.1)	**67.0**

Total Diagnostic and Treatment   4,046.0

Guide to Resources for Healthcare Information

Aerobics and Fitness Association of America
15250 Ventura Boulevard, Suite 200
Sherman Oaks, CA 91403
818-905-0040

American Alliance for Health, Physical Education,
    Recreation and Dance
1900 Association Drive
Reston, VA 20191
703-476-3400

American Association of Cardiovascular and
    Pulmonary Rehabilitation
7611 Elmwood Avenue, Suite 201
Middletown, WI 53562
608-831-6989

American Back School
PO Box 1193
Ashland, KY 41105-1193
800-637-BACK

American College of Preventive Medicine
1660 L Street NW, Suite 206
Washington, DC 20036-5306
202-466-2044

American College of Sports Medicine
PO Box 1440
Indianapolis, IN 42606-1440
317-637-9200

American Council on Exercise
5820 Oberlin Drive, Suite 102
San Diego, CA 92121
619-535-8227

American Health Club Marketing
28 West 23rd Street
New York, NY 10010
212-366-8947

American Health Foundation
320 East 43rd Street
New York, NY 10017
212-953-1900

American Heart Association
7320 Greenville Avenue
Dallas, TX 75231
214-373-6300

American Institute for Preventive Medicine
30445 Northwestern Higway, Suite 350
Farmington Hills, MI 48334
800-345-2476

American Institute of Stress
124 Park Avenue
Yonkers, NY 10703
914-963-1200

American Massage Therapy Association
820 Davis Street, Suite 100
Evanston, IL 60201-4444
847-864-0123

American Medical Association
515 North State Street
Chicago, IL 60610
312-464-5000

American Orthopedic Society for Sports Medicine
6300 North River Road, Suite 200
Rosemont, IL 60018
847-292-4900

American Physical Therapy Association
1111 North Fairfax Street
Alexandria, VA 22314
703-684-2782

American Podiatric Medicine Association
9312 Old Georgetown Road
Bethesda, MD 20814
800-FOOTCARE

Association for Worksite Health Promotion
60 Revere Drive, Suite 500
Northbrook, IL 60062
817-480-9574

Centers for Disease Control and Prevention
1600 Clifton Road NE
Atlanta, GA 30333
404-638-3286

IDEA (International Association of Fitness
Professionals)
6190 Cornerstone Court East, Suite 204
San Diego, CA 92121
800-999-IDEA

International Council for Health, Physical
Education and Recreation
1900 Association Drive
Reston, VA 20191
703-476-3471

International Health, Racquet and Sportclub
Association (IHRSA) and IHRSA Institute on
Exercise and Health
263 Summer Street
Boston, MA 02210
617-951-0055

National Athletic Trainers Association and
Certification Board, Inc.
2952 Stemmons Freeway
Dallas, TX 75247
214-637-6282

National Employee Services and Recreation
Association
2211 York Road, Suite 207
Oak Brook, IL 60521-2371
708-368-1280

National Fire Protection Association
1 Batterymarch Park
PO Box 9101
Quincy, MA 02269-9101
800-344-3555

National Health Federation
212 West Foothill Boulevard
Monrovia, CA 91016
818-357-2181

National Health Information Center
PO Box 1133
Washington, DC 20013-1133
800-336-4797

National Institute for Occupational Safety and
Health, Division of Safety Research
1095 Willowdale Road
Morgantown, WV 26505
304-285-5894

National Institute of Mental Health
5600 Fishers Lane
Rockville, MD 20857
301-443-4513

National Institute on Aging
9000 Rockville Pike
Bethesda , MD 20892
301-496-1752

National Strength and Conditioning Association
916 O Street
Lincoln, NE 68508
402-472-3000

National Swimming Pool Foundation
PO Box 495
Merrick, NY 11566
516-623-3447

National Wellness Institute
PO Box 827
Stevens Point, WI 54481
715-342-2969

Occupational Safety and Health Administration
230 South Dearborn Street
Chicago, IL 60604
312-353-2220

Office of Research on Women's Health
9000 Rockville Pike
Bethesda, MD 20892
301-402-1770

President's Council on Physical Fitness and Sports
701 Pennsylvania Avenue West, Suite 250
Washington, DC 20004
202-272-3421

Prevention
33 East Manor Street
Emmaus, PA 18098-0099
610-967-7723

Sport Goods Manufacturers Association
Castlewood Drive
North Palm Beach, FL 33408
407-842-4100

US Squash Racquets Association
PO Box 1216
Bala Cynwyd, PA 19004
610-667-4006

Wellness Councils of America
Community Health Plaza, Suite 311
1701 Newport Avenue
Omaha, NE 68152-2175
402-572-3590

Dimensions of Typical Exercise Equipment

Type	Function	Length (in.)	Width (in.)	Height (in.)	Weight (lb)
Leg extension	Quadraceps	56	33	42	180
Squat	Lower body	60	32	63	437
Arm curl	Biceps	41	27	38	136
Upper back	Upper back	42	30	79	190
Seated butterfly	Pectoral	45	43	62	218
Leg press	Lower body	60	27	48	225
Standing hip	Hips and thighs	40	49	65	205
Lateral shoulder raise	Deltoids and shoulders	41	31	63	170
Military press	Upper arm	48	36	60	147
Tricep	Triceps	48	27	60	130
Lateral pull-down	Upper back and shoulders	48	41	73	156
Hip abductor	Hip abductor	67	37	38	193
Lower back	Lower back	58	28	45	195
Abdominal	Abdominal muscles	38	38	50	116
Seated leg curl	Hamstrings	56	33	42	185
Biaxial chest press	Upper arm	47	42	76	167
Leg curl	Hamstrings	70	31	27	143
Seated calf	Calves, ankles, feet	46	30	48	168
Seated chest press	Chest	46	35	79	155

Typical Wellness Center Exercise Program Schedule

A.M.	P.M

Day	Start	End	Program
MONDAY	6:15	7:30	Turbo step
	8:30	9:15	Armed and dangerous
	9:15	10:15	Sizzle step
	9:30	10:30	Wave walk
	10:15	10:30	Ab lab
	10:30	11:30	Classic interval
	4:30	5:30	Low and pump
	5:30	6:00	Guts and butts
	6:00	7:00	Walk and sculpt intervals
	6:00	7:00	Cardio challenge
	6:15	7:15	Water works
	7:00	7:30	Stretch and relax
	7:00	8:00	Kamikaze step
	7:00	8:00	Box aerobics elite
TUESDAY	7:15	8:00	Guts and butts
	8:00	8:45	Express step
	9:15	10:15	Step and pump
	9:15	10:15	Water works
	9:15	10:15	Walk and sculpt intervals
	10:15	10:30	Back in action
	10:15	10:45	Guts and butts
	10:30	11:00	Stretch and relax
	10:30	11:15	Water arthritis
	5:30	6:00	Guts and butts
	6:00	7:00	Step and pump
	6:00	7:00	Wave walk
	7:00	8:00	Cardio challenge

Day	Start	End	Program
WEDNESDAY	6:30	7:30	Step and pump
	8:30	9:15	Low and pump
	9:15	10:15	Aero step intervals
	9:15	10:15	Sea circuits
	10:15	10:30	Ab lab
	10:30	11:00	Classic cardio
	11:00	11:30	Classic step
	12:15	1:00	A la carte step
	4:30	5:30	Sizzle step
	5:30	6:00	Guts and butts
	5:30	6:15	Water arthritis
	6:00	7:00	Cardio intervals
	6:00	7:00	Box aerobics
	6:00	7:00	Walk and sculpt intervals
	6:15	7:15	Tidal waves
	7:00	7:30	Stretch and relax
THURSDAY	7:15	8:00	Sea circuits
	8:00	8:45	Express step
	9:15	10:15	Wave walk
	9:15	10:15	Step and pump
	9:30	10:30	Walk and sculpt intervals
	10:15	10:30	Ab lab
	10:30	11:00	Stretch and relax
	10:30	11:15	Water arthritis
	5:30	6:30	Kamikaze step
	6:00	6:30	Armed and dangerous
	6:15	7:15	Sea circuits
	6:30	7:00	Guts and butts
	6:30	7:45	Aero/double step
	6:30	7:30	Sport circuit

Day	Start	End	Program
FRIDAY	6:30	7:30	Sport circuit
	8:30	9:15	Guts and butts
	9:15	10:15	Cardio intervals
	9:15	10:15	Tidal waves
	10:15	10:30	Ab lab
	10:30	11:00	Classic cardio
	11:00	11:30	Classic step
	4:30	5:30	Sizzle low
	5:30	6:30	Aero step intervals
SATURDAY	8:00	9:00	Kamikaze step
	9:00	9:30	Armed and dangerous
	9:00	10:00	Wave walk
	9:15	10:00	Classic step
	9:30	10:30	Cardio challenge
	10:00	11:00	Fit moms
	10:30	11:15	Water arthritis
	10:30	11:30	Slide and step
	11:30	11:45	Ab lab
	4:15	5:15	Workout before you go out
SUNDAY	8:30	9:30	Step and pump
	9:00	9:45	Water works
	9:00	9:30	Armed and dangerous
	9:30	10:15	Guts and butts
	9:30	10:30	Total body conditioning
	9:45	10:30	Tidal waves
	10:15	10:30	Back in action
	10:30	11:15	Water arthritis
	10:30	11:30	Double step
	10:30	11:15	Water arthritis
	10:30	11:30	Double step

Index